The Electric Chair

The Electric Chair

An Unnatural American History

by

CRAIG BRANDON

McFarland & Company, Inc., Publishers
Jefferson, North Carolina, and London

Library of Congress Cataloguing-in-Publication Data

Brandon, Craig, 1950–
    The electric chair : an unnatural American history / by
Craig Brandon.
        p.   cm.
    Includes bibliographical references and index.
    ISBN 0-7864-0686-0 (library binding : 50# alkaline paper) ∞
    1. Capital punishment—United States—History.
    2. Electrocution—United States—History.   I. Title.
    HV8699.U5B69   1999   99-31128
    364.66'0973—dc21   CIP

British Library Cataloguing-in-Publication data are available

Manufactured in the United States of America

*McFarland & Company, Inc., Publishers
    Box 611, Jefferson, North Carolina 28640
    www.mcfarlandpub.com*

Table of Contents

Preface

J ust before 7 A.M. on March 25, 1997, Pedro Medina, a 39-year-old Cuban immigrant who had spent the last 14 years of his life on Florida's death row, was escorted into the execution chamber in Florida State Prison for his first look at the electric chair. The three-legged chair had killed more than 200 people in the Sunshine State since prisoners carved it out of an oak tree in 1923. In recent years it had developed a reputation for malfunctioning.[1]

In 1990, after technicians mistakenly replaced a natural sponge in the head electrode with a synthetic one, six-inch flames had erupted from the chair during the execution of Jesse Tafero. Instead of the 2,000 volts that were supposed to kill Tafero instantly, only about 100 volts got through. Instead of a single dose of electricity, the technicians had to use three, torturing Tafero to death over a period of several minutes.

Medina had watched news reports of Tafero's death on television, as had the dozens of other prisoners on Florida's death row. The state temporarily suspended executions so it could check out the chair's connections. Now prison officials said they were certain everything was in proper order. Medina certainly hoped so.

He was one of 125,000 Cubans who came to the United States in 1980 in the Mariel boat-lift seeking freedom and new opportunities. Three years later a jury found him guilty of stabbing Dorothy James, a 52-year-old Orlando elementary school gym teacher and his former neighbor. Police found him in north Florida a few days later driving her Cadillac. A knife believed to be the murder weapon was found in the car.

The case had been appealed many times in those 14 years. Medina insisted he was not the murderer, and the victim's daughter thought he was telling the truth. After the last appeal was turned down, the date was scheduled for his execution.

"I am still innocent," he said as he was strapped into the chair. A metal electrode surrounded by a wet sponge was attached to his calf through a slit in his trousers, and a leather mask containing the other electrode was pulled down over his head. When the warden gave the nod the switch was pulled, directing 2,000 volts through Medina's body.

Once again the chair malfunctioned. Blue and orange flames up to a foot long erupted from the mask and flickered for six to ten seconds, filling the execution chamber with smoke and the stench of burning flesh. One of the security guards had to open a window to let in some fresh air. At 7:10 Medina was declared dead.

"It was brutal, terrible. It was burning alive, literally," said witness Michael Minerva, who heads the state agency that represents indigent death row inmates.

"We do not have any idea at this point what caused the flame," said Kerry Slack, the official spokeswoman from the Florida Department of Corrections.

Many of those who read the story the next day were disgusted and outraged. Opponents of capital punishment called for an investigation. The official Vatican newspaper condemned Medina's execution as a barbaric act, but Florida attorney general Bob Butterworth said that Florida's electric chair was just doing its job: making executions as brutal as possible so potential murderers might think twice before pulling the trigger.

"People who wish to commit murder, they better not do it in the state of Florida because we have a problem with our electric chair," he bragged.[2]

Leo Alexander Jones, the next inmate scheduled to die in the chair, didn't see the humor in that remark and filed a lawsuit claiming the chair was obviously defective and had caused "wanton pain" to Medina. Using it again, he said, would be cruel and unusual punishment and therefore unconstitutional. A month later Florida judge A. C. Soud tossed out the claim, saying Florida's chair had merely suffered from a "human error" and was once again ready for its next occupant.

On October 20 the Florida Supreme Court upheld the constitutionality of death by electrocution by a one-vote margin, 4–3. The three dissenting justices, injecting a bit of common sense into the decision, wrote, "Execution by electricity is a spectacle whose time has passed.... Florida's electric chair, by its own track record, has proven itself to be a dinosaur more befitting the laboratory of Baron Frankenstein than the death chamber of Florida State Prison."[3]

What few people realized was that history was repeating itself. One hundred six years earlier, in 1890, nearly the same chain of events took place at Auburn Prison in upstate New York when William Kemmler became the first man ever to die in an electric chair. There was the same stench, the same smoke, the same sickened reaction on the part of the witnesses, and even the same horrified reactions from Europe using exactly the same word: *barbaric*. Back then it was the nine U.S. Supreme Court justices who said they could find nothing at all "cruel" about causing such severe pain that the victim's body lunged against the straps so hard they often broke, nothing "unusual" about frying a human being to death with 2,000 volts of electricity until the death chamber reeked with smoke and the stench of burning flesh.

Today, after more than 100 years and more than 4,300 executions by electricity, the electric chair is still torturing its victims, nauseating its witnesses and inspiring demands for it to be abolished.

During the 1930s and 1940s nearly half the states routinely used electric chairs to rid society of murderers and other criminals. Hundreds of men, women and teenagers were killed in them. Today only four states use the electric chair as their only method of capital punishment. Three others offer it as an alternative to lethal injection. States like New York, New Jersey and Louisiana have taken the chair out of the execution chamber and put it on display in museums, where, like the stocks and the scaffold, it is viewed as a gruesome relic of a less civilized age.

"The electric chair was flawed from the very beginning," Steven Hawkins of the National Center to Abolish the Death Penalty told *USA Today* shortly after Medina'a death. "That's how it started and that's how it's ending."

"It's just a matter of time" before the last of the states pull the plug on the chair, predicted Deborah Denno, Fordham University law professor, reacting to Medina's death.[4]

Tennessee and Kentucky switched from the electric chair to lethal injection in 1998. Florida may yet hold the key to when the chair is finally shut down for good. If Florida switches to lethal injection, as the attorney general has suggested, then the remaining three states, Alabama, Georgia and Nebraska, are expected to follow. The U.S. Supreme Court has said it is willing to consider a case challenging the constitutionality of the electric chair and could eliminate the chair for good with a stroke of a pen. It seems likely that the electric chair, a barbaric anachronism from the nineteenth century, might not survive long into the twenty-first. Yet politicians in Florida have been slow to pull the plug, fearing that to do so would make them seem soft on crime.

How did such a strange device come to be invented? Why has it survived from the era of the horse and buggy into the era of the space shuttle? Those are questions this book will attempt to answer.

Although it was conceived by a group of well-meaning humanitarians in the 1880s as a substitute for the brutal practice of hanging, the electric chair's midwife was greed, the kind of pure, unadulterated greed for which the Gilded Age was famous. In this case the robber barons were inventors and entrepreneurs: Thomas Edison and George Westinghouse, who used the electric chair as a cruel weapon in their high stakes, cut-throat competitive marketing campaigns against each other. At stake were the contracts to deliver electricity to every city in the nation.

Without Edison's secret, behind-the-scenes manipulation the electric chair might have remained at the blueprint stage. The two electrical entrepreneurs spent hundreds of thousands of dollars influencing the legislation and court challenges that led up to the first use of the chair. Among their tactics were secret deals and stolen letters, but there is also solid evidence of bribery, payoffs and kickbacks.

The electric chair story is also full of strange characters, like the engineer who electrocuted hundreds of dogs, cats, cattle and horses in experiments to determine the exact voltage necessary to kill a human being. Another is the first executioner, who wore disguises, carried his equipment around in a suitcase and never allowed his picture to be taken. Another is the man who became the foremost expert on the electric chair in the 1980s, who rebuilt chairs and trained operators, only to lose his position when it was discovered that he had written a book denying the Holocaust and had no engineering degree and no engineering license.

It's the story of the famous people who died in the electric chair: the man who assassinated President McKinley, the man who killed Charles Lindbergh's infant son, the anarchists Sacco and Vanzetti, cold war spies Julius and Ethel Rosenberg and the infamous serial killer Ted Bundy.

It's the story of a century-long campaign waged in the nation's courts. On one side have stood humanitarians, armed with increasing evidence that the electric chair was torturing and burning its victims; on the other, the judges who have refused to acknowledge that the electric chair is cruel and unusual and therefore a violation of the Eighth Amendment.

It's a story that seems, at last, to be coming to its final chapter. With the Edison and Westinghouse battle long forgotten, people like Pedro Medina are still paying the price of their competition when they are tortured to death in a device that should have been relegated to the museums decades ago. The good intentions of the humanitarians of the 1880s, who wanted to use the latest technology to eliminate the barbaric practice of hanging criminals from a rope, ended up creating an even worse horror that refuses to go away.

Richard Bartlett, chairman of the New York Temporary State Commission on the Revision of the Penal Law in 1962, summed it up well:

"The electric chair is the ultimate symbol of irrationality, brutal vengeance, senseless discrimination.... It is like a cancerous growth which infects the entire body of our penal system."[5]

There have been many helpful people who assisted me in collecting the information for this work. I am indebted to librarians and custodians of historical societies around the nation who saved clippings and documents and allowed me free access to them. Many of these libraries and historical societies are working under severe budget cuts and deserve the public's support. I would like particularly to thank Lois Merry of the Document Delivery Office at Keene State College, who spent hundreds of hours locating obscure documents and books for me. Thanks also to the New York State Library in Albany, the Buffalo Erie County Historical Society, the Corning Historical Society, the Thomas Edison Archives, the Dewey Library at the State University at Albany, the Dartmouth University Library, the Oneida County Historical Society, the Albany Public Library, Dick Case, Al Stoops, Emily and Ben Brandon, Larry Syzdek, Sarah Cohen, Jane Spellman and the staff and library of the *Times Union,* and many others whom I have no room to mention. I would also like to thank two people I have never met, Deborah Denno and Theodore Bernstein, whose published works on this topic opened many doors that I would not otherwise have thought to knock on. I would also like to include a statement by Hugo Bedau, one of the world's leading authorities on capital punishment, which sums up what this book is about. In 1997 he wrote that "death in the electric chair was and remains one of the most barbaric ways to kill a person. Why it remains authorized by a dozen states is unclear."[6]

—1—
The Genie of
the Gilded Age

O
n the morning of August 6, 1890, the attention of much of the
world was focused on a small room in the basement of an old
stone prison in Auburn, New York, a small city just west of Syracuse. Although some of this attention was little more than morbid curiosity about the gruesome experiment that was about to be performed there,
an unusual collection of amateur inventors, wealthy entrepreneurs, medical doctors and legal scholars had more than a casual interest in it. Professional reputations would rise or fall, millions of dollars would change
hands and the fates of thousands of condemned criminals, most of them
not yet born, were hanging in the balance.

William Kemmler, the illiterate ax murderer scheduled to die that day,
had in some ways less riding on the outcome of the experiment than the
witnesses seated in wooden folding chairs in the execution chamber or
those waiting by the telegraph offices around the nation for news of the
results. Kemmler had long since confessed to his crime and had accepted
the inevitability of his death. He had long since become little more than
a pawn in a great political, legal and marketing game between two of the
most famous entrepreneurs in America, Thomas A. Edison and George
Westinghouse, who had battled over his case for more than two years. If
the experiment was a success and Kemmler died a swift and painless
death, it would help Edison sell millions of dollars worth of electrical
lighting equipment to cities across America. If it was a failure and Kemmler's death proved to be unusually gruesome, it would hurt George Westinghouse's sales pitch that his new alternating current generators were
safe as well as efficient.

In the dynamo room, a few hundred yards from the execution chamber, the generator that would create the voltage to power the electric chair

George Westinghouse, who owned the U.S. patents for an alternating current system for urban street wiring, bankrolled early legal opposition to the electric chair because New York planned to use one of his generators to power the chair. (New York State Library)

had Westinghouse's name on it. He had not sold it to the prison, however. In fact, he had done everything he could to keep his generator out of Auburn Prison. New York's Department of Prisons had purchased the generator on the used equipment market, shipped it to Rio de Janeiro in Brazil, then shipped it back to New York in order to get around the Westinghouse Electric Company's determined efforts to make sure a Westinghouse generator was never connected to the electric chair.

The state had gone to all that trouble because the electrician it had hired to design and purchase the equipment for the electric chair was in league with Edison, Westinghouse's chief rival, and was determined to use the electric chair to discredit Westinghouse's electrical systems. At stake were millions of dollars in contracts and franchises with every city in the United States. City governments, businesses and even private residents wanted electric service installed in their cities to replace the dirty, dangerous and inefficient gas lights. The city councils and businessmen around the nation knew they needed to buy electrical generators, lighting fixtures and transmission wires to set up these systems, but most of them knew little or nothing about electricity. You turned a switch on the wall, and suddenly a glass globe lit up with no perceptible flame and no perceptible source of fuel. There were just some wires connected to a machine blocks away. It seemed more than a little like magic.

What they did know about was safety. Electricity was, after all, the stuff that lightning was made of, and it could kill you if you were struck by it. They wanted to install the new light systems, but only if they could be assured they would be safe. For over a year Edison and the electric lighting companies he controlled had been telling these would-be electric customers that Westinghouse's equipment was dangerous. Very dangerous. It was so dangerous in fact that New York State, which was planning to kill its condemned prisoners with electricity, had specifically selected a Westinghouse generator for the job because New York knew it was the most deadly. So, Edison had argued, if you want a safe system you would be a fool to choose a Westinghouse generator. Edison had gone so far as to suggest that the process of using the electric chair to kill a condemned person be called "westinghousing."

Alarmed that he might lose millions of dollars in contracts to Edison, Westinghouse began a counterattack. At first he relied on cold science, explaining that although his electric system used higher voltages than Edison's, this voltage was reduced before it entered buildings and was therefore not dangerous. But most Americans had only the vaguest notion of what a volt was or a dynamo or a transformer, so when it came down to making a choice

Thomas Edison, who owned the U.S. patents for a direct current system, fought an all-out public relations war against Westinghouse for urban electrification contracts worth millions of dollars. (New York State Library)

it was Edison's word against Westinghouse's. There Edison had a clear advantage. By the late 1880s Edison was a legend in his own time. Newspapers called him a wizard, a genius inventor and the world's leading expert on electricity. Would Thomas Edison mislead the public just to make a few million dollars? At the time, most people took him at his word. New evidence shows otherwise.

When New York began testing its new electric chair on dogs, cats, cattle and horses in 1889 it invited reporters to witness the instant death that resulted from "westinghousing." Increasingly alarmed at the success of Edison's misinformation campaign, Westinghouse filed lawsuits against him and New York State only to see them endlessly delayed in the court system. When New York sentenced the first man to die in its brand new electric chair, he tried a different tactic, hiring one of the most prominent lawyers in the country, one with excellent political connections, to appeal the murderer's case. Killing a man with electricity, Westinghouse's lawyers contended, was cruel and unusual punishment and therefore a violation of the Eighth Amendment.

Westinghouse contributed an estimated $100,000 in legal fees to take the case all the way to the U.S. Supreme Court in hopes that New York State could be forced to go back to hanging its condemned prisoners. The justices listened to the arguments that the electric chair was cruel and unusual, but in the end they just scratched their heads. Like most Americans, they knew nothing about dynamos or volts or electric cables. They found it impossible to determine if something was "cruel" when it had not even been used yet. In a unanimous decision the high court told Auburn it was up to the state to decide if it wanted to "westinghouse" its condemned prisoners instead of hanging them.

So on that August morning the two electrical geniuses of the age waited for the news from Auburn. Edison waited in his laboratory in West Orange, New Jersey, where dozens of animals had been killed with a Westinghouse generator the year before to show its lethal power. Westinghouse waited at his home in Pittsburgh. The U.S. Supreme Court was no longer in session, so the justices waited in their homes around the country to see if they had made the right decision in permitting electrical death sentences. The lawyers who had argued the case in the state and federal courts waited for the news. The members of the New York State Legislature who had passed the law 20 months before and the governor who had signed it waited for the news. The doctors who had taken sides on the issue and participated in the experiments, the hundreds of electrical technicians who were building the Edison and Westinghouse electrical systems across the country and, most of all, the murderers who had been sentenced under the new electric chair law were waiting. All of them wanted to know what would happen when the switch was thrown in the basement of Auburn Prison and 1,600 volts of electricity were sent along a wire and into the brain and along the spinal column of the man who had been wired into the electrical circuit.

Gathered outside the gates of the prison that morning to provide news of the results of the great experiment were nearly 100 reporters from newspapers all over the country. When the New York State Legislature passed the electric chair law it had included a section that prohibited reporters from describing the details of executions. Despite that, two reporters, one each from the Associated Press and United Press, had been invited as official witnesses to the experiment and were seated in the execution room. A makeshift telegraph station had been set up across the street from the prison to send the news around the world as soon as the results of the experiment were known.

The reporters and their editors knew there was no denying the significance of the event about to take place that morning. History was about to be made. Never before had anyone deliberately attempted to take the life of a human being by sending an electric current through his body.

Even those involved in planning and constructing the apparatus in the prison basement admitted they were not entirely sure what would happen when the switch was pulled and the electricity turned on. For two years electrical engineers and doctors had struggled over the issue of just how many volts and just how many amperes of electricity would be required to kill a human being. It was an important issue. If they used too much current they might burn the condemned man's body in an unsightly way that would surely turn the stomachs of the witnesses and threaten the future of the technology. If too little electricity was used the condemned man might be rendered unconscious and come back to life a few minutes or even hours later, as sometimes happened with people who had been struck by lightning. Despite all the experiments with dogs, cats, sheep and horses, the technicians admitted they would be holding their breaths when the current was turned on. No one could say for sure what would happen.

Although there was hard evidence that if you pushed enough electricity into someone that person would eventually die, there was the nagging issue of what the victim of such a shock might feel. Was it, as some argued, an instantaneous death? Or was the twitching and wiggling that had been observed in some electrical shock victims evidence of unspeakable suffering? Doctors had argued both sides of that issue. Several of them were witnesses in the execution chamber and would watch Kemmler carefully, with a scientist's objectivity, as the electricity was turned on. Later they were scheduled to perform an autopsy on Kemmler's body to prove, once and for all, which theory was correct.

Also watching closely were thousands of stakeholders in the debate over capital punishment, not just in New York State but in other states and countries waiting to follow with their own electric chairs if the experiment proved successful. For decades there had been a growing movement to outlaw executions and replace them with life in prison. Just as it seemed that the movement to abolish hanging had reached a critical level of support, the wild card issue of electrocution had been thrown into the game. Abolitionists found their ranks split between those who believed that any form of execution should be illegal and those who believed that a new, more humane kind of execution might be the best solution. The hard-core abolitionists knew that if the condemned man in Auburn Prison died a peaceful and graceful death, their cause might be set back for decades, perhaps permanently.

Similarly, the hard-core advocates of the death penalty knew that much was riding on the outcome. Since the issue of electrocution had first been raised, many criminals had been quoted as saying that they would rather be hanged than die by electricity because electricity was by far the most awful death they could imagine. Wasn't that, the pro–death penalty forces said, the perfect deterrent? Wasn't it true that the more gruesome the punishment, the less likely it was that a murderer would strike the fatal blow? The abolitionists also understood that if Auburn Prison's basement became a chamber of horrors, the resulting public outcry might turn against not just electrocution but all forms of the death penalty.

How did such a strange experiment come about?

For some inventions it is impossible to trace the origins back to the first thought, the instigating incident that set the chain of events into motion. The invention of the electric chair is not one of those. In this case it is possible to pinpoint the exact date and time of the incident that led to the great experiment on the morning of August 6, 1890, in Auburn.

The process began just after 10 P.M. on August 7, 1881, almost exactly nine years before that humid morning of anticipation at Auburn Prison. That was the final day in the life of George L. Smith, a 30-year-old alcoholic dockworker from Buffalo.

The Brush Electric Light Company, which built and maintained Buffalo's high voltage "arc" street lights, had a generating plant on Ganson Street. Buffalo was one of the first cities in the world to use the lights, which harnessed high voltage to produce an incredibly bright light, like that used today for searchlights and lighthouse beacons. Installed just the year before, the lights were a wonder of modern technology, turning night into day in downtown Buffalo, allowing stores to stay open into the evenings. People came from hundreds of miles away just to see this marvel, which helped give Buffalo bragging rights as a center of technology and progress.

Just inside the front door of the Brush plant was a 4,800-pound generator that produced electricity equal to 225,000 battery cells and spun at 700 rounds per minute. It was one of many such generators in the plant, and because it was located near the door a three-foot-high metal railing had been built around it.

Despite this railing, some of the local folk who had heard all about the wonders of electricity had made a habit of visiting the generators when the technicians weren't looking. They found if they held onto the railing a certain way and joined hands across the room they could feel a tingling sensation as a tiny bit of electricity escaped from the generator and passed through their bodies.

Smith had probably done this and decided he wanted to experience it that evening after a night on the town. He sneaked past the door of the plant, but G. W. Chaffee, the manager of the plant, noticed him and chased him out. A few minutes later Smith was back, and because Chaffee was busy adjusting one of the generators he did not see him right away. Someone heard Smith shout that he was going to stop the generator. He placed his left hand on the armature of the generator near the brush on the left side of the machine. Nothing happened. Then he brought his right hand down on the other side of the machine.

The attendants who had been trying to reach him to chase him out again watched as Smith's body suddenly became rigid and collapsed onto the railing. When they tried to pull him off they found his hands were stuck fast to the brushes and they could not get him loose. They had to stop the generator before they could pull Smith's body away from the machine.[1]

It was seen at once that Smith was dead. He was a healthy and strong man with a wife and a child, but the witnesses said he had died the moment he touched the brushes. At a coroner's inquest the next day the cause of death was listed as "paralysis of the nerves of respiration."

As with any new technology, people had mixed feelings about the new uses of electricity that were being developed. Although most people saw electricity as a wonderful power, a culmination of progress and science that would change their lives for the better, they also had a healthy respect and even a fear of it. It was, after all, invisible, mysterious and sometimes deadly. There had already been numerous reports about innocent victims who had come into contact with electric wires and died a horrible death.

Each of the five daily Buffalo newspapers printed a brief item about Smith's unusual death, using it as a kind of cautionary tale about the dangers of the new wonders of electricity. Each quoted Chaffee about how swiftly and painlessly Smith had died. There was no legal reason to turn Smith's death into a coroner's case, since there was no hint of foul play, but the city authorities ordered one anyway out of curiosity and in an attempt to determine if there was a need for rules to protect the public from a safety hazard.

The inquest might have been routine and could have been filed away in some drawer forever, but this was, after all, the Gilded Age, when nearly every American was an amateur inventor or scientist. Each city had its informal societies that met in salons once a week to discuss the newest developments in technology that guaranteed the constant march of progress, profit and an increased standard of living.

Buffalo, a city that prided itself as a center of progress, had many such societies, and one of them included the county coroner, Dr. Joseph Fowler, who performed the autopsy on Smith. After filing his report, he

shared with his fellow amateur scientists the amazing results of his investigation. Smith seemed to have died so quickly that there was not a hint
of pain, burning or tissue damage. It seemed that the electricity, like a
bolt of lightning, stopped his heart instantly.

Among the members of the learned group who listened intently to
Fowler's fascinating report that night, was a Buffalo dentist, Alfred Porter
Southwick, a true renaissance man of the Gilded Age, who, besides filling
teeth and building crowns, was a published expert on such diverse topics
as the design of steam-powered tugboats and the best methods of oral
surgery required to correct cleft palates. Southwick, who lived on Niagara Street not far from Fowler's office, suggested to his friend after the
presentation that there might be some kind of practical use for this unex-
plored aspect of electricity. Perhaps, Southwick suggested, it might be
used at a reduced voltage as a form of anesthesia for medical operations.
Or it might be useful as a form of euthanasia for unwanted animals at the
city pound.[2]

Neither man could have speculated where that inquiry would take
them, but the conversation that August 1881 evening in a salon in Buffalo
led directly to the invention of a device that would take the lives of more
than 4,000 people in the United States and many more around the world.

As a dentist who kept up with the latest developments and theories,
Southwick was well versed in the various procedures being proposed to
reduce pain during dental work. For a dentist, reducing pain was essential. The less pain patients felt, the more likely they were to come back
the next time they had a problem with their teeth. A dentist who could
perform work in the most painless manner was certain to acquire many
new patients. The prices charged by dentists at this time showed the value
of painkillers. An advertisement in the *Buffalo Courier* showed that one
dentist charged 25 cents to extract a tooth but added 50 cents more for
the use of gas to kill the pain. So Southwick took a professional interest
in Fowler's description of Smith's most unusual death. Was there a way
that electricity could be used as a dental anesthetic? Or perhaps there was
some other practical use for this instantaneous and deadly force. In war,
perhaps? Or the extermination of unwanted wildlife?

Southwick soon became so obsessed with the idea of using electricity as an agent of death that he spent much of the 1880s, the prime years
of his life, advocating for it with leaders of government and industry. It
was an unlikely task for the descendant of a Puritan family that came from
England to America on the *Mayflower* and settled in Salem, Massachusetts. These ancestral Southwicks ran afoul of the strict laws in Salem and
were banished to Shelter Island in Long Island Sound, where both parents

died of exposure in 1660. The poet John Greenleaf Whittier found this pathetic story so intriguing that he wrote the ballad "Cassandra Southwick" about it.

Southwick was born in Ashtabula, Ohio, on May 18, 1826, and received a high school education, apparently the only formal education he ever had. He moved to Buffalo in his early 20s and took a job as steamboat captain, using his small boat as a tug to pull the barges on Lake Erie that used the Erie Canal as a shortcut to the Atlantic. In 1855 he was appointed chief engineer of the Western Transit Company, which operated steamships on the lake.

Alfred P. Southwick, who first came up with the idea of executing convicts with electricity. (New York State Library)

During the 1850s he became an apprentice in a Buffalo dentist's office. This was a common practice at a time when few doctors or dentists went to medical schools. Dentistry was considered a trade that was best taught in the office of an older expert. He opened his own practice in 1862, but it was not a very lucrative profession. Besides the quarter that he earned for each tooth extraction, he received only $8 for an entire set of false teeth.[3]

Despite his lack of formal education, Southwick was soon on intimate terms with many of the prominent doctors, scientists and businessmen of the city. Together they formed the Buffalo Club after the Civil War to promote the city's industry and future. Buffalo was a city that had been made by technology, transformed from a tiny port city on Lake Erie into one of the busiest ports of America when it became the western terminus of the Erie Canal in the 1820s. It was a city that welcomed scientists and engineers. Southwick was an avid reader and writer who could converse on equal terms with those who had more formal educations. He was one of the founders of the Dental Society of the State of New York in 1868.

Not satisfied with the more mundane dental practices, Southwick turned his attention to oral surgery and specifically the congenital defect known as cleft palate. This is a deformity in which the roof of the fetus's mouth fails to grow together during development, leaving a space. The condition creates a deformity of the face, makes it difficult for the victim to eat and makes it almost impossible for victims to speak. Although surgeons had operated on children with the deformity for centuries, Southwick developed new techniques and artificial implants that were so innovative that the Dental Society of the State of New York invited him to deliver a paper on them in 1877.

In this paper he showed a remarkable use of Latin medical terms for someone who had only completed high school, and he demonstrated a thorough familiarity with the history of dentistry. Although no one knew for sure what caused cleft palate, he said, he formed a theory based on an article he had read about a professor who raised two tigers from cubs. To make them more tame he gave them little meat, feeding them mostly on vegetables. They grew to full maturity on this diet, but when the female had cubs they died because the roofs of their mouths had not formed properly. After the tiger parents were given more meat in their diets a second litter of cubs was perfectly normal.

"Congenital cleft palate," Southwick concluded, "is evidently the result of perverted or defective nutrition, which results from a variety of causes, more or less obscure."

Southwick's colleagues gave little credence to his theory of the cause of cleft palate but did appreciate his research on its treatment. Southwick's innovative technique was to surgically implant a single hard piece of material into the mouth to form a substitute palate. Until this time the common practice was to use two pieces of soft material that moved when the patient's mouth moved, but Southwick found that this material deteriorated quickly and slipped out of place. The advantage of his device was that it was more permanent and inexpensive enough that even the poorest families could afford it. The paper shows that Southwick had humanitarian concerns as well as scientific ones.

"As far as my observation goes," he told the dentists, "the major portion of all applicants wanting relief of this kind are more troubled with fissures, congenital or otherwise, in the pocketbook. So by simplifying the mode of treatment and bringing it within the reach of all, we are doing the greatest good to the greatest number."[4]

Southwick's other work, the work that made him famous, seems also to have been guided mainly by his humanitarianism, however misguided some later thought it to be. Why would a dentist spend so much time and energy on the idea that electricity could become a useful agent of death, work that seemed to have nothing to do with his livelihood? To understand the reasons, it's important to understand something of the ideas of progress and technology that existed in the Gilded Age.

In many ways the Gilded Age view of technology was the culmination of ideas first proposed during the Enlightenment, that reason could triumph over superstition and that the forces of nature could be conquered and forced to do humanity's bidding. After the Civil War many returning soldiers who had traveled far from their homes and seen other cities and other climates dedicated their lives to improving their communities. Many of them were convinced that the factories and technologies of the North were among the main reasons the largely agricultural South had been defeated. These veterans, mostly Republicans who loved to join societies like the Odd Fellows and the Grand Army of the Republic, held the view that science and technology were the keys to power, success and wealth. Technical advances were a tangible and measurable proof of human progress and reinforced the Enlightenment's idea of the universe as a vast machine.[5]

Such technical marvels as the transcontinental railroad, the submarine and ironclad ships, new advances in medicine and surgery and improvements in the breeding of plants and animals not only had an impact on those who used them but also contributed to the widespread belief that science and technology were on the verge of solving every problem and turning the earth into a paradise that could not have been dreamed of in earlier eras.

Historian Thomas P. Hughes has compared the century that began in 1870 in America to Italy in the Renaissance, the era of Louis XIV in France and the Victorian period in Britain. In each case there was a critical mass of science, available capital and progressive ideas that changed society in ways no one could have expected or predicted. In each case fortunes were made by those who invested in the new technology. Within a few decades the Gilded Age in America produced the incandescent light, the radio, the airplane, the gasoline-driven auto, the telephone, the phonograph and motion pictures. Other historians of technology have called this period "the second creation of the world" as the values of technology—order, system and control—became the values of the culture and had a vast influence on politics, business, architecture and art.[6]

This unquestioned faith in technology during the Gilded Age meant that inventors held a special status. Alfred North Whitehead said that the greatest accomplishment of this era was "the invention of a method of invention." Despite the advances in technology, virtually anyone with a new idea could become an inventor. Anyone who tinkered around in a cellar or garage could come up with a discovery or invention that could change the world and make him or her rich.[7]

In July 1896 the editors of *Scientific American* took a look at this remarkable change in the country by noting that the number of patents granted by the U.S. Patent Office had doubled each year since 1866 and reaching a peak of 26,292 in 1890, the year the electric chair was first used. There were tens of thousands of amateur experimenters, scientists and tinkerers like Southwick conducting experiments in their spare time. Some of them, no doubt, were hoping to get rich, but most of them were driven by their own curiosity and so intoxicated with the idea of perfecting the world through science that they let their day-to-day lives suffer as a consequence.[8]

The editors of *Scientific American* called it "an epoch of invention and progress unique in the history of the world…. A gigantic tidal wave of human ingenuity and resource so stupendous in magnitude, so complex in its diversity, so profound in its thought, so fruitful in its wealth, so beneficent in its results, that the mind is strained and embarrassed in its effort to expand to a full appreciation of it."

While this interest in science and progress affected everything from medicine to astronomy and magnetism to animal husbandry, electricity held a special place in the minds of scientists in the last quarter of the nineteenth century. Although American interest in electricity dates back to Benjamin Franklin and his kite, it was only in the 1870s that a series of inventions led to an explosion of ideas for the practical uses of the flow of electrons that makes electricity work. For decades scientists had been experimenting with batteries and wires. Even though most believed there was some potential in it, electric research had more to do with theory than practicality.

Early in the century scientists understood much about this potentially useful form of energy, but to the general public it was still closely identified with magic. Most laypeople, even at the end of the century, did not have the slightest idea what electricity was, how it was produced or what made it perform its miracles. All they knew for sure was that it was the power of the lightning bolt, the very weapon of Zeus and Thor, that had somehow been harnessed by brilliant scientists like Edison and tamed to make motors run and lights burn brightly.

By the end of the century it seemed that the uses for electricity were endless. It could conquer the darkness of night, capture voices inside machines, make pictures move, push elevators to the top floors of sky-scrapers, power trolleys and automobiles and turn the most powerful motors.

During the latter half of the nineteenth century, many major hospitals had departments of electrotherapy that used electricity to treat paralysis, rheumatism, gout, arthritis and sciatica. The electrodes were soaked in salt water and attached to the affected area. In some cases doctors used "general electrotherapy," in which the patient stood on a large copper electrode while the other electrode, attached to a moist sponge, was passed over the entire body, causing muscular contraction. This was used to treat insanity, hysteria, skin diseases, drunkenness, opium poisoning and nervous exhaustion. It was also said to relieve pain, improve sleep and aid digestion. This same method of using a moist sponge to bring the electrode into contact with the skin was adopted by the inventors of the electric chair. Many quacks with portable electric batteries roamed the country, offering to cure cancer and mental illness with shocks.[9]

"The public has the notion that if there is anything under the sun that electricity can not do, it is not worth doing," said a contributor to *Scientific American* on March 7, 1900.

The public's ignorance, fear, awe and admiration of electricity were important factors in the development of the electric chair. In many ways late–nineteenth century attitudes about electricity were similar to late–twentieth century attitudes about nuclear energy or computers. On one hand electricity represented progress and an increased standard of living. On the other hand it was a terrible, sinister and dangerous force.

"The belief is a growing one that electricity in one or more of its manifestations is ordained to effect the mightiest revolutions in human affairs," wrote Thomas Ewbank, U.S. commissioner of patents in 1849, predicting that it would revolutionize transportation, communications and manufacturing. Instead of seeking gold in California, he advised, fortunes would be made by those who spent their time "digging in the mines of the motors."[10]

The first widespread uses of electricity were for communications, first with the telegraph (which used electrical batteries) and then with Alexander Graham Bell's telephone in 1876, the same year that Thomas Alva Edison, the true spirit of the era, founded his research lab in Menlo Park, New Jersey. The first commercially used electric lights appeared in the late 1870s. These were arc lights, extremely bright lights produced by jumping the electric current between two carbon electrodes. The power was produced by stream-driven generators.

When John Wanamaker of Philadelphia first turned on the arc lights at his general store on December 26, 1878, they attracted crowds who described "twenty miniature moons on carbon points held captive in glass globes." The first arc light street-lighting systems were set up the next year. When Wabash, Indiana, turned on its first streetlights in 1880, thousands of people came from miles away to see them. Newspapers reported that "men fell on their knees, groans were uttered at the sight, and many were dumb with amazement."[11]

By 1880 these arc streetlight systems were installed in many of the larger cities of the United States, including Buffalo, where the generating plant had attracted the attention of George L. Smith.

In October 1879 Edison developed the incandescent lamp, which lasted longer than arc lamps, required a much lower and safer voltage and led directly to the use of electric lighting in homes. This development, as we will see, had a direct impact on the invention of the electric chair. At a time when homes were still lighted with gas jets, candles and fireplaces, the electric light was a revolutionary development that attracted the interest of men like Southwick, who discussed it at meetings of the various scientific societies.

Among those who shared this interest in the development of electricity was Dr. George E. Fell, another Buffalo physician who had long been interested in the effects, positive and negative, of electricity on the human body. Fell had already made a name for himself as the inventor of the "Fell motor," a device used to revive people who had been injured in accidents by forcing air down their throats and into their lungs.

It was at one of these scientific meetings, some months after they discussed Smith's autopsy, that Southwick and Fell shared their discoveries with Colonel Rockwell, the head of the Buffalo Society for the Prevention of Cruelty to Animals. Rockwell told them that the BSPCA had been looking for a quick and painless way to dispose of the hundreds of stray dogs and cats collected by the city each year. Rockwell had been drowning the animals by placing them in bags and submerging them in Lake Erie. When Southwick and Fell described the findings of the Smith autopsy, Rockwell agreed that electrocution might be a better means of killing the animals than poisoning or shooting, two other methods that had been suggested.[12]

Southwick read all the information about electricity he could find, learning about which kinds of materials conducted electricity most efficiently, the characteristics of the various kinds of electricity, how the current could be safely handled without the experimenter being shocked and how much current might be necessary to kill an animal. Beginning in 1882 Southwick and a group of his friends began a series of experiments using a small electric generator.

After the turbine, dynamo and other apparatus were set up and tested, the major problem they faced was how to attach the electrodes to the animal. How could the animal be made to hold still long enough? Where on the body should the wires be connected? After considering a number of techniques, they built an apparatus that consisted of a large pine box, the size and shape of a coffin, lined with zinc plates. They attached a copper bit to an ordinary leather dog muzzle so that the electrode could be forced between the dog's teeth. They attached one wire from the generator to the zinc lining of the box and the other to the copper bit in the muzzle. They put the dog into the box, attached the muzzle, filled the box with water and turned on the circuit.

The first results were unacceptable. Sometimes the dog didn't die, and sometimes the dog's body was burned so badly the room was filled with the stench of fried meat. They made a number of modifications to the equipment, changing the voltage, changing the amount of water, using different kinds of wires. They tried attaching the electrodes on different parts of the dog's body. Rockwell had a never-ending supply of animals to use as subjects of these experiments and offered them in the interest of science.

Eventually they moved their operations into a former police station in the downtown section of the city that was near enough to the arc light wires that they could use the city's high voltage lines instead of their lower power dynamo. Now they had thousands of volts to use in their experiments instead of a few hundred. They had to take greater precautions than before.

Eventually, through many months of trial and error on hundreds of animals they began to get consistent results and were able to set up a regular procedure to rid the city of its stray dogs by setting up a holding pen, a kind of death row, adjacent to the electrical death chamber in the old police station.

Although they were regularly successful now, the scientists continued to try different voltages and different amounts of current. They tried placing the electrodes on various parts of the dogs' bodies, searching for the fastest and most painless means of death. They kept careful notes of their experiments and published them in scientific journals.

Southwick's articles calling electrocution "the safest and kindest method of killing" drew widespread attention, not just from the SPCA and advocates of kindness to animals but from a wide cross section of the scientific community that was interested in anything that had to do with electricity. The studies about the biological effects of various voltages were widely read and commented on in scientific circles.

As Southwick, Rockwell and Fell got better at finding just the right amount of current and the correct location for the electrodes, they began to talk with their scientific friends about an expansion of the uses for their technique. If electricity could be used to get rid of unwanted animals, why couldn't the same apparatus be used to get rid of unwanted human beings? Could electrocution become a humane replacement for the gallows? At first this idea was dismissed as far-fetched and possibly cruel, but Southwick continued to advocate for this idea in scientific journals in 1882 and 1883, where it attracted the attention of scientists around the country.

The idea of using technology to develop a substitute for the gallows was not a new one. As early as the 1870s members of the Medico-Legal Society of New York and some scientists in Europe had suggested using a lethal injection as a means of capital punishment. It was described as a quick, painless and certain means of death that had many advantages over the ancient practice of hanging. It was Southwick, however, who seems to have first come up with the idea of using electricity for this purpose and was known at the turn of the century as "the father of electrocution."

Southwick, who had used the body weight of dogs to calculate the amount of electricity that was needed to cause death, began to make new calculations based on the average weight of human beings. It was little more than a mathematical problem, he explained, based on size and weight, and the voltage and amperage could be calculated fairly precisely. Then he took a look at the kind of apparatus that might be necessary for putting it into practice. Killing a person, he recognized, required a bit more dignity than killing an animal, so placing a man into a water-filled coffin and forcing a copper muzzle into his mouth was not the answer.

During his animal experiments, Southwick had discovered that it was not necessary to fill the box with water to force the electricity through the dog's body. The body's own fluids were enough to conduct the electricity from one electrode to the other. All that was really necessary was to find two places on the body to attach the electrodes so that the current passed through the main part of the body, including the head and the spine.

There were many ways this could have been done, and they all probably would have worked about as well. The victim could have been clamped to a wall that had the electrodes already in place, or a person could be made to stand on a metal plate with the second electrode attached to the victim's head. One early diagram published by the Medico-Legal Society showed a man in a kind of cabinet with electrodes attached to his head and feet. Or the electrodes could have been attached to a table, like

Before the electric chair was designed, engineers came up with this idea for an "electric closet." The electrodes would have been connected at the head and to a plate the man stood on. (*New York Medico-Legal Society Journal*, 1888)

a hospital gurney, on which the condemned man would be forced to lie down and be strapped in.

As a dentist, however, Southwick was most familiar with a particular way of treating his patients, and that's why there were never any serious proposals for an "electric chamber," an "electric table" or an "electric wall." Southwick knew from experience that a chair had many advantages when dealing with a patient who had mixed feelings about the procedure that was about to take place. A chair put the patient in a position that made it easy for the dentist to reach his or her body. It was possible to strap the patient in if necessary. If the patient lost consciousness the body tended to stay where it had been placed.

As the idea of electrocution as a replacement for the gallows entered public debate in the middle part of the 1880s, the use of electricity for this purpose, thanks to Southwick, became synonymous with a chair. It was the first mention of an "electric" chair.

The early illustrations of the chair show it to resemble a dentist's chair more than a barber's chair or a dining room chair. The victims were always shown in a reclining position with the executioner standing over them holding the switch. Southwick suggested that one electrode be attached to a metal helmet that would be placed on the condemned person's head and the other electrode to a footrest, allowing the electricity to flow from the scalp to the foot when it was turned on. It would simply be a matter of strapping the convict in, attaching the electrodes and pulling the switch.

It was, of course, only a theory, and there was no way for Southwick to test it because there was no supply of stray humans as there was of stray dogs. Understanding how an idea advocated by an obscure Buffalo dentist with no experience in capital punishment could change the history of criminal justice in the United States requires a look at the state of capital punishment and the ancient art of hanging as it existed in the 1880s.

—2—
The Hangman's
Terrible Legacy

While Southwick and his friends continued their experiments on stray dogs in Buffalo in 1883 and the public's fascination with all things electrical continued to grow, there was one more link in the chain of events that led directly to William Kemmler's appointment with the electric chair in Auburn. Although it ebbed and flowed as events and public attitudes changed, the movement to abolish the death penalty had been gaining strength throughout the nineteenth century. The "anti-gallows movement," as it was sometimes called, was a disorganized collection of progressive ministers, intellectuals, reformers, newspaper editors, legislators, philanthropists, wives of millionaires and even a few misguided fanatics, all united in what they knew to be a noble cause.

The energy that drove this movement was the public's disgust with the brutality of hanging, the method of capital punishment used by nearly every county sheriff in states that had not outlawed the practice. During the first half of the century hangings were conducted in public, often in town squares or public parks, as a kind of morality lesson for those who might be tempted by the criminal life. By the 1880s most states had outlawed public hangings, largely in response to the public outcry, but they were still conducted in private, usually within the grounds of the county jail, sometimes on a scaffold and sometimes using a sturdy tree that had been grown inside the jailhouse grounds for that purpose. Because hangings were conducted at the county level during this period, there are no reliable statistics about how many criminals were hanged, but estimates are that there were several hundred a year.

Editors had discovered that sheriffs usually permitted newspaper reporters to witness these executions, and the detailed and gruesome stories that were printed about them, more than any other factor, gave new life to the abolitionist movement. Every time a graphic description of a hanging was printed in a newspaper, the local abolitionist movement was flooded with volunteers and contributions.

And a horrible death it was. The best a condemned person could hope for was a broken neck as the rope yanked him or her by the neck up into the air. But in the vast number of cases, the neck was not broken and the victim's agony lasted several minutes, sometimes as long as a dozen minutes, as he or she was slowly strangled to death. The bodies of most hanging victims wiggled and convulsed during this time, in what newspaper reporters called "the dance of death."

In the United States the usual method of hanging was to throw the rope over the arm of a wooden pillar that was constructed on a scaffold in the jail yard. A weight was tied to one end of the rope, and the other end was tied around the victim's neck. When the sheriff gave the nod, the hangman would let the weight fall from the scaffold to the ground, which would pull the rope up over the arm taking the condemned person into the air by the neck. Among the hangman's jobs were to estimate the weight of the victim so an adequate counterweight could be selected for the job.[1]

A different method was used in England, where the rope was tied to the top of the beam and the victim was forced to stand over a trapdoor. When the trapdoor was thrown open the victim fell through the hole, suspended by the neck.

Despite its brutality, hanging was the official method of capital punishment used by every state that had not banned it, as well as in Britain and the former British colonies. Although its origins are obscure, it is known to have replaced crucifixion as the official method of execution during the reign of the Roman emperor Constantine. Its use in England dates back to the origins of common law. By the eighteenth century there were over 100 offenses in England that carried the death penalty, including pickpocketing. These codes were inherited by America along with other English laws. In the Massachusetts Bay Colony the civil code prescribed the death penalty for convictions of witchcraft, idolatry, blasphemy, bestiality, sodomy, man-stealing, false witness and cursing.

Until the middle of the nineteenth century hangings were not only performed in public but were turned into a kind of public festival, where all were invited to become witnesses to justice in action. Young children were let out of school for the day and encouraged to attend as a kind of moral lesson: this is what happens to bad little boys and girls. Descriptions of these early–nineteenth century hangings read more like county fairs than acts of the criminal justice system. Vast numbers of people came to town from the distant corners of the county to see them. In 1827 so many people attended a hanging in Cooperstown, New York, that a viewing stand collapsed, killing two people and injuring many more. The execution of murderer Jesse Strang in Albany in 1827 drew a crowd estimated at between 30,000 to 40,000 people!

Such vast crowds of people were bonanzas for merchants, who set up booths along the streets offering food, drink and souvenirs. Homeowners and landlords with a good view of the scaffold sold admission to upstairs rooms. Some even sold standing room on their rooftops. Printing offices did their part by turning out "broadsides," small posters or handbills sold by boys in the streets, that described in great detail the condemned person's crimes and the lives of the victims. Sometimes these broadsides contained pictures and a forged version of the victim's confession, often in verse.

These hanging festivals were so popular that public officials were encouraged to prolong the ceremonies as long as possible, not only to increase the moral impact of the execution but to encourage spectators to stay longer and spend more money in the shops and souvenir stands. The condemned were often dressed in special costumes and led on elaborate processions, taking a roundabout route from the jail to the gallows. A band was sometimes employed to play requiem-like tunes and was often accompanied by the local militia in full uniform. Ministers delivered public prayers and led the crowd in the singing of hymns. The condemned person uttered final words to the boos and catcalls of the crowd before the hood was placed over his or her head. Then the mysterious figure of the hangman appeared, also hooded to protect his identity, to release the weight that sent the condemned off the ground and swinging at the end of the rope. Although some victims died instantly, it was more common for the ceremony to last several more minutes as the victim thrashed about in the air. When all movement stopped, the sheriff's deputies cut the body down and the doctor would appear to make the official pronouncement of death and listen to the wailings of the condemned person's family.

In the early nineteenth century, public executions were so common and so much a part of the culture that they were taken for granted. Words associated with hanging were part of the common language, with people referring to "gallows humor" and "hangman's noose" and "I'll be hanged!" Because hanging was such a public form of death, all kinds of legends and superstitions were associated with it. Hanged men used to be buried at the crossroads to ensure that their ghosts did not return to haunt the town. One of the tarot cards used in the telling of fortunes featured "the Hanged Man," usually shown to be a man hanged by his feet rather than his neck. The card is said to indicate the influence of evil forces outside the person's control.

Although there was no denying that hanging was a terrible death, advocates of the practice maintained that it was appropriate, since one of the functions of capital punishment was to avenge the wrong that the criminal had done to his victims and to act as a deterrent to those who might be tempted to commit similar crimes.

There were always those who felt otherwise, that hanging was simply a public brutality that had no place in a civilized society. By the middle of the century the abolitionists had scored some important victories. Michigan outlawed hanging in 1846, followed by Rhode Island in 1852 and Wisconsin in 1853. These states substituted life in prison for the death penalty for those convicted of serious crimes like murder.

Vermont and Maine passed laws that did not abolish hanging outright but required a one-year waiting period and a specific order from the governor before an execution could take place. This worked as a kind of de facto abolition, since few governors were willing to issue such execution orders. In many other states bills to abolish capital punishment were introduced and defeated by margins narrow enough to indicate a deep rift in public opinion.

The movement to abolish capital punishment was a favorite topic of newspaper editorials, Sunday sermons and public speeches. It was closely connected with other humanitarian efforts of that era, such as temperance, women's rights and especially slavery. Both sides of the debate made public figures of its leading writers and speakers. Edward Livingston of Louisiana was the most influential spokesman opposing hanging and the Rev. George B. Cheever of New York City was the foremost advocate of preserving the gallows.

When they could not get states to outlaw hanging, abolitionists often succeeded in getting legislatures to reduce the number of crimes that required the death penalty. Crimes like housebreaking, larceny and adultery were gradually removed from the list. By the middle of the century it was unusual for criminals to be executed for crimes other than murder, rape or kidnapping.

Both sides of the debate often used the Bible as the basis for their arguments, sprinkling their speeches with chapter and verse from the Old and New Testaments. One side argued that God demanded vengeance: an eye for an eye and a tooth for a tooth. The other side cited passages that outlawed the taking of any human life for any reason: "Thou shalt not kill." Many of the pamphlets and books published as part of the debate resembled theological tracts.

Edward Livingston, a former mayor and congressman from New York City who moved to Louisiana, broke this pattern when he used logic and reason in his arguments in favor of abolition. He suggested that the death penalty was not a deterrent to murder because in most cases the condemned had acted in a fit of passion in which there was no rational thought. He also documented cases in which innocent men had been executed by mistake and turned the deterrent argument on its ear by maintaining that juries, forced to choose between the death penalty and acquittal, often let guilty criminals go free rather then send them to the gallows.

Several New York governors, including Daniel D. Tompkins at the beginning of the century and Enos Throop a generation later, took the bold step of declaring their opposition to the death penalty. There was little support in the legislature, however, until 1832 when the Assembly appointed a committee to "inquire into the expediency" of the total abolition of hanging. Silas M. Stilwell of New York City, the chairman of the committee, recommended abolition in his report later that year. An abolition bill was introduced but never made it to a final reading. This was, however, the first of many such bills that would be introduced during the next century and a half. Two years later a similar bill was defeated in the Assembly by a vote of 49 to 37.

That same year another bill, introduced by Carlos Emmons of Erie County, called for executions to be conducted in private, out of the public's view. The bill was opposed not only by the advocates of capital punishment, who thought that public hangings were necessary to act as a proper deterrent to future criminals, but also by the abolitionists, who feared that if hangings were conducted in private the public outcry against them would diminish and their movement would suffer. With both sides opposing it, the bill failed.

In 1835 a nearly identical bill outlawing public executions was passed by the Senate and approved 66 to 20 in the Assembly. It was signed into law on May 9, 1835. Just as the abolitionists had feared, the immediate result was to diminish the public's opposition to the death penalty. Without public hangings there was no ready supply of new recruits to the movement. As far as the public seemed to be concerned, hanging was fine as long as they did not have to watch it.

In the 1840s Assemblyman John L. O'Sullivan of New York City, a fervent opponent of capital punishment, nearly succeeded in abolishing the practice. Aided by the New York Society for the Abolition of Capital Punishment and powerful newspaper editors like Horace Greeley and William Cullen Bryant, he waged a public relations battle in written and spoken form throughout the state. Their greatest opponents were ministers like Cheever, who preached from the pulpit that murderers deserved to die.

O'Sullivan advocated many of the humanitarian reforms of the time, but he singled out hanging as the one on which to focus his greatest efforts. In 1841 his committee produced a report that attacked hanging on both religious and secular grounds. This report was reprinted many times and mailed all over the country by opponents of capital punishment. Accompanying the report was an abolition bill that seemed certain to pass. O'Sullivan had more than enough votes lined up, but a number of pro-hanging clergymen came to Albany to lobby against the bill at the last minute. These clergymen convinced some assemblymen to stay home instead of attending a special night session at which the vote was to be taken. O'Sullivan could not stop the vote from taking place, and the bill was defeated 52 to 46.

During this period the battle over the death penalty was fought mainly from the pulpits, with more orthodox ministers crying out for justice and the necessity of the gallows while the more liberal clergymen preached compassion and human rights. Typical of the more orthodox ministers was the Rev. John N. McLeod of the Reformed Presbyterian Church of New York City, who preached that abolition was "most offensive to Jehovah" and warned that if hanging was outlawed then the practice of war might well be next.

"Men cannot disregard God's institutions without bringing injury on themselves," he preached. "The power of capital punishment and the exercise of that power, are necessary in society to assert, exemplify and vindicate the existence and sovereignty of God."

But it was Cheever, author of the influential anti-abolition book *Punishment by Death,* who was the unofficial leader of those battling to preserve capital punishment. Besides the religious arguments and biblical quotes that had been used for decades, and the arguments that a deterrent was needed to protect society from wanton murders, Cheever used both reason and logic in arguing his cause. He wrote, for example, that if murderers and burglars were to be punished the same way—with life in prison—it would encourage burglars to kill their victims so they could not testify against them.

Cheever and other ministers waged a full-scale lobbying effort in Albany for much of the 1840s, and when O'Sullivan's bill came up for a second vote in 1842 it was defeated by nearly the same margin as the year before, 54 to 45.

Public opinion turned against the abolitionists during the Mexican War in the late 1840s, apparently because during a time of war it becomes more difficult to advocate compassion for one's enemies. After the war the issue of slavery took over as the principal reform movement of the day. There was also an increase in crime during this period, some of it connected with an influx of immigrants, and that tended to influence public opinion in favor of hanging.

In 1860, however, the legislature passed a de facto abolition bill, like the one in Vermont and Maine, not as the result of any reform efforts but due almost entirely to the attention drawn to a frail, young and attractive woman named Mary Hartung. She had been married to a gruff saloon-keeper in Troy, New York, and stood accused of poisoning him. She was tried and convicted of murder, even though much of the evidence indicated that the murder had been the work of her lover.

Newspapers all over the state printed her picture and told her story in great detail, sometimes describing what her death on the gallows might be like. Gov. Edwin D. Morgan received a number of formal appeals to spare her life, but he told the newspapers that he could find no legal grounds for his interference. The case was then brought to the legislature where both houses voted to ask Morgan to reconsider his decision not to issue a pardon.

While the governor and the legislature battled back and forth on this issue, the anti-gallows advocates, who had been losing public support for nearly a decade, saw an opportunity. Although they had succeeded in getting bills introduced over the past several years, none had come close to being passed. This time there was a victim to rally around, and they took up Hartung's cause in newspaper columns and public speeches. Voters were urged to sign petitions to "Save Mrs. Hartung" by abolishing the gallows. As the date of her execution neared, the reformers stepped up their efforts.

The anti-gallows bill that had been introduced at the beginning of the session was amended so that it was more like the de facto Maine and Vermont laws that had, in effect, outlawed executions there. New York's law would require a one-year waiting period between conviction and execution, and the death warrant required the signature of the governor. This bill passed 94 to 9 in the Assembly and 20 to 8 in the Senate. The next day it was signed into law by the governor, thereby sparing Mrs. Hartung.

Or so they thought. In their haste to help Mrs. Hartung, the legislators found they had violated the state and national constitutions by passing an ex post facto law. The Constitution prohibited passing laws that set a punishment for a crime that was different from the one that was in effect at the time that the crime had been committed. In other words, if hanging was the punishment for murder when Mrs. Hartung poisoned her husband, then she had to be hanged no matter what laws the legislature passed afterwards. The court of appeals threw out the law the following

September and declared it null and void. Hanging was once more legal in New York State.

During the 1861 session an amended bill was introduced to correct the defects in the law. Assemblymen opposed to the gallows attempted at the last minute to substitute a bill that would abolish capital punishment outright, but this was defeated. By the end of the session the Assembly abolished the defective 1860 law but was unable to agree on a substitute. The courts complained that the legislature's intent was no longer clear, and the matter remained clouded for two years.

Finally, on April 10, 1862, Governor Morgan signed into law a bill passed by both houses that abolished the previous reform efforts and brought back the gallows. With the country at war once again, support for abolition of capital punishment was once more declining.

After the Civil War the movement to abolish hanging gained new energy from an unexpected place. Ever since public hangings had been outlawed in favor of quieter jail yard executions, the antihanging groups had been hampered by the fact that few members of the general public had actually witnessed one. A lot of gruesome accounts circulated, of course, but that was not the same as actually being there.[2]

Beginning in the late 1870s, newspaper editors around the country, always in search of stories that would increase their readership, discovered executions. Newspapers had always run stories about them, of course, but until then they had been brief and straightforward observations. Now, a new kind of execution story, full of detailed descriptions of sobbing mothers, the sound of the snapping of necks and the swaying of the bodies on the gallows, began to be published, first by the big city newspapers and then by small local papers as well. The new telegraph wire services allowed execution stories from far and near to be printed in every newspaper in the country. As big city newspapers began to compete more energetically with each other for readers and advertisers and the costs of equipment and salaries increased, so did the publishers' efforts to find the kinds of stories that increased readership and attracted advertisers.

Stories about executions were a perfect way to do this. They had always been popular, of course. Broadside sheets of ballads about murders, some containing verse or confessions, had been published for centuries. The vast crowds that used to flood into the public squares to witness public hangings now flocked to the newsstands to read the gruesome details of the terrible murderer's final moments. The *New York Times*, which was far from the worst exploiter of this trend, published 50 long and graphic descriptions of hangings in 1882 and another 41 in 1883.

On July 22, 1882, for example, the *Times* ran a long descriptive story about the demise of James F. Walsh, "a weak, illiterate fellow scarcely over 19 years of age," who was hanged in Brooklyn for the murder of Barbara Groenthal, a domestic servant. Walsh, a paint factory worker, was convicted of stabbing her with a knife after she refused his advances. After describing a last-minute meeting between Walsh and his sobbing mother, the *Times* reporter described the execution in detail: "The gallows—the same which has frequently been used in the Tombs yard and at other prisons—had been erected in the extreme end of the corridor and before Walsh's mother retired from the jail she went to the gallows and closely examined the structure. She betrayed no excitement as she looked at it and stepped into the executioner's box and gazed at the ropes and weights with the utmost composure."[3]

The reporter then told about a last meeting with two priests, who conducted a mass in his cell. Walsh's final meal was described along with what he wore to the gallows. Then there was a discussion of how his possessions would be distributed and a reading of the death warrant.

According to the *Times*, between 300 and 400 spectators were allowed into the jail yard to watch. They were kept 50 feet away from the gallows, but stood on the ground around the scaffold and were allowed to stand on the balconies of the three upper tiers of cells. Desks were arranged for the reporters on the galleries of the second tier of cells. There were many more potential spectators outside the prison, kept under control by a detachment of police. At 10 A.M. the ceremony began:

> The hangman placed the black cap on Walsh's head, the noose around his neck, and pinioned his arms. Then the Sheriff and his Deputies formed in procession and with Walsh walking between the two clergymen, the march to the gallows was begun. The clergymen read from their prayer books. Walsh was very slender and taller than the clergymen. His face was as white as the whitewash on the great walls of the jail. His eyes were closed and he did not open them to look about him either on the way to the gallows or when he reached it. The clergymen supported him and his lips moved as though in prayer, but his words were inaudible a few feet from him.
>
> When he stood under the beam, Sheriff Stegman said to him: "Do you wish to say anything?" and Walsh, evidently thinking that he was addressed by one of the clergymen, answered, "No, Father, nothing at all."
>
> The crucifix was held to Walsh's lips and he repeatedly kissed it. Then the noose was adjusted, the knot was placed under his left ear and the signal was given. There was no waste of time about any of the arrangements. The next sound was the executioner's ax on the rope holding the weight and Walsh's body darted at an angle, like a rocket toward one of the upright posts and swung back and forth with great force to a position under the center of the beam. His lower arms went up towards his

face and there was a movement as though he was trying to clasp his hands together. Then his hands slowly dropped to his sides, his breast was thrown forward momentarily and there were no other convulsions.

The rope was cut at precisely 10:05. Seven minutes later Dr. A. W. Shepard, the county physician, felt Walsh's pulse and reported that it beat 40 to the minute. Two minutes later there was no pulse and at 10:32 there was no action of the heart. Dr. Shepard said that unconsciousness and insensibility occurred almost instantly at the time the rope was cut and that Walsh was dead within nine minutes.

An autopsy showed that despite the fact that this had been "the easiest death on the gallows according to those who had witnessed many hangings," Walsh's neck had not been broken and he had strangled to death.

There were endless ways of constructing these stories. The condemned man was dead, so the press was free to say anything it wanted about him. Sometimes the murderer or rapist was described as a terrible monster and the execution article became a story of justice, with the victim finally getting revenge. Or, in another variation, perhaps there was some doubt about whether the murderer was actually guilty. That made an even better story. Would some unexpected witness show up at the last minute? Would the governor spare him at the last minute? Would the condemned man finally confess?

The morbid attraction of these kinds of stories and the public's hunger for them created a huge market. Then as now the public could not get enough of this kind of thing, and newspapers found they could print column after column of them without fear of ever boring their readers. This morbid fascination with executions is not unfamiliar in our time, over a century later, when reporters wait outside the prison walls, interview the families of the victims and print every possible detail of the crimes and the murderer's personal life.

One of the unintended effects of this attention was a renaissance for the antihanging movement. When executions were conducted in public they sometimes drew crowds in the tens of thousands, but now millions of people around the world read about each one only a few hours after the body was cut down from the gallows. Anyone with a few pennies could have the kind of gallows-side seat that was in so much demand during the days of public executions.

The details of executions, once confined to the jail yards, had now been brought into the homes of nearly every American family. The stories inflamed the old controversies over capital punishment and polarized the public's attitude. The more conservative readers found in them a kind of comfort in knowing that justice was being done, that murderers were being punished and that future criminals were being given a graphic warning. Other readers were so horrified and disturbed by them that they signed anti-gallows petitions and wrote their legislators urging them to ban the practice.

Some newspaper editors who were in favor of capital punishment ran editorials defending the practice. The *New York Times* editors said on December 17, 1887, that "only a small minority of Americans are in favor of abolishing capital punishment, but they are so vocal and persistent that several states have abolished the death penalty. These experiments do not seem to be a success.

"It is easy to argue that imprisonment for life ought really to be more terrible than death on the scaffold, but as a matter of fact it is not so terrible or so deterrent.... There is always the hope of escape. Few of these convicts take their own lives, which they would do if they truly thought death was better than imprisonment."

Newspapers with a flair for sensationalism like the *New York World* or the *New York Sun* were not above exploiting the public's fascination with executions. The more conservative newspapers like the *New York Herald* felt compelled to join this trend. For example, in its November 12, 1887, edition, the *Herald* gave this account of the public hanging of four anarchists named Parsons, Engel, Spies and Fischer who killed two policemen in Chicago:

> Then there was a click, a rattling crash, and in a second four white heads hung on a level with the scaffold. Parsons' body hung motionless for a minute. The drop was about four feet six inches and the shock to the medulla of the vertebrae of the neck paralyzed motion. Then some grotesque struggles supervened, and the lithe frame of the anarchist swayed frightfully at the end of the rope. His neck was not broken, and the horrors of a death from strangulation occurred. The folds of the shroud heaved and twisted agonizingly, and the less hardened lookers-on pitied the dying anguish of the sufferer as his chest heaved in the involuntary efforts of the lungs to obtain air. The convulsions continued a few minutes. They suddenly ceased. All was still, and Parsons' soul went thence to test the question whether "humanity" is the God-head of the universe.
>
> Engel's fall must have broken his thick, short, bull neck. The heavy body severely tried the cord when the drop occurred, but the sheriff's test of strength had been wisely conducted.... Fischer hung limp for a few seconds, and then some weak convulsive throbbing partially disarranged his white face cap. A horrible spectacle was presented by the instantaneous glimpse I was enabled to obtain of the anarchist's mouth. The tongue protruded and was clenched between the teeth. A purple

shade suffused the lower portion of the face and the horror of a dying agony by strangulation was apparent.... Spies' body went through some ghastly contortions at the noose's end.... His head wagged toward the people on the floor as if imploring aid. The struggle grew sharper and sharper until finally, when the spectators began to wonder if they would ever cease, the form straightened out and, so far as human vengeance is concerned, the spirits of the murdered policemen were appeased.

Another theme ran through these graphic stories of hangings in the 1880s, and one that was to have a direct connection with the invention of the electric chair. Many of them were bungled. Ideally, the initial shock of the fall was supposed to break the condemned's neck, but strangulation was a common occurrence. Because hanging was such an uncertain and inexact means of death, it took a skillful executioner to make sure everything went well. The knot had to be tied correctly and carefully placed near the condemned's ear. The equipment had to be in proper shape to ensure that the rope would not break and the trap door would open properly. There were also precautions to be taken to help ensure that the prisoner would not be tortured. There were many cases when the convicted man managed to stand on the edge of the trapdoor or grab onto the hangman at the last minute.

During the time when executions were held in private this did not matter much because it could all be done over again and no one would know. But with newspaper reporters watching so carefully, bungled hangings quickly became a national sensation, fanning public dissatisfaction with the whole process.

On July 13, 1882, for example, the *St. Paul Pioneer Press* in Minnesota printed this account of the hanging in Sioux Falls, Dakota Territory, of Thomas Eagan, a convicted wife killer:

> The black cap was adjusted and a nervous Sheriff sprung the trap prematurely, the body striking the ground with a sickening thud. The heavy weight of the prisoner—180 pounds—proved too much for the rope, which had not been properly tested. The contortions of the prisoner were terrible as he gasped and groaned upon the ground. When the first shocks of amazement on the part of the executioner and his attendants had subsided they leaped from the platform, seized the struggling prisoner, dragged him back through the jail, up the platform and back on to the drop, the rope in the meantime dangling after them. The severed rope was tied together, the prisoner dumped on the drop, the trap was sprung as before and with the same result. This ghastly spectacle was again repeated for the third time, the prisoner in the meantime gradually losing consciousness. At the third break, the physicians pronounced the prisoner dead and the spectators felt as much relief as the victim. This was the first execu-

tion in the Territory of Dakota and it will probably be the last of that kind....[4]

The execution of convicted murderer Col. John Bridges near Louisville, Kentucky, on July 1, 1882, demonstrated another way that hangings could be bungled. According to a wire report printed in the *New York Times*, the hanging occurred before "the largest crowd ever assembled in this county."[5]

> It was a plain wooden structure with a spring trap. At the foot of the gallows the doomed man exhibited considerable nervousness, but met the ordeal bravely. Bridges took his stand on the trap, the black cap was drawn over his face, the noose adjusted on his neck, Sheriff Boyd with a quick motion of his foot sprung the trap, and with a dull, heavy thud the body fell. At the instant of the fall the noose, which had been very carefully adjusted, slipped. The poor wretch struggled terribly and succeeded in freeing his hands and feet from the cords with which they had been pinioned. He made a desperate struggle to get upon the gallows again, but was pushed back, and suffered a horrible death by strangulation.... There was no demonstration at the scaffold, except that one or two Negro women fainted, and some groans were heard.

Even the most enthusiastic supporters of the death penalty found these reports appalling. Capital punishment was not supposed to be public torture. While abolitionists wanted to outlaw it, advocates cried out for more expertise on the part of the hangman. The bungled hangings that drew the most attention were the ones in big cities, like the hanging of Augustus D. Leighton at the Tombs in New York City on May 18, 1882. The report printed in the *New York Times* the next day explained the precautions that were taken. The reporter noted that a new rope had been purchased for the occasion and that the weights used had been adjusted to prevent a strangulation like one that had occurred on the same gallows a few months before.[6]

The weights relied on to break the neck of Sindram weighed but 35 pounds and proved too light," the *Times* reporter wrote. "To guard again the repetition of the blunder which occurred in that execution, 416 poun of solid iron were attached to the rope from which Leighton was to ha The hangman, a medium-sized man with sandy mustache and goatee, wearing a slouch hat, sauntered up and down on the prison yard i chilling air of the cloudy morning. He was joined occasionally by h and assistant, the man who was to cut the rope holding the weigh thus give the death blow to the waiting wretch within the prison."

A large crowd gathered outside the Franklin Street entranc prison, even though all they could see were the high prison wall

100 people with special passes were permitted inside. Then the man in the slouch hat tied Leighton's arms and legs, put the black cap over his head and adjusted the noose.

The reporter went to great lengths to describe the hangman's procedure for placing the noose right under Leighton's chin, "the theory of the hangman, based on personal experience, being that the knot would slip round and under the right ear when the noose was suddenly tightened by fall of the weights."

"But when the rope was cut and Leighton sprung six feet into the air as the weights fell, it was apparent that he was not to die cleanly: Leighton hung with his head thrown back and the knot pressing on his throat. The body at first hung straight and rigid, but the wheezing and heavy breathing of the man could be heard by the spectators 20 feet away. Suddenly the right foot began to twitch and then the right leg was raised into the air and turned and twisted as though the man was suffering torments. It was very apparent that Leighton was strangling to death, and everybody but the doctors turned away from the sickening sight. For fully three minutes the contortions of the body continued, and then it straightened out, and the only sign of life visible was the heaving of the breast and the occasional twitch of the hand."

It became increasingly difficult for advocates of capital punishment
defend these public tortures, and many began to suggest alternatives,
h as the guillotine that was used in France or a firing squad, as was
in some other countries. Physicians and scientists, however, sug-
there might be a way to use technology as a substitute for hang-
y suggested that a condemned man might be given some kind of
lethal injection to cause death. Science had solved so many
rn problems, why not this one? This attitude was clearly
ublic opinion. The *New York Herald* commented about it in
blished on August 10, 1884:

entenced to die for murder was slowly strangled in Brooklyn
y, to the great horror of all who witnessed and all who read
on. An almost similar occurrence took place in Maryland
y and during the year many such blundering executions
hen they occur there is a spasm of disgust and anger and
dropped. It is time that the public came to some sen-
the subject. If it is desirable that the infliction of
hould be terrifying, then there ought to be system-
hat end. In such case the old method of drawing
revived; or we might torture our criminals slowly
s, our predecessors, used to do. Indeed there
he infliction of capital punishment could be
that is the wish and desire of the public.

On the other hand, if the American people have ceased to believe that mere rigor and cruelty are deterrents ... then beyond doubt society is under obligation to see to it that capital punishment is not lingering torture....

The gallows, however, is certainly a clumsy and very uncertain mode of killing. It cannot be compared, as regards promptness and certainty, with the guillotine or the garrote, for example. The guillotine, in fact, is, save in one respect, an ideal instrument of justice. The exception is that it mutilates the body and sheds the blood; considerations not by any means fatal to its superiority, but still regarded as objectionable by many minds.

But Science stands ready to provide Justice with a number of perfectly expeditious, neat and non-disfiguring homicidal methods. It is quite easy to devise a plan by which the death of a murderer would be instantaneous, and into which neither the horrible nor the grotesque would enter. At present the usage is simply barbarous. Such revolting scenes as that at the execution of Jefferson are not uncommon and sometimes worse things happen. A few years ago at an execution in California the culprit's head was pulled off. Such scenes fill the public mind with a sense of indignation against the officers of justice....

Such executions ... only produce the impression that a judicial murder has been committed. But if death of the prisoner were painless and prompt; if the execution were freed from the revolting accessories of the gallows ... it cannot be doubted that the moral effect would be very much greater than now. And if we accept the doctrine that society has nothing to do with revenge, it is difficult to perceive how adherence to the gallows can be excused or defended, since it is clear that instrument is conspicuously inefficient, and that those who die by it are exposed frequently to protracted physical suffering.

The conservatism which clings to a notoriously bad habit only because it is a habit, is not deserving of respect, and in the case of the gallows this appears to be the main explanation of the reluctance to make a change. Such a change, nevertheless, is demanded in the name and interests of civilization; and seeing that improvement in the mode of inflicting capital punishment is easily accessible, public opinion ought to insist upon reform without further delay.

The editors did not specify which alternatives to the gallows they had in mind, but members of the New York Medico-Legal Society, made up of New York doctors and lawyers, had published in their journal results on experiments in Europe in which animals had been given lethal injections of drugs that brought about nearly instant and painless death. They had suggested that this might be an alternative to hanging.

Southwick had by this time published the results of his own experiments with dogs and began to suggest in his writings that electrocution might be the best solution to the problem of finding a replacement for the gallows. Quick and painless, he wrote, electrocution would be the modern way of executing criminals. It could be accomplished without the spilling of blood and without torture. It was, he insisted, the most humane of all the methods being considered.

Just as news of Southwick's work was reaching the scientific community and just three months after the *Herald*'s urgent plea for reform, the most famous bungled hanging story of all made headlines around the world.

John "Babacombe" Lee attracted international attention from lurid newspaper reports describing him as "the man they could not hang." Lee, 18, was a former British sailor who took a job as a servant and laborer at a seaside mansion called "The Glen" on the south coast of England. Miss Keyse, the owner of the Glen, had been a maid of honor at the marriage of Queen Victoria and the royal family had once stayed at the house. On November 14, 1884, the house caught fire and Miss Keyes was found stabbed to death. Lee, the only man in the house at the time, was tried, convicted and sentenced to hang at Exeter Prison.[7]

On Sunday, February 22, 1885, the day of his execution, he received his last rites, wrote some final letters and was led out to the prison yard, where a shed with a rope dangling from the roof beam awaited him. The executioner, named Berry, showed him a spot to stand over the trapdoor. Berry then put a leather strap around his ankles, and Lee could see reporters looking into the shed through the windows while the minister read the prayers for the dead. Then Berry placed a pillowcase with an elastic opening over Lee's head so he could not see.

"I had thought I looked my last on the light of day," wrote Lee in his memoirs, as published by *Lloyd's Weekly News* in England and many other newspapers. Then the rope was placed around his neck and Lee could feel it being pulled tight, pinching the skin on his neck. Berry asked if he had anything to say.

"No," said Lee. "Drop away!"

"I held my breath and clenched my teeth. I heard the chaplain's voice. I heard the clang of the bell. I heard a wrench of a bolt drawn, and—My heart beat! Was this death? Or was it only a dream? A nightmare? What was this stamping going on? Good heavens. I was still on the trap. It would not move!"

The trap door had opened only about two inches and then had stuck fast. It had rained the day before, and the wood had apparently swollen from the moisture. Even the weight of the executioner would not allow it to open. For six minutes Lee stood there on the tips of his toes in the dark while members of the death party jumped on the door together in an attempt to get it to open.

"Such an ordeal would be enough to kill most men, I suppose," said Lee later. "But I remained perfectly quiet and at last I was led off the trap."

Berry removed the cap, rope and straps and Lee was taken to a small room adjacent to the shed. Meanwhile a guard held the rope and jumped on the trap door, which finally opened.

"I could hear them pulling the bolt backwards and forwards," said Lee, "and each time there was a thud as the trap was released and fell inwards. You can imagine that these preparations were not pleasant to listen to. Nevertheless they did not break down my courage. They simply made me more anxious to get it all over."

At the end of four minutes, Berry came to Lee and apologized for the problems then led him back into the shed. Berry replaced the strap, the hood and the rope. Then the bolt was thrown once again.

"When the drop gave way I felt as though my terrible fall into space had begun," said Lee. "The shock took away my breath. I wanted to put out my hands and grasp something. It seemed as if my heart was leaping out of my body. But death had not come yet. I sank two inches just as before and there I remained."

Again the executioner and the guards jumped on the trapdoor, but it would not budge. They screamed at each other but nothing happened. Finally Lee was led back from the trap door. The cap was left over his head and the rope around his neck.

"I had prayed to be delivered from these men's hands," said Lee, "and something told me He was answering my prayer. But it was terrible to have to stand there and listen to the attempts that were being made to make the scaffold go."

Guards were called in to saw away a portion of the door where it was sticking. They used saws and an ax. Lee could see none of this, but he heard the sounds of it. After five minutes he was placed on the trap for a third time and the bolt was drawn. There was a jerk and the trap door stuck fast with Lee standing on his toes. There was a stamping on the boards and then, finally, the rope, hood and strap were removed. Lee went back to the adjacent room where he was offered a glass of brandy, which he refused.

"My poor fellow," said Berry with tears in his eyes, "you have had to suffer."

When Berry attempted to take off the straps on Lee's arms he resisted, saying he wanted to be hanged, that he wanted it to be over.

It was then that the chaplain looked him in the eye and said, "I suppose, my poor fellow, you know that by the laws of England they can't put you on the scaffold again?"

Lee said he had never heard of this law and he was too upset to understand what it meant. An ancient law, that had apparently never been enforced, forbade more than three attempts at hanging. The intention seemed to have been that after three attempts at hanging it was supposed that some kind of divine intervention had taken place and the condemned man was under some kind of protection that should not be interfered with.

Within minutes the news of Lee's fate was telegraphed to newspapers all over the world, where it created a sensation. Questions about the reliability of hanging were brought up in the House of Commons. In New York this news appeared on the front pages of newspapers and added tremendous ammunition to the two now quite separate groups of reformers: those who felt that capital punishment should be abolished and those who felt that some more reliable method of execution needed to be found.

Three days later, the *New York Tribune*, in commenting on Lee's case, said, "The horrible story of the three-times-repeated failure to hang a murderer in England ought to direct public attention wherever the gallows is in use, to the untrustworthiness of that method of inflicting capital punishment. If a careful collation were made of all the cases of like failure which had occurred in the English speaking countries even during the past 20 years the record would shock the least sensitive. If also the cases in which death on the gallows had resulted from slow strangulation, the inhumanity of the punishment would appear incontestable."

Two years later, on February 29, 1887, the newspapers reported the unusual hanging of a woman, Roxalana Druse in Herkimer, New York. No woman had been hanged in the state in 39 years, and her death came just as opposition to the death penalty was reaching a crescendo. Despite the bitterly cold weather, hundreds of local people gathered outside the stone jail on Main Street across from the courthouse.[8]

Mrs. Druse had been convicted of shooting her husband then taking an ax and chopping off his head. She then cut his body into pieces and burned them in the stove. Her case had become famous, not just because she was a woman but because she wrote poetry from her jail cell while waiting for her appointment on the gallows. On the day of her execution she gave out copies of her last work:

> Who will care when I am gone.
> And the birds' music hushed,
> In the twilight dim and gloomy?
>
> Who my name will softly whisper,
> Who for me will kindly pray,
> When at last death has its way?

Mrs. Druse, who had long, dark hair, wore a brand-new dress to the gallows. It was described as being of black satin with ruffles at the bottom and especially narrow so that she could maintain her modesty while being suspended from the gallows. The satin blouse was tight fitting, and there was a bouquet of roses, a gift from her daughter, pinned to it.

The gallows consisted of two upright poles and a cross pole. It had been painted black when it arrived in Herkimer from another county, but the deputies had painted it white, apparently in an attempt to make it more suitable for a woman, but the *Times* reporter said it only "rendered it more deathly looking." There were 12 notches carved in the side of one of the upright poles, one for every person who had died on it.

The rope and the noose were already hanging from the scaffold when Mrs. Druse was led to a wooden platform beneath it. Only 12 official witnesses and a number of reporters and deputies had been permitted inside the jail yard, which was covered in snow in the bright sunshine.

Sheriff Delavan D. Cook stood next to the scaffold and asked Mrs. Druse if she had any last words, but she deferred to Dr. Powell, the minister who had visited her many times in her cell. He said he had a message that he wanted delivered to "the whole world" through the reporters who had gathered there.

"I am not here as a party to this ghastly scheme," he said of the execution. "I have no manner of sympathy with it. It seems to me out of place in the civilization of our day and incompatible with the sweet spirit of our Christian religion and I can but hope that the humane people of our beloved land will from this dark day sweep the law of punishment by death into everlasting oblivion!"

Then the black cap that had been attached to the back of her dress was pulled over her face, and the witnesses heard her shriek. The noose was put around her neck, and the sheriff gave the signal. The weight at the other end of the rope was let go, and she hung there suspended in the cold sunshine. As with many hangings it did not go quickly or smoothly. Her neck was not broken and it took 15 minutes for her to strangle to death.

By then the question of whether the gallows should at last be abolished was being debated in public speeches, in government halls, from pulpits, in newspaper editorials and in homes.

Dr. Lyman Abott, editor of the *Christian Union* newspaper in New York City, said it was the duty of every civilized community to abolish capital punishment, but Dr. Harold Crosby, another prominent New York City minister, said the fear of death is a deterrent to criminals and when it is abolished crime increases.[9]

"That capital punishment has failed of its purpose of late years is the fault of the law, not of the system," Dr. Crosby told the *New York Herald.*

Dr. George H. Houghton, minister of the Little Church Around the Corner in New York City, said the scriptures clearly supported the death penalty in the passage, "He who sheds man's blood shall his blood be shed."

Anthony Comstock, the crusader against evil in many forms as head of the Society for the Suppression of Vice, said he was strongly opposed to abolition of the death penalty.

"It would never do to do away with capital punishment," he said. "If imprisonment for life were to be substituted for the death penalty, murders would, in my opinion, increase at a fearful rate. Imprisonment for life would in fact be no punishment for our criminal classes. If we hung quicker after conviction and without so much delay it would be better. A prompter way of dealing with criminals would be for the good of the community."

William F. Howe, a criminal lawyer in New York City who had defended hundreds of murderers, said he was opposed to capital punishment because of its impact on juries. Unless they were certain of a defendant's guilt, he said, they did not want to send him to the gallows.

"Out of 600 cases which I have defended where homicide was charged," he said, "I have lost but eight. That shows how difficult it is to convict in these cases. Capital punishment should be abolished. There is no use for it. It is not detersive; never has been and never will be. I favor imprisonment for life. There should be no power to pardon in these cases. Let the convicted murderer be sent to a living tomb and kept there. That would be punishment indeed."

Belva Lockwood, one of the few women lawyers in New York City, said she was uncertain of her views on capital punishment but was definitely opposed to hanging. Of the alternatives that had been suggested up to that time, she said she favored electrocution.

City recorder Smythe, who was in charge of the criminal records in the city, called the abolition of capital punishment "stupendous nonsense." "The men who propose [abolition of capital punishment] know nothing whatever of the kind of men who would be encouraged by a law that would do away with the death penalty.... My experience is that it would work disaster on the community. I am not sure that it would be safe to walk the streets of New York were capital punishment abolished.... Capital punishment may not prevent men from committing murder when they are in a condition of great mental excitement, but it will prevent cold blooded and deliberate murders. And for that reason alone the law should stand."

Two of the city's judges who dealt with criminals were unwavering in their full support of the death penalty. Judge Barrett said that he lived in "a somewhat sentimental age" but that he "had no doubt that the abolition of capital punishment would result in multiplying homicide to such a degree as would startle the community. I go further and say that capital punishment is essential to the preservation of human life." Barrett said he thought capital punishment was favored by most people, and he based that opinion on the comments of jurors that he interviewed before murder cases. "Few men care to sit as jurors in murder cases," he said. "Only one fifth of those men who are called to serve on juries claim to be opposed to the death penalty, although by such a claim they would be excused from duty."

Judge Cowing said he was not only in favor of capital punishment but added that he thought it might be a good idea to bring back the whip as well. "It is the fashion just now to consider that it is cruel to inflict physical pain on a criminal," he said. "Now I believe that by the infliction of a certain amount of physical pain on a certain class of our criminals the community would be benefited. If some of the younger criminals who are constantly coming before me again and again in court were to be thoroughly and publicly whipped by the authorities they would not come before me so often…. Human life cannot be held too dear and when it is wantonly taken life should be exacted for life."

Dr. Thomas DeWitt Talmage, pastor of the Central Presbyterian Church in Brooklyn, whose sermons were reprinted in newspapers all over the country, was the only person interviewed who mentioned electricity as an alternative. Although he had once been in favor of capital punishment, he said, he believed that the execution of murderers was unnecessary in a society that had prisons that seemed to be escape proof.

"This much I will say," said Talmage, "if we are to inflict the death penalty we should do it in the least painful manner. I have long favored and publicly advocated killing by electricity. Indeed, I think there is even a better method. If an overdose of some powerful anesthetic were given to the condemned man so that he would quietly fall asleep and never awaken again in this world I would be in favor of that plan. It is not necessary to inflict pain and the inflicting of it serves no purpose. If we are to have the death penalty inflicted at all let there be no horrors. Whether we should have it inflicted at all is a question with which I am in debate with myself."

Most prophetic of all were the editors of *Harper's Magazine*, who, after describing a hanging, wondered what Americans from the year 2000 would think about the practice from their more civilized time:

We are led to wonder if the time will ever arrive when the gallows shall be placed as a curiosity in museums and sightseers shall flock to gaze upon it and marvel how a people who gave evidence of so much civilization and refinement ... could have employed such a machine.... Will posterity shudder at a model of a gallows set up in complete working order on a shelf? Will the American of the year of our Lord 2000 be so far in advance of us? We venture to hope so.

In the meanwhile, since without present lights we find nothing better to do with a murderer than to hang him, why may not merciful ingenuity devise some method of execution that shall not so very closely resemble the revolting act which the criminal expiates? It is perhaps a little significant that the gallows is the only piece of machinery that has stood stock-still in this era of progress. There it stands, the same clumsy, inefficient, inhuman thing it was when it first lifted its ghastly framework into the air of the dark ages. If we must use it, let us see to it that it be adjusted with at least as much accuracy as the average apple peeler."[10]

Clearly the public was ready for a change, but should capital punishment be abolished or could a better method be found? The stage was set for the entrance of Dr. Southwick's invention.

— 3 —
The Death
Commission

T he obsession of an obscure Buffalo dentist, even one with influential friends, would normally have had little impact on the state legislature in Albany. But in 1885, the year that the story of "Babacombe" Lee's terrible experience made headlines around the world, there was a growing sentiment for reform. The world of scaffolds, nooses and hangmen was beginning to seem out of place in a country that had outlawed slavery, built a transcontinental railroad and was making daily inroads in science, medicine and mechanical inventions.

Opposition to hanging, however, did not necessarily mean opposition to the death penalty, and many politicians and ministers were careful to make that distinction. There was a delicate political game being played. The increased publicity about hangings, especially the bungled ones, was giving new ammunition to the reformers who had for decades been attempting to abolish capital punishment. Abolitionist groups that had been dormant for years were suddenly signing up new members. At the top levels of government, especially in New York, abolitionists seemed much too radical to be taken seriously.

Meanwhile the hard-core defenders of capital punishment, who believed that the death penalty was essential to protect law and order, avenge murderers and act as a deterrent, dug in their heels and insisted that the death penalty was supposed to be cruel and brutal. That was the whole point, they said.

In the 1880s a third group arose that thought of itself as providing the obvious and rational compromise between the two extremes. They agreed with the abolitionists that it was time to "abolish the rope" but didn't want to abolish the death penalty. They wanted to find a new method of execution that was reliable, fast and painless. Most middle-of-the-road

47

intellectuals, professionals, jurists and doctors seemed to favor this compromise as the best solution to the problem. This reduced what had been a major ethical problem to a mere technological one: find a better way to execute condemned prisoners.

It was in this ideological climate that Southwick proposed his revolutionary idea. Although the hard-core abolitionists saw no difference between strangling a man to death and frying him with a bolt of artificial lightning, it made all the difference in the world to the growing segment of the population that saw technology and progress as the solution for every problem. If electricity could light their streets and send their voices over wires to distant cities, if steam engines could send trains across the country and around the world, if new inventions could ease the burdens of factory workers in every walk of life—why couldn't technology provide a solution to the problem of capital punishment?

Southwick's articles in scientific journals earned him the support of the inventors and entrepreneurs who read them during the early 1880s, but these readers were only a tiny minority of the population. To gather the kind of support necessary for the monumental task of changing the law for a practice that dated back to the time of the Romans required money, political clout and a public relations apparatus, none of which was available to Southwick. What he did have were some influential friends, especially State senator Daniel H. MacMillan.

MacMillan was a graduate of Cornell Law School who went into private practice in Buffalo in 1869. His firm, MacMillan, Glock, Pooley and Depew was one of the most powerful in the state, with clients that included the wealthy Vanderbilt family. He ran for the Senate in 1885 and was elected for a single term, after which he returned to his legal business. He was a member of the New York Republican Committee and a delegate of the Republican National Conventions in 1888, 1892 and 1896.

A strong supporter of the death penalty, MacMillan understood the implications of Southwick's proposal. If the death penalty could be made more humane, he reasoned, it would deprive abolitionists of their best argument against it. Although he was a Republican, MacMillan was a close acquaintance of David Bennett Hill, a Democrat from Elmira who had a history of advocating social reforms. In the 1870s, while a member of the Assembly, Hill introduced a bill that would have outlawed the use of prison laborers on construction projects. He was elected lieutenant governor in 1882 on the same ticket as Grover Cleveland, and one of the duties of that job was to preside over the Senate, where he met MacMillan. When Cleveland was elected president of the United States, Hill took over as governor and was reelected in 1884.

During a series of dinners in Albany restaurants where they discussed state issues, MacMillan showed Hill some of Southwick's articles suggesting the use of electricity to replace hanging. Over a period of time Hill was converted to the idea that electrocution was the humanitarian alternative and possibly the only way to save the death penalty from the abolitionists. Hill was such an enthusiastic convert to the cause that he included it in his State of the State message in 1885, just days after being sworn in for his first full term as governor. He made it a major part of his agenda for the coming session: "The present mode of executing criminals by hanging has come down to us from the dark ages and it may well be questioned whether the science of the present day cannot provide a means for taking the life of such as are condemned to die in a less barbarous manner," Hill said. "I commend this suggestion to the consideration of the Legislature."[1]

Hill's public endorsement meant that the idea was no longer just an ideological debate. It had been accepted by the chief executive of the most powerful state in the union. Although Hill did not mention Southwick or electrocution, the idea had by then been raised often enough that people knew what he was talking about. The time seemed right to make a change.

The *New York Tribune*, which had editorialized in favor of a more scientific alternative to hanging the previous August, praised Hill for making the proposal a few days later: "Hanging as a means of execution is notoriously uncertain in its operation.... There is no reason to doubt the ability of modern science to devise a mode of swift and really painless execution. Electricity would certainly furnish the means; and it is unquestionably a duty on the part of the Legislature to take Governor Hill's suggestion on this head into consideration, for there should not be permitted the existence of a doubt as to whether condemned prisoners suffer needlessly in paying the final penalty."[2]

A few weeks later, after the news reached New York about John "Babacombe" Lee's terrible experience at Exeter Prison, the *Tribune* editors used it as a further prod for reform: "The suggestion made by Governor Hill to the Legislature of this state regarding capital punishment has not as yet been acted upon, but such occurrences as that at Exeter should quicken the interest in the proposed reform sufficiently to produce at least a serious investigation of the subject."[3]

Although there was little hope that the English were ready for such reform, the editors said, it was time for Americans to take the lead:

A people whose institutions and traditions prepropose them in favor of all human rights ought long ago to have recognized the responsibility

Gov. David B. Hill of New York, who proposed that a more humane method of capital punishment be found to replace hanging. (New York State Library)

that rests on society for the swift and painless execution of capital sentences. The repudiation of the old doctrine that society is an avenger occurred long ago, yet the retention of the gallows appears to indicate that the medieval spirit of retribution still survives, and that there is an unexpressed reluctance to part with it altogether.

But while we must admit the anachronism of execution by hanging, we must equally admit the possibility of instituting a more certain, swift and painless mode of killing our criminals. Science is full of resource in this direction, and either by potent drugs or strong currents of electricity can certainly solve this problem without difficulty. There is therefore no reason whatever for delaying the reform demanded while every failure on the scaffold speaks trumpet-tongued against the barbarity and wanton humanity of the existing practice.

Many of the more conservative legal and medical groups were not so willing to accept the need for reform. *The Lancet*, the respected medical journal published in London, took a look at the proposed alternatives to hanging, lethal injection and electricity, and was not impressed. "Electricity is another agent suggested. We doubt the possibility of applying this agent so as to destroy life instantly. We confess that looking at the matter all around, we incline to think that hanging, when properly performed destroys consciousness more rapidly, and prevents its return more effectually than any other mode of death which justice can employ. It is against the bungling way of hanging that we protest—not against the method of execution itself. That it is, on the whole, the best, we are convinced."[4]

Despite their enthusiasm and the support from many of the newspapers, Hill and MacMillan could not persuade the legislature to take any action during the 1885 session, even though they both introduced, for purposes of debate, bills that called for amending the state's penal code to allow forms of execution other than hanging. For many lawmakers the idea seemed too radical, and although scientists, intellectuals and newspaper editors were in favor of it, most of their constituents didn't consider it an important issue.

The next year MacMillan tried a different tactic. Instead of a bill to change the law he introduced a resolution to set up a special blue ribbon commission to look into finding alternatives to hanging. A bill establishing "A Commission to Investigate and Report the Most Humane and Practical Method of Carrying into Effect the Sentence of Death in Capital Cases" was approved without debate on May 13, 1886.

Appointing a commission to study an issue is an age-old method legislators use to show their constituents that they are concerned about an issue without taking a stand on it, but that does not seem to have been MacMillan's intent. In trying to persuade his fellow legislators about the merits of Southwick's proposal he found the lack of hard information a significant obstacle. Although there was a lot of discussion in medical and scientific journals around the world about the relative merits of electrocution and lethal injection, no one had until then taken the time for a comprehensive investigation of the relative merits of each method.

The resolution approved by the Senate left the selection of the members of the commission up to the Senate Committee on the Whole, which is not surprising, since the chair of that committee was the same as the resolution's author: MacMillan. In our own century, such a blue-ribbon commission would have been expected to include a wide range of experts in many fields to provide a number of different viewpoints and representation from various special interest groups. There were suggestions for criminologists, doctors, scientists, legal scholars electrical engineers and humanitarians.

The three people MacMillan appointed to the commission didn't represent anything even close to this kind of approach to the issue. In fact, the selection seemed all but certain to guarantee that they would recommend that electricity be substituted for hanging, and that was probably MacMillan's intent all along. Not a single eyebrow was raised when he announced the appointment of his close friend and the state's leading proponent of capital punishment by electricity: Alfred Porter Southwick.

From our perspective a century later this seems like a remarkable example of stacking the deck on an issue, like appointing the chairman of General Motors to a committee deciding what kind of cars the state should buy, yet this issue was not even raised at the time. MacMillan identified Southwick as a scientist who had written a number of articles about the use of scientific and humane methods that could be used to replace the gallows. That was true, but by this time Southwick was hardly open-minded about the issue. There were a number of medical doctors who had written about lethal injection as an alternative to hanging, yet none of them were appointed to the commission.

From the beginning there was one solid vote in favor of electrocution, a huge head start for the idea. The other methods that were considered probably never had a fair chance because the other two members of the commission were more neutral and had other concerns. They were Matthew Hale of Albany, a noted legal scholar, and Elbridge T. Gerry, of Manhattan, a famous humanitarian.

All three of the commissioners were blue bloods. Southwick's ancestry has already been described. Hale was the grandson of Col. Nathan Hale, the Revolutionary War hero from New Hampshire. His mother was a direct descendant of Miles Standish and John Alden of the *Mayflower.* Gerry was the grandson of the first Elbridge Gerry, a signer of the Declaration of Independence and vice president of the United States.

Hale, 56 at the time of his appointment, was born in Chelsea, Vermont, graduated from the University of Vermont and served in law firms in New York City and upstate New York. He was elected to the state Constitutional Convention in 1867 and served on its judiciary committee. Later that year he was elected to the state Senate and formed a series of law firms in Albany. He was one of the organizers of the New York State Bar Association and served as its president.

A Republican who later became an independent, Hale was much sought after as an attorney for important Constitutional law cases to be argued before the court of appeals. Among his prominent clients were the owners of various railroads, the Central National Bank of Boston, the Adelphi Club of Albany and the Albany Police Department. He was charter member and trustee of the Fort Orange Club and belonged to the Reform Club of New York City, the Commonwealth Club of New York, the National Urban League, and the New York State Civil Service Reform League.

Hale had a reputation as an orator and was a regular speaker at Bar Association meetings. He was said to have one of the most extensive libraries in Albany. He was a chubby man with a large forehead but was known as a great wit. His role on the commission was to act as legal adviser. Because it was understood that the commission would eventually propose legislation to amend the capital punishment wording in the state penal code, it was important to have an expert on Constitutional law to deal with these issues from the beginning.

Gerry, 48 at the time of his appointment to the commission, was also a lawyer. A graduate of Columbia, where he was president of the Philolexian Society, he practiced law in New York City and specialized in cases involving the wills of the well-to-do. He also took time to defend at least one murderer. Like Hale, he was a member of the 1867 State Constitutional Convention.

Gerry's principal work was as a humanitarian, founding both the American Society for the Prevention of Cruelty to Animals and the

Left: Matthew Hale, the legal expert on the Gerry Commission, which was appointed to find a more humane alternative to hanging. (The *Albany Times Union*) *Right:* Elbridge T. Gerry, chairman of the Gerry Commission. (New York State Library)

Society for the Prevention of Cruelty to Children in 1874. He was president of the latter group at the time of his appointment to the commission. This society investigated thousands of cases of child abuse each year and placed hundreds of children in foster homes. He also served as governor of New York Hospital and was probably best known as commodore of the New York Yacht Club. Many newspapers in fact referred to him as "Commodore Gerry" because of this association. As one of the foremost humanitarians in the state, he was a natural to serve on the commission and was elected chairman at its first meeting.

Missing from the commission was a true scientist or a medical doctor. Although Southwick assumed that role, he was a dentist and amateur electrician with no formal training in either field. The lack of this kind of experience on the commission became a serious problem when the debate about electrocution reached its climax three years later. If the commission's report had contained more scientific background, it also might have prevented the series of bizarre animal experiments that were to be staged later in an attempt to determine which kinds of death were most efficient and least painful.

Although the commission's mandate was quite narrow—to find the best and most humane method of capital punishment—the three commissioners chose to interpret it as broadly as possible, producing what turned into a 95-page encyclopedia of torture and death that traced the origins of capital punishment back to biblical times.

Gerry said in an interview after the report was issued that the commission collected 700 separate books and articles, including encyclopedias, histories, books of travel and works on law and medical jurisprudence.[5] Through this research the commission was able to identify 40 different methods of execution that had been used in recorded history and described their workings in meticulous detail in the report. Although the commission did not take the revival of most of these practices seriously because they were so inhumane, Gerry said they were included to give the legislature a complete overview of the topic.

The list of the methods of death described by the commission reads like something out of Edgar Allan Poe. Among them were beating with clubs, decapitation, blowing from cannon, breaking on the wheel, burning at the stake, burying alive, crucifixion, dismemberment, drawing and quartering, drowning, exposure to wild beasts, flogging, the garrote, the guillotine, hari kari, impalement, the iron maiden, poisoning, pressing to death, running the gauntlet, shooting, stabbing, stoning and strangling. In fact, nearly half of the final report was taken up with this extensive inventory of torture and death, complete with literary and historical references and elaborate descriptions of victims' demise.

Besides its research into the history of capital punishment, the commission's other main source of information was a questionnaire sent out to the state's most prominent experts on law and medicine, including judges, district attorneys, sheriffs and doctors. Although several hundred of these forms were sent out, only about 200 were sent back. The questionnaire asked five questions:

1. Do you consider the present mode of inflicting capital punishment by hanging objectionable? Please give the reasons for your opinion.

2. Were you ever present at an execution, and, if so, will you kindly state details of the occurrence bearing on the subject?

3. In your opinion, is there any method known to science which would carry into effect the death penalty in capital cases in a more humane and practical manner than the present one of hanging? If so, what would you suggest?

4. The following substitutes for hanging have been suggested to the Commission. What are your views as to each?

    1. Electricity.

    2. Prussic acid, or other poison.

    3. The guillotine

    4. The garrote.

5. If a less painful method of execution than the present should be adopted, would any legal disposition of the body of the criminal be expedient, in your judgment, in order that the deterrent effect of capital punishment might not be lessened by the change? What do you suggest on this head?

What is most interesting about this survey, and about the entire work of the commission, is that nowhere does it even mention the option of abolishing capital punishment. Many states had already done that, and it was certainly an option that should have been part of the survey if the commissioners really wanted to make a full report.

Despite the fact that abolition was not given as an option, several people responding to the survey said they favored abolition of the death penalty. The commission chose to ignore them, dismissing the whole idea in the final report, with a one-sentence, offhand remark: "as this subject was not referred to your commission, we have paid no attention to it in our report."[6]

Although the commissioners could argue that a consideration of abolition was not part of their mandate, it was certainly a valid option and deserved more than this casual rejection. The commission's reluctance to deal with it demonstrates its own prejudices. Gerry, in particular, must have had some mixed feelings about the death penalty. He was a leading advocate of the humane treatment of animals by giving them a painless death, and he was a pioneer in the field of child abuse. He must have seen that disposing of human beings in such a way raised serious ethical questions.

The commission did not publish and apparently did not even compile the results of its survey, choosing instead to provide only selective quotes and general responses. It is possible, however, to reconstruct some of the results of the survey from the surviving documents. Of the 200 responses received, 80 favored retaining the gallows, 87 preferred electricity, 8 favored poison, 5 the guillotine, 4 the garrote, 7 various other methods, and 8 were undecided. On the face of it, these results look like a slight plurality for electricity, but a closer look shows that only 43 percent favored electricity to 40 percent for hanging. This is hardly an outcry for reform, and that may have been why the commission chose to downplay the survey results in its report.

Even the selected quotes from the survey that the commissioners chose to include in the report show a lack of enthusiasm for reform. It is fair to assume that those who expressed strong feelings against electrocution did not find their opinions quoted in the report.

Several of those responding to the survey suggested compromises. One suggested hanging for men and electrocution for women. Another suggested that two degrees of severity be established, with hanging going to the most aggravated cases and electrocution where there were mitigating circumstances. Many said they thought electricity was so dangerous that it might injure the law officials who were attempting to use it. Others said they thought death by electricity was too uncertain and that the prisoner might be revived a few minutes or a few hours after the execution.[7]

Dr. N. E. Brill of New York City, in a lengthy response to the commission, said the size of the dynamos that would be necessary to electrocute convicts would be more than some counties could afford. He also submitted newspaper reports of victims of accidental execution who were revived minutes and hours after the accident, even though they seemed to be dead. Even those struck by lightning, which was much more powerful than any man-made dynamos, often survived, he said: "If lightning does not kill, surely we cannot expect death to result from artificial electricity," he said, adding that he preferred the guillotine to either hanging or electrocution.[8]

This question about the seemingly unpredictable nature of electricity's effect on the human body would become even more controversial over the next two years, but in their report the commissioners said that many people who had seemed to recover from electrocution had not received the full current, only a portion of it. Again, the lack of a real scientist on the commission was a serious problem on this issue. A deliberate use of the current would ensure a more reliable result, the commission predicted.

"We have satisfied ourselves from careful consideration and inquiry made of experts in electricity that these objections are unfounded," the commissioners said in their report. "We think there is no practical difficulty in constructing an electrical apparatus which can easily and safely be managed, and which will be absolute in its working and will effect the instantaneous and painless death of the convicted criminal."

Among the supporters of electricity in the survey were Dr. C. H. Chittenden of Binghamton, who said that "electricity would produce instantaneous death if properly applied. I would prefer it to the drop or weight."

Dr. Lewis Balch of Albany, who was in favor of retaining the gallows, said he thought electricity would "require a skilled workman to have charge of the batteries to insure their proper working.... [T]his ... death would be instantaneous, perfectly painless, with no distortion."

J. Henry Furman of Tarrytown said he thought electricity would produce "immediate and painless death without mutilation of the body." He went on to make more practical suggestions that were quite similar to those eventually endorsed. He suggested that a metal chair be used with electrodes attached to the brain and the base of the spine and that the technician be "invisible to the condemned person."

Dr. A. P. Jackson of Oakfield, who was an advocate of hanging, said he thought electricity would be "a most admirable substitute, probably the best known to science, fulfilling all the indications in the most humane, practical and painless manner."

Dr. Alfred Carroll of New Brighton said he was in favor of a change because hanging was not a sufficient deterrent to crime. What was needed, he said, was some really gruesome punishment to make criminals think twice. "To the most dangerous of the criminal class the scaffold bears no associations of disgrace," he said, "it is rather a heroic culmination of a career of proud and daring defiance of law, almost to be emulated by the survivors ... and invite the imitative ambition of less distinguished evil-doers."

"Nothing save an overstrained sentimentalism could be opposed to such a measure," he said of electrocution, "and I feel confident of its preventive efficacy in an enormous number of depraved minds." He suggested giving the bodies of executed criminals to medical colleges for dissection.

After its initial exploration of the various means of capital punishment, the commission turned its attention to the use of electricity, as no one doubted it would do with Southwick as one of the members. As part of this research, the commission asked many prominent experts for their opinions.

Professor Elihu Thompson of Lynn, Massachusetts, one of the foremost experts on electrical theory in the country and later the founder of the Thompson-Houston manufacturing company, gave specific instructions on how best to use the current to make death as quick as possible. In a hint of the great controversy ahead, he suggested that alternating current would bring death more quickly than direct current. This current could be supplied by a battery, a water motor, or even a small machine run by hand, he suggested. The entire apparatus would cost between $100 and $200.

Thompson did not think that a metal armed chair, as suggested by Southwick, would be the best way to apply the current because it would be difficult to attach the electrodes. Instead, he suggested attaching one electrode to the head and the other to the feet. The electrodes should be attached with wet sponges, he suggested, to reduce burning and assure a good electrical contact.

Thomas A. Edison, the most famous electrician of all, was contacted by letter at least twice by Southwick. In his first letter, on November 8,

1887, Southwick asked Edison for his opinion about the best way to use electricity for executions. In his first reply Edison indicated that he did not believe in capital punishment and preferred not to be involved in the commission's work but said he would "join heartily in an effort to abolish capital punishment."

Southwick didn't give up and wrote to Edison again on December 5, telling him that "science and civilization demand some more humane method than the rope," which he suggested was "a relic of barbarism." If Edison, the most famous electrician in the world, would endorse the idea, Southwick said, it would "help much with the legislature."

At this point Edison did a complete about-face on the issue for reasons we will explore more fully in the next chapter. In his second letter to Southwick, on December 9, Edison said the best way to dispose of condemned men would be to use alternating current, which, of course, was not the method he used in his street-lighting projects but was exactly the kind of current used by his major rival, George Westinghouse. Edison wrote to Southwick:

"The best appliance in this connection is, to my mind, the one which will perform its work in the shortest space of time, and inflict the least amount of suffering upon its victim. This, I believe, can be accomplished by the use of electricity, and the most suitable apparatus for this purpose is that class of dynamo-electric machinery which employs intermittent currents. The most effective of these are known as 'alternating machines.' manufactured principally in this country by Geo. Westinghouse.... The passage of the current from these machines through the human body even by the slightest contacts, produces instantaneous death."[9]

This endorsement of electric execution by Edison was crucial to the commission's final recommendation. Although Southwick had made up his mind long before he was appointed, at least one other member of the commission, Gerry, said it was a major factor in his decision. At a public hearing on the work of the committee in 1889, Gerry testified that he thought Edison knew more about electricity than anyone else in the United States and that Edison's endorsement was the major factor in persuading him.[10]

As we will see in the next chapter, Edison had important financial concerns that influenced his decision to change his mind and support Southwick's proposal and was not in a position to give an unbiased view. His decision to use the electric chair as a tool in his marketing rivalry with Westinghouse can be dated to sometime in late November or early December 1887.

Dr. George E. Fell, Southwick's friend and fellow amateur electrician from Buffalo, submitted to the commission a lengthy report of the experiments that he and Southwick had conducted in previous years. He also described some new experiments conducted in July 1887. In an attempt to determine exactly what was causing the dogs to die, Dr. Fell performed operations on some of the dogs before they were killed. This involved removing the chest walls so that the heart and lungs of the dog could be seen during the execution. At the second the current was turned on, he said, the heart stopped beating.

"Nothing could be more sudden," he said. His conclusion was that if electric current was used on a prisoner it would cause instant death and that the prisoner could not be brought back to life through any artificial means.

"Prior to these experiments I held the view that electricity might prove the best agent for executing criminals," said Dr. Fell in his report; "after they were made I enthusiastically supported it as the only agent which this age had any right to use for this purpose."

Despite the lengthy list of alternatives to hanging and the lack of consensus from the survey, Gerry said it was clear almost from the beginning that there were really only five alternatives to hanging that might prove acceptable. They were the garrote (in which a collar is placed over the convict's head and is given a strong twist, breaking the neck), the guillotine, shooting, poisoning and electrocution.

Although it would seem that the garrote and the guillotine could not have been seriously considered by someone like Gerry, with a reputation as a humanitarian, he said they brought death nearly instantaneously and therefore painlessly. They were eventually rejected, he said, because they disfigured the body and, in the case of the guillotine, were much too bloody. Even if the execution were held in private, the commissioners felt, the guillotine would be "needlessly shocking to the necessary witnesses" and "found utterly repugnant to American ideas."

Shooting by firing squad, although appropriate for the military the commissioners believed, was too bloody to be used in civil cases. In addition there had been cases when the condemned had not died instantly. This kind of execution was also too closely associated with the governments of tyrants and military rulers, they said.

Gerry said later that his own personal preference was for death by poison, which he said would be preferable to electricity. He had voted for this method, but Southwick and Hale had voted for electricity. The problem with poisons, Gerry said, was that many of them could not be administered properly without the assistance of a doctor, and it would be virtually impossible to find a doctor willing to perform a task that seemed to violate the doctor's oath to preserve life at any cost.

Lethal injection, a method only used extensively in the late twentieth century, was considered by the commission but rejected. In this case the suggestion was to inject prussic acid through a hypodermic needle into the condemned man's blood stream. This had been suggested by several European doctors as the most humane method. The commissioners rejected it on the advice of some doctors who felt that it was hard enough to get patients to submit to injections. If hypodermic needles became associated with death, it would be even harder to get them to cooperate. Many doctors wrote to the commission objecting to the use of a hypodermic needle because of the negative impact it would have on their efforts to get the general public to accept its use.[11]

The commissioners had no trouble coming up with examples of bungled hangings and described a number of cases in detail, most of them from Britain. They included the case of Nathan B. Sutton, who was hanged on January 7, 1888, in Oakland, California: "The drop was nearly five feet and the fall was so great that the man's neck was torn by the rope, the spectacle prompting many of those present to avert their faces."

After examining issues such as whether hanging encouraged juries to find defendants, especially women, not guilty, the practice of giving brandy to convicts just before hanging and the practice of hanging several people at one time, the commission concluded that: "[t]he time has come when a radical change should be effected.... [W]hile the general voice of the press has strongly urged for some time past the propriety of such a change, yet it is only after a careful weighing of the reasons and objections thereto that a correct result can be had. The deprivation of life is, in itself, the most serious loss which any human being can suffer. To aggravate that loss by any method which even incidentally increases the pain of dissolution, or renders the execution of the law more terrible, is justifiable only upon the argument as to its deterrent effect. As already shown, that has been tried for ages without success."[12]

In the autumn of 1886 Gerry was called away to Europe and could not take part in the final preparation of the report. As a result it was not ready for its scheduled release in January 1887. The legislature then granted the commission an additional year to submit its report.

The final report, submitted to the legislature on January 17, 1888, recommended, without qualification, that electrocution should be substituted for hanging as the official method of capital punishment in New York State. "Perhaps the most potent agent known for the destruction of human life is electricity," the report concluded, because electricity was painless, certain and instantaneous. "It is the duty of society to utilize for its benefit the advantages and facilities which science has uncovered to its view."

The recommended execution apparatus, as described in the report, was similar to Southwick's original idea of using a semi-reclining chair, like a dentist's chair, with metal plates attached to a headrest and the footrest. The chair could be built for $50, with an additional $250 to $500 required if the chair was to be attached directly to the generating plant rather than just to the overhead transmission lines used for streetlights. If it was necessary to build an independent generating plant, that would cost an additional $250 to $500.

"The cost of maintenance of either of the foregoing plans would be merely nominal," the report said; "after the plant is once established, the expense of conducting an execution would be infinitesimal."

Instead of each county conducting its own executions, as had been the practice until then, the commission recommended building electrical execution chambers in the state prisons in Auburn, Sing Sing and Dannemora prisons. These chambers could be built for a one-time cost of about $1,000 each.[13]

The commissioners also went somewhat beyond the bounds of their mandate to make some further suggestions regarding executions. They urged the legislature to outlaw the practice of conducting elaborate funerals for executed criminals. Because hanging is "both a degrading and revolting means of death," the commission found, it has a certain deterrent effect, but criminals who commit capital crimes "are usually the most ignorant and brutal in the community." They tend to be "superstitious" about what happens to their bodies after death. The commission therefore endorsed the idea suggested by one of the doctors that the bodies of criminals be given to scientists for their use, not only for the betterment of science but because it would act as a stronger deterrent than the execution itself.

"Very many bravos who will, without flinching, walk from the cell to the scaffold and who are certainly very indifferent to the infliction of death itself would hesitate long to commit crime … if they are certain that after execution their bodies were to be cut up in the interest of medical science," the commissioners wrote. They said that in New York City the bodies of hanged men had been given up to friends who "indulge in the most drunken and beastly orgies" when the dead man's "evil deeds are glorified into acts of heroism."

The commission recommended that the date and time of the execution be kept secret so the friends and relatives of the victim would not be able to gather outside the gates of the prison. Instead of burial services, they recommended that the prisoner's body, after the scientists had completed their necessary studies of it, be "buried without ceremony in the prison cemetery or graveyard with sufficient quicklime to ensure their immediate consumption."

As a further means of lessening public sympathy for the victims of execution, the commission made one of its most controversial recommendations: banning the press from witnessing executions and even from writing about them at all. Newspapers immediately attacked this as censorship and a violation of freedom of the press. It was also, of course, a way to slow down the movement to ban executions, which was being fed by these gruesomely detailed accounts.

The commission recommended that "instead of the sensational reports of the execution which always appear on the same day or the day following in the public prints giving a detail of the agonies and struggles of the dying wretch, a simple statement would be substituted to the effect that the sentence of the law had been duly carried into effect."

The only reason for reporters to be present at executions, they said, was to produce sensational and dramatic articles describing "with painful fidelity every detail of the horrible scene," which can create among readers "a vicious and morbid appetite" that "has been known to stimulate others to the commission of crime."[14]

The commission concluded its report with a proposed comprehensive bill, drawn up by Hale, that would amend the state's Criminal Procedure Code to enact all of their recommendations, including the substitution of the electric chair for hanging, setting up execution chambers in three state prisons, requiring that the dead bodies be submitted to scientists for experiments and then buried without funerals, and the restrictions on the press about what could be published. Reporters who violated that section of the law could be charged with a misdemeanor.

The bill was introduced in the Senate the same week by Sen. Henry Coggleshall of Waterville, an upstate Republican. MacMillan had already retired from the Senate and therefore could not introduce the bill himself, but Coggleshall was a close and trusted friend. Reaction from the public was generally favorable.

Sheriff Hugh Grant of New York City, who was in charge of executions there, said he favored the idea of turning responsibility for them over to the state, noting that every county in the state used the same hangman and many of them had to import a gallows because they did not have one of their own. It made sense for the executioner to be directly employed by the state rather than have each county deal with him independently. As for the use of electricity, Grant said that was up to people who had more knowledge of the subject than he did.

Joel O. Stevens, the undersheriff who worked with Grant, said he thought the whole idea of using electricity was much too experimental. He thought hanging was a quick and painless method, tried and true, and there was no reason to change.

Warden Walsh of the notorious Tombs Prison in New York, where the prisoners were hanged, said he had never attended an execution and would not attend one even if he were paid $5,000. He said any method that would lessen the horror of executions would be desirable.

A condemned prisoner in the Tombs, referred to only as Lyon, said his first preference would be to die by firing squad, but he would prefer electricity to death by hanging.

Mayor Hewitt of New York City said that if he had been forced to pick, he would rather die by electricity than hanging. He was particularly opposed to the ban on newspaper coverage of executions, saying it amounted to censorship, even though he himself always skipped over newspaper articles about executions.[15]

The *New York Times*, in an editorial published on December 17, 1887, when it received a leaked copy of the report, endorsed the use of electricity over the rope, saying that hanging was, and always had been, a barbarous practice, even when it was performed well. Many thought that hanging should be retained because it was so horrible, thereby discouraging future criminals, the *Times* editors said, but by that reasoning it would make sense to bring back such practices as disemboweling and quartering.

> But the progress of civilization has made those whom it has affected sensible that it will not do for the community in executing justice upon a bloodthirsty savage to be as bloodthirsty and as savage as himself. The greatest contrast ought to be observed in all circumstances between the commission of crime and its expiation. The terrors of the law should be retained while the mere horrors are abolished.
>
> …An execution … ought to be certain, swift and painless. At its best, hanging does not fulfill these requirements, while when it is bungled it becomes a spectacle which revolts civilized spectators or readers and inspires them with indignation rather at the law and its ministers than at the law breaker who is answering for his offenses.
>
> Electricity supplies an agency which meets all the necessities of the case and puts out of the question the lingering struggles and contortions which so often deprive executions of their solemnity. There should be no doubt of the acceptance of the Legislature of the report of the Commission. It will be creditable to the State of New York to be the first community to substitute a civilized for a barbarous method of inflicting capital punishment, and to set an example which is sure of being followed by the rest of the world.

On January 17, 1888, after the report was released, the *Times* also endorsed the idea of moving executions from county jails to state prisons, but questioned the idea of refusing to allow any funeral or burial services for condemned convicts. Such a change did not punish the criminal but his unoffending survivors, the editors said. On the question of censoring news reports of executions, the *Times* said the commissioners probably had the best of intentions, but such a change would do more harm than good. "It would be better for everybody concerned if newspapers gave but a bare announcement of the execution of ordinary murderers, but when a murder is really an important historical event it is as absurd to condense to a mere announcement the expiation of the crime as the account of the crime itself. To make a mystery of an execution like that of Guiteau [the assassin of President Garfield] for example, or of the Chicago Anarchists is a proceeding too much in the line of a despotic government to be acceptable here."

Other newspaper editors were more critical of the report.

The *Albany Times*, in a January 18 editorial, said the commission had gone too far beyond its mandate in making some of its recommendations. To these editors it seemed contradictory that the commission was advocating the use of electricity as more humane than hanging and then endorsing such barbarous practices as outlawing funeral services and demanding that the bodies be used for scientific experiments. "It is a piece of legislation akin to the driving of a stake through a suicide's body and the dismemberment of the condemned after death," the editors said. "Instead of a more humane mode of execution, these provisions certainly add new pains and penalties to all that there was in the old method. The most aggravated cruelties are to be inflicted upon innocent members of the family of the condemned, and, in many cases the condemned is to have, according to his religious training, even an essential rite of burial refused him after death."

As for electricity, the editors said it was still experimental and those who experience it "will hardly come back to say whether it is more humane or not."

The editors predicted the bill would not pass either house of the legislature.

The editors of the *American Law Review* also thought the recommendations could not be taken very seriously: "The whole discussion shows into what an age of sickly sentimentality and drivel our civilization has descended. One of the objects of the law in inflicting capital punishment by hanging is and should be to deter the commission of murder by visiting upon its perpetrator the punishment of death inflicted in a revolting manner." The use of electricity, if used in "bungling hands" might be "the most horrible torture which could be inflicted on the convict." If the commission was really looking for a painless way to kill, the writers suggested, it should have recommended sinking the convict in a vat of water and "drown[ing] him like a rat."[16]

William Dean Howells was also sarcastic in his essay published in the January 14 edition of *Harper's Magazine*, but turned his scorn on those who maintained "a great deal of affectionate regard for the good old gallows." After examining the pros and cons of using electricity to replace hanging, Howells said the best minds seemed to be in favor of electricity or "the death spark" as he called it. "There is apparently no good reason why this mysterious agent which now unites the whole civilized world by nerves of keen intelligence, which already propels trains of cars and promises to heat them, which had added life in apparently inexhaustible variety, should also be employed to take it away." It was the duty of society, he said, to "kill by the humanist method known to science." He foresaw a time when the governor of the state could press a button on his desk and execute a prisoner who was hundreds of miles away. It would be so easy that even a woman or a child could do it.[17]

While Howells seemed to be speaking for the cultural elite, many common people still thought of electricity as a dark and mysterious force closely related to magic in the way it created light and made motors move and carried voices over wires. A newspaper reader in Kansas City wrote a letter to the editor opposing electrical executions because he thought the victim's soul would be destroyed. John O. Henry, an electrical engineer commenting in a trade journal on the letter, said it "reminds us of the general superstition or ignorance of the subjects we at times have to contend against and the necessity for common sense or easily understood explanations."[18]

The major dissenting view came not from the newspapers, which were mostly in favor of the new law, but from the electric industry itself. They were afraid that linking electricity to death in such a direct way would make consumers too afraid to allow electric wires on the streets or in their homes.

Thomas P. Lockwood, writing in the *Electrical Engineer* two months after the report was made public, called the Gerry Commission's recommendation "a cold-blooded proposition for the degradation of a noble science" and asked electrical engineers to refuse to become "electrical executioners." He sarcastically referred to a future "United States Electrical Execution Association" and asked, "Shall our electrical journals of which we are now so justly proud be obliged to record the invention of

new and improved systems for scientific killing? And be filled with advertisements for complete plans for electrical executions?" Electricity, he
said, was "too noble a science" to be thus lowered to such an ignoble use
as to become "the instrument of deliberate homicide.... Let us keep electricity as clean as we can.... We must draw the line somewhere, and in
the name of electricity and in the service of man, let us draw it at capital
punishment."[19]

A *Scientific American* editorial also opposed the law but much less
passionately than Lockwood did. If the hangman often failed to do his job
properly, the editors said, an electric system, because it was a "vastly more
complicated mechanism" would multiply the possibilities of failure.[20]

A question was also raised about what to call the process that the
commission recommended in its report. There seemed to be no single
word in the language that conveyed the meaning of deliberately killing
someone with electricity. The *New York Times* editors resisted the word
electrocution as a "monstrosity" and suggested instead that the process
be called "euthanasia by electricity." Gerry suggested the word *electrolehe.*

Scientific American suggested 18 possibilities: *electromort, than-
electrize, thanatelectrisis, electrophon, electricise, electrotony, elec-
trophony, electroctony, electroctasy, electricide, electropoenize,
electrothenese, electroed, electrocution, fulmen, voltacuss* and *elec-
trostrike.* Edison first suggested *dynamort, ampermort* and *electromort.*

Later on, a New York attorney with a knowledge of Latin and Greek,
Eugene H. Lewis, was asked by one of Edison's managers to make an eval-
uation of all the names from a linguistic point of view. He recommended
electricide. Then he added a proprietary comment.

"There is one other word which I think ... might be used with some
propriety. It can be used as a verb and as a noun to express kindred ideas.
The word is westinghouse. As Westinghouse's dynamo is going to be used
for ... executing criminals why not give him the benefit of this fact ... and
speak hereafter of a criminal as being 'westinghoused'; or to use the common noun we could say that ... a man was condemned to the westinghouse.
It will be a subtle compliment to the public services of this distinguished
man. There is a precedent for it too.... We speak of a criminal in France
being guillotined or condemned to the guillotine. Each time the word is used
it ... perpetuates the memory and services of Dr. Guillotine."[21]

These were fighting words, of course, and just one round of the ver-
bal attacks and behind-the-scenes dirty tricks of the greatest commercial
rivalry of the era, the so-called battle of the currents.

—4—
The Battle of
the Currents

Despite the endorsement of the governor of New York State, the recommendation of the Gerry Commission and the blessing of Thomas Edison, in early 1888 the bill to change the method of execution from hanging to the electric chair was hopelessly stalled. Although some members of the public seemed fascinated with the idea of electrocuting criminals, as shown in editorials and letters to the editor, there were just as many who felt that no change was necessary.

For politicians, fooling around with the death penalty was a hot potato. There was no political advantage in taking a stand on such a controversial issue. For every constituent who favored the proposed law there was another who opposed it. Most of the members of the state legislature in Albany thought there was no pressing need to make such a drastic change to adopt a process that few understood, one that seemed risky and untested.

Those in favor of the death penalty saw few reasons to switch from the time-honored use of the gallows. Opponents thought that shooting bolts of lightning through a prisoner wasn't any less gruesome than hanging him. Without a firm constituency, without a public outcry in favor of it, the state legislature seemed all but certain to let the bill die.

Despite that, the bill sailed through the Assembly with little opposition. Assemblyman Charles T. Saxton, a Republican from the Rochester area and chairman of the Assembly Judiciary Committee, was an enthusiastic supporter of the bill, probably because of his connections with MacMillan and Southwick. When it came to the floor for a vote, the few objections that were raised had nothing to do with the electrical part of the bill. Several assemblymen said they opposed the idea of disposing the executed person's body in quicklime and burying it in an unmarked grave.

The bill was amended to allow religious services to be performed only inside the prison walls and was approved on April 17 on a voice vote.[1]

In the Senate the support was much less enthusiastic. Eight days after the Assembly vote, the Senate Judiciary Committee cut out the section of the bill that substituted electricity for hanging and left only the other reforms that the Gerry Commission had recommended. MacMillan, the prime supporter of the bill, had chosen not to seek reelection and was no longer in the Senate. Without the support of the Judiciary Committee the bill would normally not have been brought to the floor for a vote. The electrical execution bill seemed as good as dead.[2]

There was, however, a little-used maneuver that allowed the Senate to bypass the Judiciary Committee's recommendation. On May 8, the very last day of the legislative session, when the emasculated bill was called up for a vote, Sen. Henry Coggleshall proposed that the bill be amended to put the original electric execution language back into it. When that was approved the restored bill was quickly passed by a voice vote without a single objection.[3]

What led to this unusual political maneuvering? Albany was well known at the time for its backroom politics. Although the legislative process seemed to be conducted in the ornate stone chambers of the Capitol, the real wheeling and dealing took place in the restaurants, taverns and brothels along State Street and the red-light section of town known as "the Gut."

In the era of Tammany Hall bills often took unusual courses as they were molded by political bosses or influenced by outside interests willing to trade cash for influence. The newspapers of the time took note of these sudden swings in voting patterns and unusual procedures as evidence of bribery and payoffs, which were so common in Gilded Age politics that they were taken for granted.

The bill that created the electric chair became law not because of the efforts of Southwick or the Gerry Commission but as a byproduct of one of the greatest rivalries in the history of American technology between Thomas A. Edison and George Westinghouse, Jr.

By the spring of 1888 the electrical execution bill had become just one of several battlegrounds in a self-serving public relations war as each entrepreneur sought to convince the public that his electrical lighting system was safer and more efficient than the other's. The stakes in this rivalry were tremendous. By 1888 every city in the country saw the benefits of replacing its gas lighting systems with electric ones. City councils were ready to pay millions for the expensive generating and distribution equipment needed for these systems. Because most of these city councils and their constituents knew next to nothing about electricity, they were largely at the mercy of the rival companies when it came to choosing a system made by Edison Electric Light Company or the Westinghouse Electric Company.[4]

The cost of the systems was a factor, of course, but the primary concern was safety. As the use of electricity became more common, so did the reports of people being accidentally electrocuted. If electric lights were to replace gas, the public had to be reassured that the new system was at least as safe as the old one. It was this fear of electricity that allowed the electric chair—the only electrical device designed to deliberately kill a human being—to become a piece in the grand battle between Edison and Westinghouse.

Whether money actually changed hands or some other method was used to influence the Senate, it's unlikely that Edison took any part in it personally, but his managers were certainly familiar with how it was done. By 1888 the Edison Electric Light Company and its subsidiaries all over the country had negotiated hundreds of franchises for permission to string electrical cables and build power plants. There was no bidding process for these franchises. The way one obtained a government contract in the 1880s was through payoffs, bribes and kickbacks. This process was so well-known that many politicians didn't even bother hiding it, calling it "honest graft." It was just another cost of doing business.

Historian Harold L. Pratt, who has examined the role of bribes and kickbacks in the awarding of utility contracts during this period, found that "politicians were growing rich" by collecting under-the-table "franchise fees" in return for their votes on important contracts and outright bribes paid by the utilities to secure franchises. City council members suddenly switched from backing one company to backing another "in a political culture of democratic anarchy and honest graft."[5]

So Edison's managers and salesmen, who were battling Westinghouse all over the country to obtain these franchises, were certainly not above playing by local rules. In 1888 the two companies had set up competing systems in Manhattan, where all city contracts were controlled by Tammany Hall and its boss, Richard Croker, whose influence extended beyond New York City to Albany. Governor Hill was closely tied to Croker, having sought his help when he ran for his first full term as governor. It would have been impossible to secure franchises in New York without the help of Tammany Hall.

Although there is no way to determine exactly who furthered Edison's interests in Albany by pulling the strings necessary to get the electric chair bill approved, subsequent events clearly point the finger at one man, Harold P. Brown, who was to become Edison's primary mouthpiece in the battle with Westinghouse over the construction of the electric chair.

Brown, who had no formal training as an electrical engineer, started his career with the Western Electric Company in Chicago and then worked for the Brush Electric Company, which maintained Chicago's arc street-lights from 1879 to 1884. After that he went into business for himself as a consultant and obtained several patents for systems to put arc lights and incandescent lamps on the same circuit. He was also involved in selling and building urban lighting systems and was therefore familiar with the negotiations for utility franchises.[6]

Although Edison and Brown denied on several occasions that there was any financial connection between them, a trail of paper evidence shows they kept in remarkably close contact during the years 1888 and 1890. The newspapers at the time assumed that Brown was Edison's man despite the denials. Letters between Brown and Edison and between Brown and Edison's research manager, Arthur Kennelly, show clearly that Brown was taking direction from the Edison Electric Light Company on a weekly basis, seeking advice from them, accepting the free use of equipment and accepting financial help for equipment purchases. Brown was also allowed full use of Edison's research labs in New Jersey.[7]

Even after the Senate passed the newly restored electrical execution act, there was further evidence of tampering when the Senate and Assembly leaders got together to reconcile the separate versions of the bill that had been passed by each house. The new bill, to be submitted to both houses, underwent what the New York Times called "a very curious emasculation."[8]

In the rush to complete work at the end of the legislative session, Section 10 of the bill had been mysteriously deleted, apparently by some "mistake." The deleted section read as follows: "The Superintendent of State Prisons shall on or before the 1st day of January 1889, cause an electrical apparatus suitable and sufficient for the purposes specified in this act to be constructed and placed in each of the State prisons of this State, together with the necessary appliances for the execution of convicted criminals under the provisions of this act."

Without this section, the Department of Prisons would not be authorized to purchase the equipment needed to build the electric chair. The Times reporter who covered the legislature believed that the governor would probably have to veto the bill rather than sign it in this incomplete state. Although Saxton and Coggleshall were informed of this problem they took no action to correct what the reporter called, "this curious treatment" of the bill, which was signed into law by Governor Hill on June 4.

What possible reason could anyone have had for deleting this section? At the time no one could offer any reasonable explanation. Within a few months, however, with the so-called battle of the currents raging, it became clear that this missing section of the law allowed Edison's lobbyists, especially Brown, some extra time to convince the state to require that the electric chair be powered exclusively by alternating current, the kind that Westinghouse used. This was a major part of Edison's public relations war to convince the public that AC, the "executioner's current," was too dangerous to use in homes or in domestic neighborhoods. To understand this fully, it's necessary to take a look at the development of Edison's electric companies.

When Edison developed the first practical incandescent lightbulb in 1879 he used what is called "direct current" or DC. The electrons flowed from the positive side of a generator through the lightbulb's filament to the negative side. The resistance to the current in the filament caused it to glow, creating the light. This is the kind of electricity that is used in flashlight batteries today. It worked fine for electric lights in a laboratory or even inside a large building or complex, but the design had a built-in flaw that prevented its practical use to light entire cities.

As the lightbulb got farther away from the power plant in a DC system, the resistance in the long wires caused the voltage to drop. Lamps near the generator burned brightly, but those farther away were dim. Using this system to light an entire city would require dozens of generating stations, each of which could provide power for only a few square blocks. Edison understood this limitation, and his plans to electrify cities included the construction of multiple power stations in each city so that the lights were never far enough from the generators to cause a serious voltage drop. In addition, Edison's system required thick cables made of expensive copper to help reduce the drop in voltage.

There was, however, a much better way that used a different kind of electricity called "alternating current." Instead of a direct flow of electrons from positive to negative, AC generating stations switched the polarity of the two terminals back and forth many times a second so the electrons actually moved back and forth in the wire rather than in a long chain. The voltage remained constant over long distances, so the lights at the end of the line glowed just as brightly as the ones closer to the generator.

Alternating current had another advantage in that it permitted the use of transformers that could regulate the voltage of electricity in various parts of the system. The generating stations could increase the voltage of AC electricity through the use of "step up" transformers. This high-voltage electricity could then be transmitted over long distances with little loss. Then, near the point where it was to be used, it could pass through "step down" transformers that reduced the voltage to safer and more useful levels. This is essentially the kind of system that is used in most places in the United States today.

Edison's failure to see the value of alternating current as the solution to the long distance distribution problem is curious, and some of his biographers have blamed it on Edison's advancing middle age. Several of his biographers have called this the biggest mistake of his life, a failure of the vision that had driven him to his remarkable success. He had always used DC generating equipment in his experiments and remained favorable to it even when the scientific evidence showed conclusively the benefits of AC. His failure to adopt what was obviously the better technology set up what newspapers at the time dubbed "the battle of the currents."

While Edison was drawing up his plans for DC power distribution systems for America's cities, European scientists were doing the same thing with AC. In 1886 Edison bought an option for the rights to use the European system, clearly recognizing its value, but then, over the objections of his staff of scientists, allowed the option to lapse, clinging instead to the old DC technology for which he already held the patents. He refused to recognize that his system was obsolete and pointed out a series of minor drawbacks to AC.

It's unclear if Edison really believed that DC was superior to AC or if it was more of a strategic business decision. The contracts for the DC electrical systems that Edison had set up around the country involved stock and bond exchanges instead of cash payments. Edison had, in effect, become a coinvestor with local businessmen in the systems. If they were to be replaced with AC systems Edison would lose tens of thousands of dollars. This was in addition to the millions he would lose if all new systems were built using AC equipment instead of the DC equipment that he made and sold.[9]

By late 1887 Edison and his captains embarked on a no-holds-barred smear campaign designed to discredit AC as too dangerous to be considered for lighting systems. This campaign had four major thrusts. First, Edison asked his managers to collect information about fatal accidents involving AC. Second, he authorized a series of experiments in his laboratory in which animals would be killed to demonstrate the dangers of AC. Third, he began a lobby campaign in several state legislatures to pass laws limiting the voltage permitted for power lines. This would have eliminated most of the advantages of AC.

Finally, Edison wanted New York to require that its new electric chair operate exclusively on AC, further demonstrating its lethal character. American scientists and electrical engineers without any financial stakes in the matter found AC clearly superior to DC and did not hesitate to say so in private. In public they hesitated to contradict the man who was unquestionably the most famous inventor of his time. With the scientific evidence all pointing the other way, Edison counted on his considerable reputation to carry enough influence with the public and government officials to win the contracts. Who would dare say that the "Wizard of Menlo Park," the father of the electric light, was wrong about electricity?

Edison's stubborn failure of vision set the stage for the entrance of someone willing to go one-on-one with the living legend and the acknowledged American genius of electrical technology. George Westinghouse of Pittsburgh became rich and famous after his invention of the railroad air brake even before he went into the electric business in 1885. He bought the rights to the European patents that Edison had rejected and became a major player with the purchase of the United States Electric Lighting Company in 1886. Seeing the opportunity presented by alternating current, he hired an engineer named William A. Stanley to come up with a practical AC lighting system. Stanley designed his own transformers and set up the country's first AC lighting system in Great Barrington, Massachusetts on March 6, 1886.

Westinghouse then began setting up similar systems in Manhattan, in direct competition with the Edison Electric Light Company, which had already set up a DC system. Within months, this competition for customers heated up into a full-scale national debate that was joined in by scientists and city officials across the nation. It also led to a bitter legal battle that lasted seven years after Edison charged Westinghouse with violating his patents.

Edison, while concerned about competition, also seems to have been genuinely concerned about the safety of AC after Westinghouse announced plans for using voltages as high as 10,000 volts. An electrical tragedy might hurt the entire industry, he feared.

"Just as certain as death Westinghouse will kill a customer within six months after he puts in a system of any size," Edison wrote to Edward Johnson, the president of the Edison Electric Light Company. "It will probably never be free from danger.... None of his plans worry me in the least; the only thing that disturbs me is that Westinghouse is a great man for flooding the country with agents and travelers."[10]

In late 1887, just as the Gerry Commission was preparing its final report, Edison and his managers fired another salvo against alternating current by setting up, as a demonstration, a 1,000-volt AC generator at Edison's West Orange, New Jersey, research facility. The electrodes were attached to a piece of tin on a laboratory table. Then, in the presence of newspaper reporters and invited observers, researchers forced dozens of stray dogs and cats onto the grid, where they were instantly killed. This process is so similar to the one developed by Southwick and Fell in Buffalo a few years earlier that the Edison electricians must have been aware of, and possibly even duplicated, Southwick's apparatus.

According to Edison biographer Matthew Josephson, Edison himself took part in these experiments. The dogs and cats, he said, were purchased "from eager schoolboys at twenty-five cents each and executed in such numbers that the local animal population stood in danger of being decimated."[11]

In February 1888, just weeks after the Gerry Commission issued its report and weeks before the Assembly passed the electric chair bill, Johnson collected the results of this research into a report called "A Warning from the Edison Electric Light Company." Besides the fates of the dogs and cats killed at West Orange, it reported other mishaps with high voltage lights and transmission lines. It called Westinghouse a "patent pirate" interested only in his own profit and caring nothing about the safety of his products.

Westinghouse was so furious at these charges that he threatened to sue for libel. He denied that his systems were unsafe and maintained that the high voltages were used only for transmission lines and were stepped down to the same level as Edison's own system when they entered a building. The public relations battle was in full swing.

Edison's next tactic was to lobby state legislatures to set a maximum voltage limit for electric transmission lines at 300 volts, enough to protect Edison's projects but too low for alternating current to be used effectively. Bills were introduced in Ohio and Virginia but did not pass. Meanwhile, most American cities were now choosing the cheaper and more efficient AC systems despite Edison's efforts.

In New York Edison and his team of public relations experts tried a different approach, one that would have a more lasting impact. Amidst the campaign to portray AC high voltage lines as dangerous, the electric chair became the perfect tool. If New York state was to electrocute people, deliberately killing them with high voltage, he told his managers, it was important that they use alternating current to show how dangerous it was.

In public Edison maintained his opposition to the electric chair and all forms of capital punishment, but behind the scenes, working through Brown and others, he was doing everything he could to make sure it was built to use alternating current so it could be used against Westinghouse.

Although he had probably been working behind the scenes in Albany, Brown's public debut came on June 5, 1888, one day after the electric chair bill was signed into law by Governor Hill. In a letter published in the *New York Evening Post*, Brown suggested that the New York Board of Electrical Control should forbid the use of the "damnable" alternating current in New York because it was too dangerous. For the next two years Brown surpassed even Southwick as the leading advocate of the electric chair. The only difference was that Brown insisted over and over, on every occasion and without any reservation, that the chair must use alternating current rather than direct current.[12]

Brown's lobbying campaign had a dual focus. On one hand he worked closely with the Department of Prisons, which had the job of designing and building an electric chair to be used according to the new law. At the same time he staged a number of sensational experiments, killing hundreds of dogs, cattle and horses to demonstrate how swift, certain and "humane" death by alternating current was.

The part of the new law that authorized the use of the electric chair was included in just one sentence: "The punishment of death must, in every case, be inflicted by causing to pass through the body of the convict a current of electricity of sufficient intensity to cause death, and the application of such current must be continued until the convict is dead."

There was nothing about alternating current or direct current nor anything about a chair. There was no appropriation of funds for the state to buy any electrical equipment because that part of the law had been mysteriously dropped out before it was passed. That bought Brown enough time to make sure that when the state finally got around to buying the equipment it would have Westinghouse's name on it.

Under the terms of the new law, the county sheriffs, who had been in charge of executions until then, turned the responsibility over to the state prisons. The condemned were ordered to be kept in solitary confinement broken only by visits from prison officers, relatives, physicians, clergymen or attorneys.

The judges were not to set the exact day on which the sentence was to be carried out. Instead they set an entire week, allowing the prison warden to select the actual date. Attendance at executions was limited to prison officials, clergymen, physicians and a limited number of members of the public. After the execution, a funeral would be conducted within the prison walls, and the body would either be buried within the prison walls or given to relatives for burial.

The new law proved to be just as controversial as the report of the Commission had been, with public opinion clearly split. The *New York Times*, in an editorial the day after the bill was signed by the governor, praised the legislature for allowing New York to: "have the credit of being the first State in the Union to do away with the brutal work of the hangman.... This is a step forward in the cause of humanity to which even the most violent advocates of capital punishment cannot reasonably object.... The revolting scenes that have characterized so many public executions in the past can no longer be repeated in this State."[13]

The *New York Tribune* also endorsed the new law: "No right-minded person can fail to approve the enactment of the law which puts an end in this State to the brutal and barbarous practice of executing condemned prisoners by hanging. It is creditable to the Empire State that it has taken the lead in a reform that probably in no long time must be adopted by all civilized communities.... Punishments involving mutilation of the infliction of personal violence have disappeared with the advance of civilization, and now, the gallows is to share the fate of the stocks and the whipping post."

The *Albany Times*, in an editorial on June 5, however, was not as enthusiastic about the new law: "It is a particularly gloomy comment on this law that, wide as has been the influence and agency of electricity in our concerns of daily life among the highest and lowest, the first official use to which the Empire State puts it by any due process of law, the first recognition of it in our statutes as an agency in the transaction of official business, is an agency of death."[14]

Brown's letter warning about the "damnable" alternating current was read before the New York Electrical Control Board on June 8, and local electric utilities were asked to bring their comments to a hearing scheduled for July 18 at Wallack's Theater.[15]

Among those attending this hearing were representatives of all the major electric companies and Ralph W. Pope, secretary of the American Institute of Electrical Engineers. Among the letters read at the hearing were many from engineers who thought Brown's charges absurd, stemming from ignorance or planned falsehood and designed to mislead the public about the safety of electricity. He was accused of being unduly influenced by "companies that stood to gain from outlawing alternating current," meaning Edison. Brown was not present at the hearing but read accounts of it in the *Electrical Engineer.*

To defend himself against these charges he obtained Edison's permission to use his West Orange laboratory to conduct a series of experiments that he said would prove the deadly qualities of alternating current. Edison assigned Kennelly to work with Brown and together they attached electrodes to dozens of stray dogs and tried various combinations of volts and amperes before announcing that it took only 300 volts of alternating current to kill a dog, but 1,000 volts of direct current.

Once they were satisfied that they could reproduce these results in public, Brown announced that he had scheduled a demonstration at the lecture hall of Columbia College's School of Mines for July 30. He invited the press and members of the electrical community. Assisting him in the demonstration were Kennelly and Dr. Frederick Peterson, a member of the New York Medico-Legal Society who had used electricity in his practice, performing as many as 30 electrical treatments a day for various ailments in hospitals and clinics.

Brown opened his demonstration by insisting that he had been drawn into the controversy not out of any self-interest but because of his concern that alternating current was too dangerous to be used on city streets. He denied charges that he was in the pay of any electric light company and had "no financial or commercial interest" in the results of his experiments. Of course the fact that he was using Edison's equipment and was assisted by Edison's chief of research spoke for itself.[16]

Then Brown brought in a 76-pound Newfoundland dog that had been muzzled, confined to a metal cage and previously prepared with electrode connectors on one of its fore legs and one of its hind legs. Brown connected the dog to the DC generator that Edison had loaned him and starting with 300 volts gradually increased the voltage to 1,000 volts. As the voltage increased, the observers noted, the dog's yelping increased but it remained alive. Then Brown disconnected the DC generator and connected the dog to an AC generator.

"We will have less trouble when we try the alternating current," Brown said. "As these gentlemen say, we shall make him feel better."

He connected the dog to the AC generator and turned the voltage up to 330. The dog died instantly. He then announced he would try the experiment again on another dog, but this time he would use the AC generator first to show that the dog had not been weakened by the DC current. He had just brought in the second dog when he was interrupted by Agent Hankinson of the Society for the Prevention of Cruelty to Animals, who denounced the experiments and ordered them shut down. After some discussion Brown agreed, and the second dog won a stay of execution.

This was all wonderful theater, and the newspapers loved it. *The New York Times* told the story under the headline "Died for Science's Sake."

The *Electrical Engineer* criticized the experiment as scientifically unsound and included a little ditty someone on the staff had written:

> The dog stood in the lattice box,
> The wires around him led,
> He knew not that electric shocks,
> So soon would strike him dead...
> At last there came a deadly bolt,
> The dog, O where was he?
> Three hundred alternating volts,
> Had burst his viscerae.[17]

One of Westinghouse's engineers who attended the demonstration insisted that alternating current was safe, even at 1,000 volts. He suggested that an AC engineer, T. Carpenter Smith, offered to be hooked up to the AC generator and take 1,000 volts if Brown would take the same 1,000 volts of direct current.

"This willingness on the debater's part to sacrifice both his friend and his opponent on the altar of science did not meet with approval of either of those gentlemen, and it lapsed to the manifest disappointment of the rest of the company," the *Times* reporter wrote.

The reporter overheard Brown say at the end of the demonstration that, "the only places, where the alternating current ought to be used were the dog pound, the slaughter house and the State prison."

After working out an agreement whereby the experiments would be observed by a representative of the board of health, Brown completed his demonstration on August 3 by killing three more dogs. The first was killed with 272 volts AC after five seconds, the second got 340 volts for five seconds. The third dog was still living after a jolt of 220 volts after five seconds so it was given 234 volts for 30 seconds and "died without a sound or a struggle."

The next day Brown wrote to Kennelly that he needed a vacation. He was worn out and had lost 12 pounds because of his professional battles with the electrical engineers who were dismissing him as little more than the proprietor of a traveling sideshow. In the same letter he betrayed his true motives for holding the demonstrations by promising that his work "will get a law passed by the legislature in the fall, limiting voltage of alternating current to 300 volts."[18]

In a paper prepared for the National Electrical Light Association later that year, Dr. P. H. Van der Weyde attacked Brown's experiments as unprofessional and motivated by commercial rather than scientific interests.[19]

Brown took his canine execution show on tour throughout the state

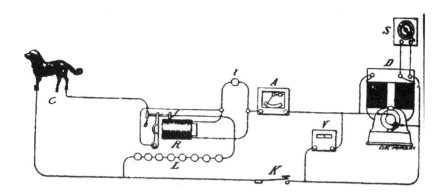

Schematic diagram for Harold P. Brown's experiments using electricity to kill a dog. (*New York Medico-Legal Society Journal,* 1888)

during the rest of 1888, killing as many as a dozen dogs in an evening after first measuring their electrical resistance and then applying a lethal dose of what he was always careful to assure the audience was the deadly alternating current.

Meanwhile, the Medico-Legal Society of New York had been asked by the Department of Prisons to suggest the best way to go about implementing the electrical execution law that was scheduled to go into effect on January 1, 1889. Without any experience or expertise in electricity, the state had no idea about how to go about constructing the electric version of the gallows. The society appointed a committee to come up with specific recommendations and appointed Dr. Peterson, Brown's assistant in the dog experiments, as its chairman. While electrical engineers around the country were blasting Brown for his obviously commercial motives, the committee took his experiments seriously and used the results in making their recommendations.

In the draft version of the committee's report on November 15, it recommended that either direct current or alternating current could be used for the executions "but preferably the latter." By the time the final report came out a month later the committee mentioned only AC.

On December 5 Brown and Kennelly staged another demonstration at the Edison labs to answer critics who had charged that the dogs in the previous experiments weighed much less than a man and were therefore invalid in determining how the current would work on a human being. In the presence of Edison, Gerry and a committee of the Medico-Legal Society, they killed a horse and two calves with alternating current ranging from 710 to 730 volts. The *Times* reporter who witnessed the demonstration wrote that

Top: A drawing for Harold P. Brown's experiments using electricity to kill a horse. (*New York Medico-Legal Society Journal,* 1888) *Bottom:* A schematic diagram for Harold P. Brown's experiments using electricity to kill a calf. (*New York Medico-Legal Society Journal,* 1888)

beginning on January 1, "the alternating current will undoubtedly drive the hangman out of business in this state…. The experiments proved the alternating current to be the most deadly force known to science."[20]

    Just a few days later, on December 12, the Medico-Legal Society committee made its official report, which was endorsed by the society as a whole and sent to the state. This report, which led directly to the design of the electric chair, made no mention of direct current as an option. It had to be alternating current.

"We think there are serious objections to the employment of any apparatus in which the prisoner takes a standing position," the report said. "The necessity of some bodily restraint is evident.... In our opinion the recumbent or the sitting position is best adapted to our purpose."

One electrode should be connected to the condemned person's head, the committee recommended, and the other "might be placed on any portion of the body," but they suggested the spinal cord.

The committee recommended that the state use either "a stout table covered with rubber cloth and having holes along its borders for binding" or " a strong chair.... We think a chair is preferable to a table."

Early designs for the electric chair envisioned a helmet and chin straps to hold the electrode to the victim's head. (*New York Medico-Legal Society Journal*)

The condemned prisoner would be tightly strapped in and a helmet containing an electrode would be securely clamped or strapped to the head. The other electrode would be attached to the spine with a strap. The cables from the two electrodes would be attached to the generator, and a switch on the wall would turn the current on and off. The electrodes would be attached with sponges or chamois skin, soaked in a brine solution to assure the best contact and reduce burning. The hair should be cut to make good contact with the head electrode. The generator should be able to produce at least 3,000 volts.

The report quoted Brown, with whom the committee seems to have been in close contact, as saying that the entire apparatus for electric executions, including the alternating current generator, could be purchased for $5,000.

Also included in the report was a long quote from Edison, about whom they said "none can be regarded as a higher authority," in which he recommended using alternating current for the electric chair because it produced "instantaneous death."

Edison spoke at one of the society's meetings, and Brown had written to Kennelly afterwards that the committee had been impressed with his comments and that they "carried great weight."

In the very last paragraph of its report, the committee recommended that "the alternating current should be made use of.... [S]uch a current allowed to pass for from fifteen to thirty seconds will ensure death."[21]

This was a major victory for the direct current side of the battle of the currents, and Westinghouse was quick to counterattack. In a long letter to the *New York Times* published on December 13 he showed why Brown's experiments with AC were unsound and then went on to explain what was really going on in Edison's labs with all those dead animals. "It is generally understood that Harold P. Brown is conducting these experiments in the interest and pay of the Edison Electric Light Company; that the Edison Company's business can be vitally injured if the alternating current apparatus is successfully introduced ... and that Edison representatives ... consider themselves justified in resorting to any expedient to prevent the extension of this system."

The experiments, he said, had been designed not to produce valid scientific information but to produce "the most startling effects.... We have no hesitation in charging that the object of these experiments is not in the interest of science or safety, but to endeavor to create in the minds of the public a prejudice against the use of alternating currents."

Quoting from the Edison Electric Light Company's annual report, he said that during the past year Edison had sold electric light generating systems capable of powering 44,000 lights, while in the month of October 1888 alone Westinghouse had sold 48,000. The attack on alternating current, he said, was an act of desperation by a company that was rapidly headed for bankruptcy.

In his reply in the *Times* five days later, Brown denied "that I am now or ever have been in the employ of Mr. Edison or any of the Edison companies" and charged that Westinghouse was minimizing the dangers of alternating current to protect his business interests. Then he went on to challenge Westinghouse to a duel by electricity.

"I therefore challenge Mr. Westinghouse to meet me in the presence of competent electrical experts and take through his body the alternating current while I take through mine a continuous current.... We will commence with 100 volts and will gradually increase the pressure 50 volts at a time. I leading with each increase until either one or the other has cried enough and publicly admits his error."

When Westinghouse ignored the challenge, Brown claimed it was because Westinghouse knew he would lose. During the next year Brown collected a number of articles and reports that supported his position that AC was dangerous and published them in a pamphlet that he sent out to the mayors and members of city governments of every city in the United States with a population over 5,000. The pamphlet, "The Comparative Danger to Life of the Alternating and Continuous Currents," calls AC "the executioner's current" because New York planned to use it for the electric chair. Brown never explained how he managed to pay for the cost of the publicity campaign, but one of Edison's salesmen, F. S. Hastings, wrote a letter to Edison in early 1889 asking Edison to direct Brown to send copies of his booklet to a list of legislators in Missouri, where negotiations for an Edison system were underway.[22]

Brown also lobbied in a number of states in favor of proposed laws that would have set 300-volt limits on the voltage that electric lines could carry, which would hamper the use of AC systems.

Meanwhile, on January 1, 1889, New York's electric execution law went into effect, despite the fact that there was no apparatus yet available with which to carry it out. According to the law, the first person convicted of murder in 1889 would be sentenced to electrocution rather than hanging.

The *New York Examiner* noted that there had been "a carnival of death and crime" in the weeks after the law went into effect and wondered if there was a connection. "There is little doubt that the criminal classes look with less horror on the new method of execution than on the gallows." It quoted another paper that had sent a reporter to interview the prisoners on death row in the Tombs prison and found that all of them would have preferred to die by electricity and regretted that the new law did not apply to them."

Southwick, who had attempted to remain neutral in the AC-DC controversy and was on the verge of being forgotten as Brown took over as chief spokesman for electrocution, attempted to grab the spotlight back again on January 6 when he announced to the press that he had invented an important piece of the apparatus to be used in carrying out the new electrocution law. It was, as one might have expected from a dentist, a chair.

This was not the first time during the debate over electrocution that an "electric chair" had been mentioned. Southwick himself suggested it in the articles he wrote in the early 1880s, and several of the correspondents who answered the Gerry Commission's survey mentioned the

An early design for the electric chair used a footrest that made it look more like a dentist's chair. (New York State Library)

use of such a chair. This was the first time, however, that anyone had attempted to work out the details of the design of such a chair. As drawn by Southwick, the chair looked very much like a dental chair and included a headrest with an electrode connected to a dynamo. The other electrode was to be attached to the metal seat of the chair. Significantly, Southwick specified in his plans that the chair must use alternating current.

After the law went into effect lawyers and judges complained that because it did not spell out the way the electrical current was to be administered and because the state seemed to have no apparatus ready for such an execution, the law might be unenforceable, and murderers might have to be set free. They suggested that the law be amended to be more specific about how executions were to be performed. Southwick said he was opposed to amending the law because any reopening of the issue "might result in the repeal of the entire law—stranger things have happened. Besides, if it should become necessary to execute a criminal before the passage of the amendment it would further complicate matters and tend to make the entire law inoperative."[23]

In late February at a convention of electrical dynamo manufacturers in Chicago, Brown's bizarre experiments and the electric chair were main topics of discussion. The manufacturers believed that the talk about electrocution was bad publicity and added to the public's fears about the safety of electricity. For this reason they passed a series of resolutions. The first declared that neither form of electricity was dangerous. They also pledged that none of them would provide any of the dynamos for "such ignoble use" as the electric chair to New York or any other state. This resolution was probably introduced by a friend of Westinghouse. By this time Ohio, Illinois and Michigan had introduced bills, modeled after New York's law, for their own electric chairs.

The New York Department of Prisons, already forced to deal with the unpleasant business of conducting electrocutions, insisted that the manufacturers' boycott was not a concern and vowed to continue to enforce the law as best it could. The kind of dynamo necessary was so similar to the kind used for electric lighting, they said, that it could be purchased on the open market almost anywhere. Once the dynamo was purchased, they said, it would become state property, and the state could do whatever it wanted with it.

Of the three state prisons that were to conduct executions, only Sing Sing had an existing electrical generating plant. Clinton and Auburn still used gas for lighting, but both of them had steam heating plants and therefore had the necessary power sources to run a dynamo.

Austin Lathrop, the state's superintendent of prisons, was clearly not happy about the way the new law was being administered. Until then, executions had been the responsibility of the county sheriffs, and he complained that he did not have the experience or the resources to take over the job.

On March 1 Governor Hill signed an amendment to the 1888 electrical execution law allocating $10,000 for the purchase of the equipment necessary to construct the electric chair apparatus. This money had been in the original bill but had been left out of the final version, during the last minute mix-up in the Senate. The new law still did not set out an exact procedure for the executions, but specified the purchase of "an electrical apparatus suitable and sufficient for the infliction of the punishment of death … together with the necessary machinery and appliances." There was no mention of alternating current, despite Brown's efforts and that of the Medico-Legal Society to get that wording included. By this time Westinghouse had his own lobbyists in Albany protecting his interests.

In an interview with the *New York Times* printed on March 9, Brown admitted that no one yet knew the exact method to be used to execute convicts. It was agreed that each prison would have its own dynamo, the device that generated the electricity, instead of using the city's electric light transmission lines. It was also agreed that the condemned man would sit in a chair, which would be connected to the dynamo.

Brown said he assumed that the chair would be made out of iron and that the electrodes would either be connected to each arm or to the head and the spine. He said the exact location of the electrodes would probably vary with the person and in the opinions of the doctors. The connections between the body and the electrodes would be covered with sponges, he said, soaked in a salty solution to make a better contact for the electric current.

As the executioner of hundreds of dogs, cattle, horses and other animals, Brown claimed to be an expert on the way high voltage jolts of electricity act upon a living creature. "There have been many curious statements concerning the extraordinary power of resistance the human body, and particularly the human head, is supposed to have," he said. "It has been asserted that the skull would interpose such a barrier to the current that its course would not be effective. Such statements I have ascertained by experiments to be quite unfounded…. There is no fear of failure from that source."

According to his experiments, Brown said, the dynamo required by the state need be no more powerful than 1,000 to 1,200 volts. "Our experiments have conclusively proved such a current to be ample to secure the necessary results and a stronger current might burn—something extremely undesirable," he said. Brown insisted, once again, that the current would have to be alternating current, since anyone shocked with direct current was likely to revive, even after a heavy dose. In one of his experiments, he said, a dog was only unconscious after being given a shock of 1,420 volts of direct current. He insisted it could have been brought back to life with artificial respiration.

"I know that there are men who have said they have taken an alternating current of 1,000 volts without feeling any evil effects from it," he said, "but they have taken it as a plumber flips molten solder from his soldering iron with the ends of his fingers…. If any man has placed his hands on the poles of a dynamo having a current of 1,000 volts flowing from it he has done it as quickly as the plumber does with his solder."

With doubts still lingering about which system to use, Brown scheduled yet another of his dog and pony shows at Edison's Menlo Park, New Jersey, labs on March 12. This time he invited a number of prominent doctors who had raised some concerns about his procedures. Among them was Dr. Carlos F. MacDonald, medical superintendent of the State Asylum for Insane Criminals, who was to spend much of the next decade observing executions in the electric chair and performing autopsies following them. He attended the experiments as the representative of Governor Hill. Also present was Austin Lathrop, the superintendent of prisons, Dr. Alphonse D. Rockwell, another prominent physician who was to write extensively about the electric chair, and Dr. Edward Tatum of Philadelphia, who had written about the process in his state.

The main question yet to be determined was where on the condemned person's body the electrodes were to be placed. Until this point, Brown had used two methods. One involved placing the electrodes on each hand, which forced the current to travel through the chest, stopping the heart and collapsing the lungs. The other method was to attach one electrode to the head and the other to the base of the spine, forcing the current to run through the brain and the spinal cord.

The goal, according to MacDonald, was to produce death as quickly and as painlessly as possible but using the minimum amount of current so as not to unnecessarily disfigure the body. The experiments took place from noon to 6 P.M. and involved killing four dogs, four calves and a horse. All of the experiments involved alternating current, since Brown insisted that his previous experiments had determined conclusively that this was the preferred method. The reporter for the *New York Times* said the current alternated at 200 to 300 times a second, which he described as a series of nearly instantaneous "knock down blows ... greatly improving upon the delivery of the notorious John L. Sullivan [a famous boxer]."

The animals were led, one by one, into a compartment of a wooden structure in the rear of the laboratory. The room was filled with coils of wire, clusters of lamps, gauges and dials that reporters said encouraged most of the visitors to keep a safe distance. The boys who had sold the animals stood by, watching as the experiments took place. The dogs were the first to go, with one electrode placed on a hind leg and the other placed either on the heart, the head or the neck. The electrodes consisted of a flat brass plate covered in felt and soaked in a solution of salt water. The ends of the wires were attached to the two electrodes. The technicians stood back while one of them turned a crank on the dynamo, creating the electric current. The intensity was measured by a set of lightbulbs. One by one they lit up, indicating that the voltage was building up to the required 500 volts.

"Are you ready?" asked the technician at the switch.

"Look out," he said, after the others assured him they were at a safe distance. Then he closed the switch. Instantaneously the dog's limbs stiffened. There was no sound, no convulsion and no appearance of pain. In 10 seconds the switch was opened again and the dog dropped in a heap.

Of the four calves killed that day only one uttered a sound. They had their legs tied before the electrodes were attached and the current was raised to 800 volts. The horse was an old, rough-coated brown beast no longer useful for pulling a plough or a cart. The 830-pound horse was killed with a jolt of 1000 volts lasting 25 seconds.

The experimenters found that the best results were obtained by placing one of the electrodes on the head and the other on one of the rear legs. By passing the electricity through the brain, it was thought, death would be instantaneous.

"To this end," the *Times* reporter wrote, "a helmet has been suggested, fitting closely and strapped on. This is thought by many electricians to be the best way. To take the place of a bandage on the hind leg, a shoe or slipper, with metallic soles, or a sort of buckskin to be strapped over the calf of the leg, or a foot tub containing water have all been proposed. All of these suggestions are under consideration, but those in charge cannot yet give any intimation of their plan."

On March 19 MacDonald wrote a letter to Brown inviting him to bring details of his proposals along with an estimate of his costs to a meeting with wardens and the Department of Prisons at which they would discuss the hiring of a consultant to build the electric chair.[24]

Soon after this Brown signed a contract with the Department of Prisons to supply, install and put into operation the electric chairs in the three prisons. Edison's mouthpiece in the battle against alternating current was now being paid by the state to actually build an execution device.

There are conflicting accounts about who actually constructed the first electric chair. Southwick and Fell both claimed later that they had designed a chair long before Brown took over as the state's official electric chair technician. As we will see later, however, even Brown's designs for the chair were modified before the chair was actually used.

While Brown conducted his experiments and drew up the initial plans for how to build the first electric chair in the spring of 1889, the state of New York was ready to sentence its first criminal. After the new law went into effect on January 1 it was only a matter of time until a real criminal was selected to substitute for the long parade of dogs, cattle and horses. From that moment on the debate about the use of the electric chair was no longer just an abstract topic; it bore a human face.

—5—
The People v.
William Kemmler

Despite all the publicity about the new electrical execution law, it's unlikely William Kemmler, a 28-year-old alcoholic vegetable peddler in the city of Buffalo, had heard anything about it. Kemmler was illiterate and spoke with a thick German accent that betrayed his origins as the son of an immigrant in the ghettos of Philadelphia. During the winter of 1888-1889 he lived in a similar kind of ethnic neighborhood, full of taverns and brothels, in a tenement on Division Street in Buffalo. Yet it was Kemmler's destiny to play one of the crucial roles in the great experiment with electrical death.

Kemmler's fate was an accident of time and place. If he had committed his crime a few months earlier or a few months later, if he had chosen some other state to run away to with his girlfriend, the world would never have heard of him. He would have remained a faceless murderer hanged from the scaffold in a county jail yard and soon forgotten.

Instead, his name and face were in newspapers all over the world, his case was heard by the U.S. Supreme Court, and, by a recent estimate, his name and the legal case that is named after him have been cited in 226 cases before the high court.[1]

Kemmler was born in a tenement at 2531 North Second Street in Philadelphia on May 9, 1860, one of eleven children of a Lutheran family, of which only five survived, William, a brother and three sisters. Although he never attended school, he could speak some English and German, but he never learned to write. His father was a butcher, and he spent his early years assisting in the butcher shop. From his earliest days he had to work for a living on the streets of Philadelphia, selling newspapers, blacking boots and doing other kinds of work. His mother died of tuberculosis at

William Kemmler, the first victim of the electric chair. (*New York Herald*)

an early age, and his father died of gangrene from an injury he acquired during a drunken brawl.[2]

When he was seventeen he took a job in a brickyard in Lamaisville, Pennsylvania, for two years, where he saved enough money to buy a horse and wagon. He returned to Philadelphia as a vegetable peddler, buying produce from farmers in the countryside and selling it in the city. He was on his way up in the world and was making a fair living, but at this point he "became a heavy drinker and brawler and his intellect grew more dense than mere ignorance had left it," according to Albert M. Dickenson of the *Saturday Globe.*

A medium-sized, slender and sandy-haired man, Kemmler was a perfect example of what temperance advocates of his time called a "life ruined by drink." When he was sober, Kemmler was capable or running a small business and maintaining something like a normal life, but when he was drunk he lost all control, lashing out at his loved ones and getting himself into terrible scrapes that were difficult to sort out later.

These problems came to a head sometime early in 1888. One of his female neighbors, who had taken a liking to him, took advantage of him during one of his drunken binges, dragged him before a justice of the peace and persuaded him to pronounce the marriage vows. When he sobered up, Kemmler tried to talk the woman into an annulment but she would have none of it, insisting that he was her husband. When his "wife's" family took her side in the dispute and threatened legal action if he failed to acknowledge her, Kemmler felt his only option was to skip town. Since he was leaving everything behind anyway, he took the opportunity to take the real love of his life, Matilda "Tillie" Ziegler, with him. Since she was also involved in an unhappy marriage, it was an easy decision for her to make. He had met Tillie through his brother, who was married to Tillie's sister.

Frederick Tripner, Tillie Ziegler's father, told the *Buffalo Evening News* on April 1, 1889, that "William, the poor boy, was married once, but he left his wife the next day. She got him drunk and he married her while he was on liquor. A little while after that he sold all of his property for

$1,200 and came away here to Buffalo with Mrs. Ziegler. They took her little girl Emma with them."

Tillie Ziegler told her friends she ran off to Buffalo with Kemmler in 1888, leaving behind her husband of eight or nine years, a cabinetmaker. She left him, she said, because he wouldn't let other women alone and because of that had contracted what she called "a bad disease." Tillie, 24, was described by those who knew her as plump and quite beautiful, with extremely fair skin, dark hair, blue eyes and a good complexion.

Kemmler changed his last name to Hort when he moved to Buffalo, apparently to keep his "wife" from locating him, and took out his peddler's license under that name. The registration shows

Tillie Ziegler, Kemmler's common law wife, who was murdered with an ax. (*New York Herald*)

that his business consisted of three horses and a cart. Henry Kemmler, William's brother, said William and Tillie returned to Philadelphia for Christmas in 1888, and they seemed to be happy. William told his brother he was making good money in his business.

"William and Tillie seemed to get along fine," said Henry Kemmler. "She said she liked William better than her husband."

But domestic tranquillity could not last long for someone like Kemmler. In early January neighbors complained about loud and violent arguments involving Kemmler and Ziegler in their little apartment at 526 South Division Street. They had a room in the rear of a house owned by Mary Reid. Neighbors said both of them had violent tempers, and they seemed to argue and fight constantly. Some said they often heard blows being struck, but no one intervened.

Just before 8 A.M. on March 29, one of these arguments took a particularly violent turn. Neighbors could hear screaming and blows being struck, but by now they were used to it and chose to ignore it. The first sign that this argument was any different from the rest came when Kemmler ran into Mrs. Reid's kitchen with his hands and sleeves covered in blood.[3]

"What have you done now?" asked Mrs. Reid, fearing the worst.

"I've killed her," Kemmler told her. "I had to do it. There was no help for it. I'll hang for the deed. Either one of us had to die."

"You don't mean it, do you?" said Mrs. Reid, who began screaming hysterically.

"Yes, I do," said Kemmler. "See my hands!"

As he held them up, the blood dripped onto the floor. Then he ran back to his apartment and returned with Tillie's four-year-old daughter, Emma, who was crying that "Papa has killed my mama."

Mrs. Reid ran for help next door while a neighbor named Asa King ran down the street to seek out Police Officer O'Neill, who was walking his beat nearby. Kemmler, despite the fact that he was probably drunk, did not resist when O'Neill placed him under arrest and took him to the police station. Meanwhile, a Dr. Blackman, who had an office at 509 Swan Street, was called to Kemmler's apartment to examine Tillie. The doctor found a room covered in pools of blood. Lying in one of them, with her face, hair, black dress and entire body covered in blood, was Tillie.

A reporter from the *Buffalo Evening News*, who arrived a few minutes later, found eggs still frying in a skillet on the stove and potatoes in the oven. The kitchen table had been overturned in the course of the fight. In the pools of blood on the floor, the reporter found Tillie's slippers, and the marks of her stocking feet could be traced on the floor. One of the walls of the apartment was covered with bloody fingermarks where she had attempted to get away from Kemmler. Nearby on the floor was a small hatchet, the kind used to chop wood for a kitchen stove.

"He must have thrown her to the floor and chopped away at her until his arm grew tired," was how the reporter reconstructed the crime from the evidence.

Dr. Blackman said it was the worst case he had ever been called to examine. Despite her multiple cuts and loss of blood, he said, Tillie's heart was still beating, so he placed her on a bed and called an ambulance to take her to Fitch Hospital. When she arrived, the doctors shaved her head so they could better examine her injuries and counted 26 gashes in her skull, some of them so deep that sections of brain tissue were seeping out. Tillie's skull had been fractured in five places. Her right arm had been cut in five places and both of her shoulders had been gashed.

The doctors considered her case a hopeless one, but they went to work to try to save her anyway. They called in the resident brain expert, a Dr. Park, who removed 17 fragments of skull from her head. Despite the doctor's efforts, Tillie never regained consciousness and died at 1 A.M. the next day.

Meanwhile, Kemmler was refusing to cooperate with Buffalo special officer Hammersmith, who was conducting the investigation. All Kemmler would say was, "I have nothing to say. Don't bother me." The next day, however, he confessed his crime to Lt. Daniel W. Berry of the Buffalo Police. Kemmler insisted he wasn't a bad man but just the victim of his "foul temper."

"I wanted to kill her, and I am ready to hang for it," Kemmler told Berry, words that would prove ironic later when Kemmler found out that New York had a unique form of punishment for him. While smoking a cigar given to him by police, Kemmler insisted he was not sorry for the crime and would do it over again if he could. He asked for a drink of whiskey, but the police turned him down.

In searching Kemmler's apartment, police found and confiscated $500 in cash. Tillie's daughter, Emma was placed under the care of the landlady, Mrs. Reid.

During the next few days, as Kemmler gradually sobered up and had time to think things over, his attitude toward Tillie softened, and he seemed to have become genuinely remorseful that she was dead. He told police he wanted his $500 savings used to pay for Tillie's funeral, including a coffin with silver handles.

He also became more cooperative with police, telling them that he had killed the woman he loved during a fit of drunken jealousy because he suspected that Tillie was having an affair with one of his friends, "Yellow" John DeBella.

The rest of the story came out at the trial, which began at 9:40 A.M. May 7, 1889. It was not a long trial because Kemmler had already admitted he was guilty of the crime, but it attracted much attention because of the brutal nature of Tillie's death. The judge assigned to the case was Henry A. Childs, 52, of nearby Medina, New York, who had studied law as an apprentice in a law office rather than going to law school. A former district attorney, he was known for his courteous personality but strict adherence to the letter of the law.

At first Kemmler's case was treated like an ordinary murder trial. No one seems to have thought that this case might become the first to fall under the new electrical execution law. Apparently everyone assumed that the first case would come from New York City, where the majority of the state's murders were committed. None of the lawyers, the judge or the newspaper people covering the trial made the connection until the trial was nearly over. There were, in fact, several references to hanging made in the early part of the trial.

Erie County district attorney George T. Quinby, wearing a new spring suit, presented his entire case in a single day. He opened his remarks with a gruesome description of the murder scene while Kemmler, sitting at the defendant's table, bowed his head, leaned on his elbows and gazed at the

Henry Childs, the judge who sentenced Kemmler to die in the electric chair. (*New York Herald*)

floor. Beside him were his two court-appointed attorneys, Charles Hatch and C. W. Sickmon.

Quinby stressed to the jury the importance of Kemmler's repeated statements to police: "Yes, I have done it, and I will take the rope for it."

"What was the motive for the crime?" Quinby asked the jury. "The defendant got it into his head that she thought too much of DeBella. He was jealous. There is getting to be a frightful number of homicides and the punishment meted out to the murderers does not seem to check the crime. It is time that such a salutary lesson should be taught as will have a deterring effect."

Was this a reference to the electric chair? If it was, no one in the courtroom and none of the reporters caught it. More likely, it was a reference to the deterrent effects of capital punishment in general. It was still days before the matter of the electric chair would be raised publicly.

Listening to these opening statements and the rest of the testimony was Henry Kemmler, William's brother, and his wife, Tillie's sister. It must have been an extremely difficult time for them, feeling as they must sympathy for both the victim and her murderer.

Quinby told the jury the only possible defense was one of insanity, and he was ready to prove that Kemmler was sane at the time he committed the act. Unlike defense attorneys in modern court procedure, defense attorneys in 1889 did not make their opening statements at the beginning of the trial, but waited until the prosecution had presented all of its witnesses.

Quinby's first witness was William J. White, a civil engineer hired by Erie County to survey the scene of the crime. He introduced a map of the murder scene and a diagram of the building. Included on it were large blotches of red ink to show where blood had been found.

"There were also blood stains upon many dishes on the floor," said White. "The table was turned over and resting upon some barrels in the corner. The tray of a trunk, filled with articles of women's wear, was also upon the floor, but the trunk was not in this room."

Next came the testimony of the doctors who performed the emergency surgery and later the autopsy on Tillie Ziegler. At an appropriate point in the testimony, Dr. Charles S. Jones took a paper box out of his pocket in which he had preserved the 17 pieces of bone he had removed from her skull. These were carefully shown to the jury.

On cross-examination, Sickmon, Kemmler's attorney, seemed intent on showing the jury that Tillie was an attractive woman and therefore one who might have been involved in an affair with another man. Many of the witnesses who had seen Tillie in life and in death were asked about her beauty.

"Was she a good looking woman?" Sickmon asked Dr. Jones.

"Average looking," said Dr. Jones.

"Features regular?"

"Yes," he said.

Dr. Roswell Park, the next witness, was the consulting physician in the case and one of the most prominent doctors in the city. The cancer institute in Buffalo is now named after him. He was asked some details about hospital procedures.

"Now why did you remove those pieces of bone?" asked Quinby.

"To save her life, if possible," said Dr. Park. "To remove the pressure from the brain."

"Were the wounds inflicted by a sharp or blunt instrument?" asked Quinby.

"Blunt."

"What do you call a blunt instrument, a club?"

"Anything without a sharp point," said Dr. Park.

"Where is that hatchet?" asked Quinby as he took the rusty hatchet from a paper wrapper and held it up in front of Dr. Park.

"What do you call that, blunt or sharp?"

"Sharp in the sense in which I meant it," said Dr. Park. "I would call the back part of the hatchet blunt."

"What did you think of the woman's case when you first saw her?" asked Quinby.

"I regarded it as hopeless," said Dr. Park. He said he noticed that parts of Tillie's throat and breast were freshly discolored but could not say for sure if the marks had been made by a human hand.

"You may now say whether wounds inflicted with this instrument would be dangerous to human life," instructed Quinby, holding up the hatchet.

"Certainly dangerous," said Dr. Park.

Sickmon, in his cross-examination, asked the same question he had asked before.

"Was the woman good-looking?"

"Not as I saw her," said Dr. Park.

"Was she not comely?"

"She might have been," he said.

Asa D. King, a gray-haired, gray-whiskered bookbinder from Boston, testified later that day that he was visiting his father, Earl D. King, at 530 South Division Street, next door to the Kemmlers, on the day of Tillie's death. After Mrs. Reid, the landlady, ran into the house screaming, he went over to Kemmler's room.

"I put on my hat," he said, "went around, opened the door of Kemmler's kitchen and looked in. A woman was upon the floor on her hands and knees, blood all over her and her hair hanging down, her body swaying backwards and forwards. I shut the door. Then I opened it again. A man stood before me. He was wiping his hands on something. They were bloody. He stepped over the body."

King then identified the defendant as the man he had seen with the bloody hands.

He remembered telling Kemmler, "This is brutal, man. Let us go for a doctor," but Kemmler stepped out of the room and walked down the street. King followed him to a nearby saloon where he saw Kemmler enter and ask for a drink.

"Do not give it to him," King said he told the bartender. "He has brained his wife and she is weltering in her blood."

"What did he [Kemmler] say?" prompted Quinby.

"He said, 'Yes, I have done it, and I am ready to take the rope for it. The sooner the better.'"

King then followed Kemmler to another saloon, all the time insisting that a doctor should be sent for to help Tillie, but Kemmler refused.

On cross-examination, Sickmon quizzed King about how Kemmler appeared that day.

"How did he look, did he stare at you?" asked Sickmon.

"No," said King.

"When you said to him, 'Man, this is brutal,' did he make any reply?"

"No."

"In the walk to the first saloon did he say anything?"

"Nothing."

"How many times did you speak to him at that time?"

"Three times I think."

"And he paid no attention whatsoever?"

"He did not speak."

"Did he look at you?"

"He did."

Mary Reid, the landlady, testified that the couple often quarreled violently. Kemmler was often drunk, she said, but it was Tillie who seemed to start most of the fights.

"She used unladylike language," said Mrs. Reid. "I never heard him speak cross to her."

After that there was some corroborating testimony from neighbors and the police officers who arrested Kemmler. The hatchet that had been found in the kitchen was introduced as the murder weapon, and the jury was allowed to examine it. Near the end of the day, Quinby presented his star witness, "Yellow" John DeBella, a yellow-faced, black-haired Spaniard who said he was a partner in Kemmler's peddling business and lived in the same apartment with Kemmler and Tillie.

He said Kemmler took out his peddler's license under the name of John Hort even though everyone knew his real name was Kemmler.

"What we called him was 'Philadelphia Billy,'" DeBella said.

DeBella said Kemmler and Tillie quarreled frequently and once he heard Tillie tell Kemmler she would not live with a drunken man and was going back to Philadelphia.

"Did Kemmler ever say anything to you about his wife wishing to return to Philadelphia?" asked Quinby.

"He did once," said DeBella. "He said, 'Women are hell. When she says she wants to go to Philadelphia and I say I will go with her she will say she don't want to go.'"

DeBella then described a fight that Kemmler and Tillie had in their bedroom that lasted all night. He said he could hear it from his room next door.

On cross-examination DeBella testified that he and Kemmler often went on drinking binges together. On one occasion, he said, Kemmler went four days without eating. Many times he had seen Kemmler wake up groggy in the morning and noted that his nerves were shaky. On the afternoon and evening before the murder, he and Kemmler had made a tour of local saloons, he said.

Lt. Daniel W. Berry of the Buffalo Police, the final prosecution witness, testifying just before court was to adjourn, said he had given a glass of brandy to Kemmler just before he confessed to killing Tillie Ziegler.

"He told me that he was jealous of DeBella," said Berry, who then read a written confession in which Kemmler stated that he struck Tillie with the ax with the intention of killing her.

The next day defense attorney Charles Hatch opened the defense by painting a picture of Kemmler as a loner who spent much of his life in a drunken stupor and was incapable of taking responsibility for his actions. Such a man was incapable of premeditation, Hatch argued, so Kemmler should not be found guilty of first degree murder but of the lesser charge of manslaughter.

"All we will try to show you," he said, "are the facts in this case that have not been brought out so far. We will show you that the defendant drank—drank to excess—since he came here. We will show you that he once tried to drive his horse over a railroad train and committed many other insane freaks; that he spent $50 one night for liquor, that he was drunk at least three times during the week of the murder, from Monday until Thursday night, that he often sat in saloons for hours at a time as he sits here in court now, speaking to no one, paying attention to nothing, with his whole moral faculties dulled.

"We will not ask you to acquit this man," Hatch told the jury. "I believe it would be monstrous to turn loose upon society a man with such propensities as are his, but will ask you to carefully consider whether at the time of the homicide he was in a mental condition to premeditate a murder. There is no explanation in the world that will show that this terrible mutilation was a deliberate plan to kill. If he wanted to murder, one blow would have been sufficient."

He then asked the jury to spare Kemmler's life and sentence him to life in prison.

"Look at the prisoner," said Hatch. "There he sits with hardly any feeling, scarcely any understanding of the terrible position in which he is placed."

Kemmler sat motionless through this with his hands clasped and his head bowed, with what reporters said was "an air of utter dejection." Meanwhile the defense was set to bring before the jury a parade of witnesses from Buffalo's saloons and skid row to testify that Kemmler was not only a drunk but an insane and crazy drunk as well.

Charles A. Spang, a tall, slim-waisted man, testified that he was a former employee of Kemmler's and often peddled fruit for him.

"Was Kemmler a drinking man?" asked Sickmon.

"Yes," said Spang, "and a very hard one at that. It was one continual drunk from the time I went with him until I quit him. The fact was that both he and I always blew everything in. My folks kicked and I had to quit him…. We used to go into every saloon we came to."

"And what would be Kemmler's condition at night?" asked Sickmon.

"Well, long before night we would both be as full as we could hold."

"How much money would you spend each day?"

"Oh, it must have been $4 or $5 a day. Once he told me he wasn't drinking, but in a few days it was the same old story. I ran my own wagon this time and would get back from my route about 3 or 4 o'clock. I'd go in the house, have a pint of beer with Mrs. Hort and the rest, turn in my money and go home. We were all drinking the day before the murder. Billy and Yellow and I got pretty full."

"What did the defendant drink?"

"He drank everything. He started in on cider and would end up on whiskey."

"Could he walk straight?"

"He could neither walk nor talk straight. He could just get along and that's all. We had some eggs to sell but we were all too drunk to sell eggs."

"What would be Kemmler's condition in the morning?"

"Shaky," said Spang. "He would want a drink. Me and him always went for a drink in the morning."

"Did you see him the morning of the murder?"

"Yes, in John Martin's saloon. He was pale and trembling. His eyes looked wild. His eyes had looked wild for ten days before that. He had been drinking pretty hard for two weeks. He seemed melancholy. When I would say, 'Good Morning Billy,' he would hardly answer."

"Did you ever see him sitting down and saying nothing?"

"Yes, for hours at a time at the market."

"How would he sit?"

"With his head down and his thumbs going round and round like this."

"How many times have you seen him sit like that?"

"Several times. He would sit on barrels outside the mission houses. His memory was bad. He would forget who owed him money. I have often seen him sit like that at home."

"From what you have seen of him for two weeks previous to the homicide, would you say his conduct was rational or irrational?" asked Sickmon.

"Unreasonable. Out of the way. He acted very funny."

On cross-examination Spang admitted that he had also been drunk frequently during this time and had, in fact, had "three or four" drinks of whiskey before he came to court that morning.

"I'm as sober as any man in the courtroom," insisted Spang.

"You say he looked wild," asked Quinby. "What do you mean by that?"

"Strange-like," said Spang. "Bad looking in the eyes, a vacant stare like. Staring at vacancy and keeping his thumbs going round and round."

Henry Kemmler, the next defense witness, said he and his brother lived in the same house together in Philadelphia before Kemmler came to Buffalo. He said Kemmler was drunk for four months and did not have any job or occupation other than drinking. He was often found on a bench in the shed in the morning. When he visited Kemmler in Buffalo, he said, Kemmler was drunk most of the time.

Thomas M. Carpenter, another city fruit peddler, said he had known Kemmler since the previous autumn. Once at his house, he said, he watched Kemmler drink a quart of whiskey "quicker'n any man I see, or half a dozen men for that matter. It was good stuff, too, no whiskey like you get over a bar. When you would meet him on the street the first thing he'd say was 'Come and have a drink.' I took him home two or three times. He would act stupid. He couldn't walk. One time him and me went on a drunk together for two days. It was on a bet for $5. He thought he could drink more than me and I thought he hadn't room enough to hold as much as I could."

Thomas Martin, a red-haired, freckled man who owned a saloon at the corner of Jefferson and Division streets, said Kemmler was one of his best customers and often was found in a hunched-over position, looking stupid and refusing to answer questions. He would sit like that for three or four hours, he said. Sometimes Tillie joined him in the saloon, either to drink beer with him or to try to bring him home. On the day of the murder, when Kemmler came in just before his arrest, he looked wild, he said.

"He turned his head from side to side. His eyes looked curious," said Martin.

After that there was a parade of over a dozen drunks, all relating to the jury in some detail their drunken carousals with Kemmler. They told of getting drunk with him three or four times a week, often to the point of being unable to walk or speak. Quinby attempted to counter this by bringing in some of the fruit dealers from the Elk Street Market where Kemmler conducted his business. Although he often seemed intoxicated, they testified, he was a shrewd business man.

John Kehoe, a rebuttal witness for the defense, testified that he had once seen Kemmler at the Olympic Theater buying drinks for the women there. He said Kemmler spent about $50 there because the drinks cost twice as much as they did at a bar.

Throughout this phase of the trial the defense kept asking witnesses if Kemmler appeared to be "irrational" in addition to being drunk. When the witnesses agreed that Kemmler did seem to be irrational, Quinby insisted that they make the distinction.

For example, John Burkhardt, a retired peddler, described Kemmler as "queer, stupid and irrational."

"What do you mean by irrational?" snapped Quinby. "You mean drunk, don't you?"

"No, I don't," insisted Burkhardt. "A man may be drunk and yet know what he is doing."

"How often have you been drunk?" asked Quinby.

"How often have you been drunk?" shot back Burkhardt.

"Answer the question," said Quinby. "Are you a drinking man?"

"I never get drunk," said Burkhardt, "but I have drank more or less since I was a boy." He insisted Kemmler was stupid and queer even when he wasn't drunk.

The defense then called Dr. T. D. Crothers, editor of a magazine called *The Journal of Inebriety* and physician in charge of Walnut Lodge, a private asylum for alcoholics in Hartford, Connecticut. He said he had specialized in the treatment of alcoholics for 14 or 15 years and had treated hundreds of cases. He also said he had examined Kemmler in his jail cell that morning.

"A man who uses alcohol in excess has a defective brain," Crothers testified. "It destroys his moral power. It destroys his will power, breaks it up. It destroys his body less than it does his mind."

He said there was a close relationship between consumption and drinking, that offspring of consumptives have a marked tendency to drink. This was relevant because Kemmler's brother had earlier testified that Kemmler's mother had died of consumption and that his father had died of gangrene acquired during a drunken binge. A man who had drunk all his life, as Kemmler had done, could not have a sound brain, he said, and would be incapable of judging the quality of his acts.

Another common characteristic of inebriates, he said, was a delusion about the fidelity of their wives. Although they would never suspect their wives of cheating while they were sober, he said, they often went into a jealous rage when they were intoxicated, usually over some little thing that would have been otherwise dismissed.

A deformity in the pupil of Kemmler's eye, he said, was a sign of brain disturbance. He had a small head, his eyes were close together and set back very far in his head. All of these were signs of brain disturbance. Kemmler also seemed unable to understand simple questions.

"I asked him if he remembered the crime," said Dr. Crothers. "He hesitated. After expressing the question two or three times in different ways, he said he thought not. I asked him if he remembered what he had bought and sold the month before the crime. He made no answer. I put the same question to him in another form and he shook his head, but did not speak. I asked him if his father got intoxicated. He said he did and got drunk every Sunday. I asked him what his father had died of. He said some brain disease in the hospital."

Dr. Crothers said he could not say for certain if Kemmler was insane and added that there was no scientific proof that drinking habits passed from father to son.

"I asked the prisoner if he wished to live," Dr. Crothers said. "He hesitated and finally said he did. I found that he had suffered with private diseases." This was never explained, but seems to have been a reference to venereal disease.

In answer to questions put to him by both lawyers, Dr. Crothers said a man who had been drunk all day might not be able to premeditate a crime, even if he had been able to perform such normal functions as ordering a horse watered, purchasing eggs for sale and fixing a door.

"He might do all of this and be morally irresponsible," said Dr. Crothers.

Quinby was buying none of this and commented within the jury's hearing that "if all men who drink have defective brains, then two-thirds of mankind has defective brains."

He then brought in his own expert witness, Dr. Phelps of Buffalo. He said he examined Kemmler the day after the murder and determined that he did not have a feeble mind and was well aware of the nature and consequence of the crime. His colleague, Dr. Slacer, was also called and said basically the same thing.

The concluding statements by both sides centered on the prime question in the case. Was Kemmler sane enough to understand the nature of the act of killing Tillie? The defense attorneys argued that someone like Kemmler, who lived so much of his life in a drunken stupor, was incapable of understanding the implications of what he was doing when he picked up the hatchet. Quinby, on the other hand, called such excuses nonsense and urged the jury to avenge Tillie's death by finding Kemmler guilty.

Judge Childs then explained to the jury that if Kemmler understood the "nature and quality" of his act then the only question was the degree of the crime, which was a question of fact for the jury to decide. For a verdict of murder in the first degree, deliberation and premeditation must be proved. If these could not be proved then it was murder in the second degree. Drunkenness was no excuse for crime, Childs explained, but was admitted by law to show lack of premeditation.

He told the jury that it might help for them to divide the case into two "chapters," with the prosecution supplying the bloody first chapter and the defense supplying the second chapter, "which might truthfully be labeled 'whiskey.'"

The jury retired at 5:40 P.M. on May 9 and began its deliberations after supper was brought into the room in the front of the courthouse. The members deliberated until 10 P.M., when Judge Childs adjourned the case until 9:30 the next morning.

The case had been drawing an increasing number of spectators all week, and by the time of the jury deliberations there were not enough seats for all of those who wanted to witness the climax of the case. When Kemmler was brought into the room the next morning he immediately fell into the same posture he had used throughout the trial, slumping down in his chair in a bowed, dejected posture.

When the jury came into the courtroom most expected them to announce a verdict, the rumor being that they had split nearly evenly between first and second degree murder on each of the many ballots taken the night before.

"We balloted all night," one of the jurors said later. Early that morning the tally was eight for first degree murder and four for second degree. So when they came into the courtroom it was not to announce a verdict but to ask for sections of the testimony to be read back to them. Included was testimony from some of the doctors, as well as some from Kemmler's drunken friends, including "Yellow" DeBella.

After the testimony was read back, Judge Childs told them it was not necessary for them to find that Kemmler had a high order of intelligence for him to be amenable. It was only necessary to know that he understood the "nature and quality" of his act and that he meant to kill.

"If this were not the law," said Childs, "half the human family would be exempt from the consequences of crime."

Sickmon objected to this statement, saying that the defendant might know the nature and quality of his act and yet might not be guilty of murder in the first degree.

"I have already charged that," said Childs, who then sent the jury back to the deliberation room until 11:15, when they came out a second time.

"Everyone was certain that they had agreed," wrote the reporter for the *Buffalo Evening News*. "Another trial that was in progress in the court room was suspended so the Kemmler jury could take its place in the jury box. The sky by this time had become overcast and the gloom of the court room was in keeping with the scene about to be enacted. A rush of people from the corridors soon filled the court room to overflowing."

"Gentlemen of the jury, have you agreed upon a verdict?" asked the clerk.

"We have," said the foreman, almost in a whisper.

The clerk then ordered Kemmler to stand while the verdict was read.

"There was a sharp clap of thunder at that instant," wrote the reporter;

"rain dashed against the windows. The prisoner started to his feet as if electrified."

Again, this is a curious choice of words, considering Kemmler's ultimate fate, but as yet there had still been nothing written or stated publicly that indicated that Kemmler's sentence would be in any way unusual or that there was any other significance to the word *electrified*.

"Guilty of murder in the first degree," said the foreman in a voice that was raised but trembling. Sickmon asked that the jury be polled, and each of the 12 confirmed that the verdict was unanimous.

Kemmler had been gazing directly at the jury, but he was sitting down again even before the jury poll was completed, assuming his usual slumped over position.

Judge Childs said he would pass sentence on Thursday. Hatch asked for a delay, but it was denied. Kemmler was handcuffed and taken out of the court in a slouchy, uneven gait to the jail.

It was not until later that day that the significance of the Kemmler case became known. Exactly who put two and two together to figure out that Kemmler was about to become the first human being sentenced to die by electricity is uncertain. It could have been that someone in Albany or at the Department of Prisons, hearing the news of the conviction, brought it to the attention of a reporter. It could have been one of the New York City newspapers waiting for a case to write about. Or it could have been that Judge Childs was officially notified by Albany in time for the sentencing. Perhaps the judge and the attorneys knew all along but were keeping the news secret for some reason.

Suddenly, Kemmler's case, which had been summarized in newspapers around the state as a typical bloody murder trial, took on new significance. From this moment onward Kemmler became the man who was first in line for "death by the wire rather than the rope," as the newspapers described it.

The new law, which went into effect January 1, was set to take effect for any murder that was committed after that date, so it was merely a matter of timing that transformed Kemmler from just another convicted murderer into the test case and set him apart from every murderer before him and after him.

Kemmler himself seems to have been notified of this after his conviction but before the sentencing, the first in history to involve electricity. Reporters who attempted to interview him about this were met with stony indifference. Playing euchre with his guards in his shirt sleeves in his second-floor cell, he was less than cooperative with reporters who attempted to interview him.

"Come and see me again," he said in answer to the reporter's questions. "I'll talk with you then."

"Suppose you are sentenced to die," asked the reporter; "would you rather be hanged or killed the new way?"

"Eh?" said Kemmler.

"Would you rather be killed by electricity?"

Kemmler shuddered.

"I'll tell you some other time," he said. "Come around and see me again, won't you?"

One of the guards was more forthcoming, saying Kemmler ate and slept well and did not seem too troubled by his fate.

"He is about forty thousand times more afraid of the battery than of the rope," said the guard. "He asked me all about the gallows, how it is made, how big it is, the length of the rope and so on, and he said if he had to go he would prefer to die that way. He didn't know anything about the new way until it was explained to him and then he said he was afraid of the battery."

The same article explained that the electric chair at Auburn Prison would be ready for Kemmler any time after June 10.

On May 13 Judge Childs returned to his courtroom to pronounce the first ever sentence of death by electricity: As Kemmler watched and listened, Childs said: "The sentence of the court is that within the week commencing on Monday the 24th Day of June in the year of our Lord one thousand eight hundred and eighty-nine, and within the walls of Auburn State prison, or within the yard or enclosure adjoining thereto, the defendant suffer the penalty of death, to be inflicted by the application of electricity, as provided by the Code of Criminal Procedure of the State of New York, and that in the meantime the defendant be removed to, and until the infliction of such punishment be kept in solitary confinement in said Auburn State prison."

Suddenly people all over the country were reading about William Kemmler and the unusual and terrifying death the state of New York planned for him to avenge the death of Tillie Ziegler. What they didn't know was that a number of very rich and powerful people also had their eyes focused on Kemmler and the machine that was to be built in Auburn. Kemmler's trial turned out to be only the first round in a long and complicated battle. His case was soon to be argued by medical societies, law schools, bar associations, the state legislature, the state's appellate courts and, finally, the highest court in the nation.

—6—
Westinghouse's Counterattack

Whe New York State authorized $10,000 for the purchase of the apparatus needed to build the electric chair in March 1889, there were no specific instructions about electrical generators, volt meters or electrodes. That was left up to the State Department of Prisons, which did not have the slightest idea about how to go about building an electric chair. What was needed was an expert, a consultant, someone who knew enough about electricity and had enough experience to build the device in a hurry. The law had gone into effect earlier that year, and the chair would be needed quickly.

Who better to fill that role than the electrician who had been demonstrating his expertise at killing all manner of animals, the foremost advocate of the electric chair, Harold P. Brown? As far as Austin Lathrop, the superintendent of prisons, was concerned, it was the perfect choice. For Brown, the appointment as the state's official electric chair technician was a perfect opportunity to further his plan to discredit Westinghouse.[1]

Brown was hired in March after a meeting called by Lathrop and also attended by the wardens of the three prisons that were to have electric chairs: Auburn, Sing Sing and Dannemora. Dr. Carlos F. MacDonald, superintendent of the State Asylum for Insane Criminals at Auburn, recommended Brown for the job. He wrote a letter to Brown suggesting that he come to the meeting with his plans and schematics for the electric chair and a detailed estimate of the costs.[2]

Brown's contract with the Department of Prisons has not survived, but some of its details can be inferred from later statements. Brown said later that his involvement was limited to the electrical devices, and he refused to actually design the chair, leaving that up to MacDonald and Rockwell. Other witnesses said that he did have a hand in designing it.

He was to be paid half of his $1,600 fee when the electric chair was set up and successfully tested and the other half after Kemmler's execution. The contract also had an escape clause that ordered the state to make the final payment even if there was a delay in executing Kemmler after the summer.

As soon as he was appointed, Brown set out to purchase three Westinghouse AC generators because, as he told Lathrop, they were the most dangerous and therefore perfect for the job. By now, however, Westinghouse was wise to Brown's plans and ordered his salesmen to refuse to sell any equipment to Brown. Unable to buy the dynamos openly, Brown tried using middlemen and indirect methods of making the purchases, but each time Westinghouse officials discovered his schemes and thwarted them. Even Brown's attempts to buy used machines from third parties were foiled by Westinghouse officials, who were determined not to let any of their generators fall into Brown's hands.[3]

Since the state refused to pay him until the dynamos were actually installed in the prisons, Brown also needed money to pay for the purchases. On March 27 he wrote to Edison, asking for his approval to seek help from a Westinghouse competitor, the Thomson-Houston Electric Company, which was involved in merger talks with the Edison Company. This letter is one of several that demonstrate how closely Brown was working with Edison.

"In view of the approaching consolidation [with Thomson-Houston] the people of 16 Broad Street [Edison Company] do not feel like undertaking the matter unless you approve of it," Brown wrote to Edison. "A word from you will carry it through, without it the chance will be lost. Is it not worthwhile to say the word?"[4]

Edison apparently said the word. Any letter that Edison sent back or any paper trail of what he did next is not recorded, but things moved along quite swiftly after that. With Thomson-Houston's advice and financial assistance Brown came up with a remarkably elaborate scheme that involved a Boston dealer in used electrical equipment, who located three Westinghouse generators in upstate New York. The dealer shipped the generators to Rio de Janeiro, Brazil, where even Westinghouse's diligent efforts failed to keep track of them. Then they were shipped back to New York in secret and finally shipped to the three prisons.

Brown had one of them shipped to Auburn under what he called "strict secrecy" because he was afraid Westinghouse might find a way to sabotage his plan before the devices arrived. Brown's delivery instructions were sent out on May 12, the day before Kemmler was sentenced in Buffalo. Whether all this stealth and secrecy was necessary or if Brown was simply suffering from paranoia remains uncertain. Also unknown is how closely the Department of Prisons was monitoring and approving of Brown's elaborate schemes.[5]

The day after Brown sent the delivery instructions to Boston he wrote another letter to Edison, thanking him for his help and informing Edison he had been "able to arrange the matter satisfactorily."[6]

At the time the world was reading about Kemmler's fate, Brown was holding press conferences explaining his plans for the construction of the Auburn electrical system. Now that the first victim had been chosen, there was a renewed public interest in his work and his equipment. During these interviews Brown was very careful to explain that the dynamos to be used by the state were *Westinghouse* dynamos and that they operated on the very dangerous *alternating* current as opposed to the continuous—and safer—direct current.

The dynamos, he explained, were designed for electric lighting and produced 1000 volts each, even though it had been found that only 140 volts (or roughly what was being used in street lighting) were enough to kill a person. The dynamos were to be connected to an "exciter" to control the current and then sent to a strong oak chair, he said.

"The prisoner will wear a metal cap to which one of the electrodes will be attached, " he explained to the press. "The other will be attached to metal shoes. There will be sponges, soaked in salt water, placed in both the cap and the shoes to control the point of contact. The warden himself will pull the switch for 15 seconds and then it is all over with the convict."[7]

Brown's detailed descriptions of how the chair would work lost him the support of at least one major newspaper. The *New York Evening Post*, which had supported the new law, changed its mind two days after Brown's interview was published. The *Post* editors said on May 14 that they had assumed the executions would be performed simply, with the push of a button, but changed their minds after reading about Brown's "terror-giving paraphernalia."

The generator that was destined to be used in the first electrocution arrived in Auburn on June 7. Brown inspected it in August and told a reporter that it was powerful enough to "knock the life out of Kemmler." With him during his inspection was a man Brown described as his "assistant," Edwin F. Davis, the man destined to pull the switch at Kemmler's execution and at least 300 more after it.

Davis was born on May 28, 1846, in West Caton, near Corning and conducted electrical experiments while still a boy. In 1884 he established one of the first telephone companies in the Corning area. His appointment as Brown's assistant was probably the work of Lathrop, a fellow resident of the Corning area.

Meanwhile, the new round of publicity was attracting its share of strange ideas. On June 6 Lathrop received a letter from a "well-educated" Philadelphia man who had suffered a financial disaster and needed a way to provide for his large family. For $5,000 he offered to become a human guinea pig, sitting in the electric chair while the power was turned on. If he died the money was to go to his family. If Lathrop agreed to the proposal he was to place an ad in The *Philadelphia Ledger* for "A.F." "It is needless to say that Gen. Lathrop has not accepted this offer," a newspaper reporter wrote.[8]

While the Westinghouse forces were unable to prevent Brown from securing one of their generators and setting it up in Auburn, they set about attacking Brown's plans on an entirely different front: the courts.

Kemmler's sentence to become the first person anywhere to be executed by electricity attracted worldwide attention and put a human face on the ongoing debate over the ethics of using the electric chair. Until then the talk of a "subject" or a "victim" of the execution had been purely theoretical. In their schematic diagrams of the proposed device, the electricians had talked of a "load" or a "resistance" that would be switched into the circuit once the dynamo was running at the appropriate speed. Now, for the first time, that part of the electrical circuit had a name and a face, and drawings of that face were reprinted in newspapers all over the world.

The advocates of the electric chair could not have hoped for a better test case. An unrepentant adulterer, an illiterate drunkard, an admitted ax murderer, Kemmler was not the kind of man around whom it was easy to generate a sympathetic audience. It was easy to make the argument that the world would be better off without him. What would have happened if there had been some doubt about the guilt of the person who was scheduled to be the first person to die by electrocution? What if it had been someone with a pleading family or someone with influential friends? What if it had been a woman instead of a man? The debate would have taken a much different course, and the outcome could have been different as well.

Despite that, Kemmler's sentencing did serve to rally support to those opposed to the electric chair. Humanitarians who had followed the debate in the newspapers through the battle of the currents and the executions of the dogs and ponies found the idea of attaching a human being to an electrical generator and pulling the switch in many ways more horrible than hanging. Many who had remained silent began to question the whole idea of legal electrocution. Although there was a very vocal group that insisted that electrocution was the more humane method, others insisted that it was nothing but barbaric torture. When these new converts to the abolitionist cause were added to the already growing movement against the death penalty, many thought there was a good chance that New York's law might be overturned before it took its first victim. In fact, as we shall see, that nearly happened.

Because of the way the new law was written and enacted there was more at stake than just exchanging electrocution for hanging. The old capital punishment law had been repealed at the time the electrocution law was passed. Therefore, if the electrocution law was found unconstitutional it would leave New York without any capital punishment law at all. In fact, supporters of the electric chair maintained that murderers sentenced to die after January 1, 1889, would have to be set free. This fact certainly helped strengthen the argument that the law should not be repealed.

Within weeks of Kemmler's arrival at Auburn Prison in the spring of 1889 a writ of habeas corpus was filed against the state by attorney William Bourke Cockran complaining that the law was in violation of the Eighth Amendment to the Constitution because it constituted cruel and unusual punishment.

Cockran was no small-time lawyer trying to make a name for himself. He was one of the most famous attorneys in the country, with clients that included New York City newspaper publishers, railroad barons, life insurance companies, private utilities and tobacco concerns. He also had excellent political connections as one of the bosses of the Tammany Hall machine in New York. After serving a year in Congress from New York's 12th District in Manhattan he had quit the year before because his law firm was losing money without him. Known for his great speeches and excellent speaking voice, Cockran had made a name for himself by defending his fellow bosses in Tammany Hall against charges of graft and corruption. It was estimated at the time that he made as much as $100,000 a year in fees, which made him the highest paid lawyer in the country.

When asked why he took Kemmler's case, Cockran maintained that he had always been an opponent of capital punishment and was acting out of conscience and a sense of duty. Yet his record clearly shows he had never shown the slightest interest in criminals or death sentences unless they involved someone wealthy enough to pay his fees. He never took another such case after he finished with Kemmler. He did, however, have an extensive track record of helping utility companies fight government regulators in court.

W. Bourke Cockran, the attorney who argued the case against the electric chair in New York State. (New York State Library)

Even in 1889 few people were fooled by his denials, and newspaper reporters soon figured out who was paying Cockran's exorbitant fees. As was revealed later, he had been retained by the Westinghouse Electric Company, which had finally figured out how to play the high-stakes marketing game that Brown and Edison had started the year before. If Westinghouse could get the law repealed and Kemmler was allowed to go free, there would be no gruesome display in Auburn of the dangers of a Westinghouse generator.

Cockran's writ was filed in Cayuga County Court in Auburn.

Although it was filed against the prison warden, seeking a stay of execution, the state attorney general, Charles F. Tabor, a Democrat from Buffalo, chose to argue against it, asking that it be dismissed.

Judge S. Edwin Day granted a temporary stay, ruling that Cockran's suit seemed to have some merit but said he didn't have enough information to determine if electrocution was cruel or unusual. He therefore took the unusual action of appointing an administrative referee to conduct a series of hearings around the state to gather the necessary information. These hearings, under the supervision of court referee Tracy C. Becker, attracted considerable attention and served to polarize the debate.

Becker, 34, was a graduate of Albany Law School and served as assistant district attorney in Buffalo for four years before going into private practice. At the time of his appointment he was a professor of criminal law and medical jurisprudence at the University of Buffalo, so he was an excellent choice, but the hearings he presided over had a hidden agenda.

Although they appeared to be fact-finding sessions designed to gather information, they turned into a platform for Cockran to cross-examine Brown, Edison and other supporters of direct current and the electric chair. In front of the newspaper reporters, Cockran, who was one of the best cross-examiners in the country, made Westinghouse's opponents appear to be ignorant, silly and even corrupt. Westinghouse was going to get his money's worth.

Just as Edison had hired Brown to be the front man for his attacks on alternating current, Westinghouse used Cockran for his counterattack on Edison. Kemmler had become little more than a pawn in the high-stakes marketing war between the two powerful companies.

The hearings began on July 9 in Cockran's law offices in the Equitable Building in New York City. Cockran had a two-pronged strategy for convincing the judge that the electrocution law ought to be thrown out. The first part was to bring in witnesses to discredit the experiments that Brown had conducted the year before by showing they were conducted unfairly to make alternating current look more dangerous than it was. The second part was to cast a shadow of doubt over the certainty that electricity could cause death. To show this, Cockran was able to gather a remarkable number of witnesses who had been struck by lightning or knocked unconscious by electrical wires. Among those attending the hearings were George T. Quinby, the district attorney who had prosecuted Kemmler, and Deputy Attorney General William A. Poste, who represented the state.

The first witness Cockran called was Brown himself, setting up a confrontation between the proxies for the two electrical giants that Westinghouse must have anticipated with great relish. This round clearly went to Cockran, who got Brown to admit that he was not a member of the Institute of Electrical Engineers and that he had no formal education in electrical science nor any background in the ethics of capital punishment. In preparation for his testimony, Brown had written to Edison to ask for advice, and Kennelly wrote back advising Brown to focus on the fact that electrocution, if done properly, would not mutilate the condemned man's body.[9]

After Brown described his animal experiments in detail, Cockran asked him how it was possible to use the results of those experiments in determining what would happen when a man was executed. How did he know how much current to use?

"Suppose, however, that a mistake was made and an insufficient power was applied, what would be the effect upon the criminal?" Cockran asked.

"In that case, the subject would be rendered unconscious and would be unable to feel any pain," Brown said. "The electrodes used would be kept moist so that the flesh would not be burned."

"Is unconsciousness the inevitable result of a powerful electric shock?"

"Yes," said Brown.

"Is it possible to inflict torture upon a subject without causing unconsciousness?"

"Yes, if the current were applied at a very low pressure, say 100 or 150 volts."

"At 400 volts?"

"No, I think such a pressure would result in fatality."

In answer to another question, Brown said it was not possible to generate a man-made electrical force that was anything close to the power of a lightning bolt.

"Yet you have heard of a human being having been struck by lightning and not being killed?" asked Cockran.

"Yes," Brown said. "I have."

When Cockran asked him about his association with Edison, Brown claimed it was a personal one, based on favors Edison had done for him when he was conducting his experiments on animals.

During the next few days Cockran brought in several Westinghouse electricians who testified that their experiments with animals and electricity conflicted with those of Brown. Their main point was that human bodies had different resistances to electricity, and therefore it was impossible to determine how much voltage would be needed for the electric chair. A few hundred volts might be enough to kill one man, they said, but would only stun someone else. They also raised the horrible possibility that the electric chair might only stun its victim, who would appear to be dead but could then come back to life sometime after burial.[10]

One of the first witnesses, Franklin F. Pope of Newark, said he was a Westinghouse technician who had experimented with electricity for 30 years. If a dozen people held hands and a weak electric current was passed through from one side to the other, he testified, some would not be able to stand the shock and would let go while others would feel nothing. Further, he said, the Wheatstone Bridge, the device that was commonly used to measure the electrical resistance of objects, could not accurately measure the resistance of living things, especially human beings.

To back up this opinion, he described an experiment he had performed a few days before at the Western Union Telegraph Company in New York. While measuring his own body's resistance, he said, he found that it varied greatly with the strength of the current. At one volt, he said, his resistance was 6,300 ohms, but at 10 volts it was 5,140 ohms. At 50 volts it was 3,850 ohms, and at 100 volts it was 3,500. He speculated that the variation was due to some kind of chemical reaction by the electricity on the fluids in the body.

Pope said the Westinghouse dynamos that had been purchased by the state could produce a maximum of 1,050 volts, but the special committee of the New York Medico-Legal Society which had investigated the issue at length, had suggested a voltage of 1,000 to 1,500 volts ought to be used.

There followed a lengthy discussion of lightning as opposed to the "artificial electricity" produced by a dynamo. Pope said lightning was much more powerful than any current that had been produced by man. The longest spark he had ever witnessed from a dynamo was about 16 inches long, he said, while a lightning bolt could stretch for a half mile. Despite the high voltage produced by lightning, he said, people struck by it often survived. Cockran then commented that if heaven's thunderbolt was not fatal in every instance then man's certainly could not be.

In an electrical execution, Pope testified, the body of the victim was likely to be burned and the brine-soaked sponges that had been used by Brown to prevent this would be of little use. A strong current, he said, could boil water in a few seconds and would scald the victim's flesh.

In answer to questions from Quinby and Poste, Pope said he had seen only two or three persons who had been killed by alternating current. Although it was possible that such a death could be painless and instantaneous, he said, it was by no means certain. He insisted that even if the

Westinghouse dynamos were altered so that they could produce a higher voltage, there was no certainty that the victim would die.

The next day, after an invitation from Edison, the hearing was moved to his laboratory in West Orange, New Jersey, for further experiments to measure the human body's resistance to electric current. The experiments were to take place in the same labs where Brown had performed many of his animal experiments. Cockran could not attend that day and sent his assistant, T. D. Kenneson, who brought with him an electrical expert from the Westinghouse Company named John H. Noble. One of Edison's assistants named Wirt gave the group a tour of the facilities. When the group entered Edison's phonograph room, Brown, pointing at Noble, objected in an attempt to preserve Edison's trade secrets. An argument broke out between Brown and Noble that threatened to turn into a fistfight until Becker, the trained referee, worked out an agreement that allowed Noble to stay.

Wirt offered himself as the subject of the first experiment. With his hands immersed in a solution of zinc sulfate to make them conduct the current better, four one-volt batteries were attached so that the current passed through his body from one side to the other. The current was so weak that he did not feel it, he said, and his resistance was measured at 1,310 ohms. Next to plunge his hands into the solution was Deputy Attorney General William A. Poste, whose resistance was measured at 1,200 ohms.

Charles F. Hatch, the attorney who defended Kemmler at his trial, was measured in a different way. An electrode six inches by four inches, covered in felt, was saturated with salt water and placed on his head. Then he was asked to stand in his bare fee on a metal plate on the floor. His resistance was first measured at 9,870 ohms, but it dropped to 8,170 a few moments later.

Brown insisted that all of these measurements were unnecessary because the 1,050 voltage of the Westinghouse dynamos were more than enough to cause death. The only use for measuring a convicted man's resistance, he said, was to make sure the electrical contacts were sound against the prisoner's body.

When the hearings resumed a few days later, Cockran focused on Brown's earlier experiments. Daniel L. Gibbons, a member of the New York Board of Electrical Control who had been present at the School of Mines at Columbia College, said in some cases the animals had not died instantly.

"In such cases the animals seemed to suffer the most horrible agony," he said. "It was the most frightful sight I have ever seen. The creatures uttered cries as if suffering the most excruciating pain, and when the current was turned off they fell down as if exhausted by their ordeal."

Theodore Moss, another member of the board, testified that the animals' torture was so heartrending that he was forced to leave the room. Although Brown had carefully measured the voltage during the experiments, he said there had been no attempt to measure the amperage, or volume, of electricity that was used.

"The effect of a current is different on different people, just as whiskey is," he said. "Some it might kill, while there may be others to whom no amount of electricity would be fatal. In some cases the strong current would paralyze the nerves and stop the beating of the heart or cause polarization of the blood. If this latter occurred I think a person could probably be brought back to life by passing through him another current which would neutralize the effects of the first.... My conclusion is that no electrical current can be generated by methods now known to science that would kill in every instance."

After attacking Brown's experiments, Cockran returned to his other main point, that electricity was a wildly unpredictable force that sometimes killed and sometimes created a death-like state from which victims often recovered. Among the witnesses called was Alexander G. McArdle, a former employee of the Signal Service Bureau in Washington who had spent several years studying the effects of lightning strikes on human beings. Often when this happened, he said, the victim was knocked unconscious, but death was not at all certain. It was possible for the bolt to pass down one side of a person and not affect the other half. Asked about the electric chair, he said that if the current was allowed to continue the victim was likely to be burned to a crisp, even if a sponge was used where the electrode contacted the skin.

One of the most entertaining witnesses was Charles Tupper, who owned a restaurant at 226 Eighth Avenue. He told the story of his dog, Dash, a cross between a Scotch collie and a St. Bernard, who had the misfortune to step on a telegraph wire that had fallen to the street, coming into contact with an electric light wire. Dash jumped four feet into the air and fell back on the wire unconscious. He lay across the wire for about 15 minutes, Tupper said, because the spectators who gathered around to watch were afraid to pull him off.

Finally, one of the spectators threw his coat on the ground to act as a kind of insulator and stood on it while he lassoed Dash with a rope, pulling him off the wire. Dash fell to the ground with his eyes closed and Tupper assumed his dog was dead. But following the advice of one of the spectators he took Dash to a nearby backyard, where he half buried him in the ground in hopes of drawing off the electricity.

When Tupper went back to the brickyard six or eight hours later, he discovered that Dash's eyelashes were twitching and noticed other signs that there was still life in the old dog. Within a few days Dash was back to normal. After Tupper finished his story, Dash himself was brought into the hearing room, and Becker examined the wounds on Dash's nose and legs that had been caused by the electric wire.

Dr. Frederick Peterson, a specialist in nervous and mental diseases who had assisted Brown in his experiments, testified that he had used both alternating and direct current on his patients for several years as part of his therapy and found the former the most dangerous. It was so painful, he said, that he rarely used it. When he did he never applied the electrode to the head because it caused dizziness and nausea.

After Brown's experiments he had done autopsies on several of the dogs and found that the blood was darker than normal and that some of the nerves and capillary vessels had been broken. No one knew for sure why electricity caused death, he said, but he assumed that there was both a mechanical and a chemical reaction. In every case he witnessed, he said, the dogs died painlessly, and it was only when an insufficient current was used that they gave evidence of being hurt. A condemned man would probably lose consciousness as soon as the power was turned on, he said, and his death would be entirely painless.

John H. Noble, the Westinghouse technician who attended the resistance testing at the Edison labs, testified about an accidental shock of 1,000 volts he once received. The current passed from one hand to the other, and the only injuries were a few burns that healed within weeks.

Francis W. Jones, chief electrician of the Postal Telegraph and Cable Company of New York, explained that the measured resistance of a human body was an important part of the calculation in determining how much voltage was necessary to kill a condemned man. If the resistance of the criminal's body was too high, he said, the dynamo might not be able to generate enough voltage to kill him. By using various currents and configurations in experiments on his own body, he had found that the resistance could be as high as 80,000 ohms and as low as 31,000 ohms. In measuring other men he found that the resistance varied from 40,000 ohms to 7,120 ohms.

"I had read that 2,500 ohms was man's average resistance, " he said, "but my tests showed this to be a wrong calculation. If, as Dr. Peterson says, one ampere is needed to kill, it would require as many volts to make a fatal current as the criminal has ohms of resistance. Therefore I do not think you could generate an absolutely fatal current for a man with a resistance of 40,000 ohms. You would need a current with the voltage of 40,000 to kill him and it is entirely out of the question to produce a current with a pressure as great as that."

On July 18 Elbridge T. Gerry, the chairman of the state commission that had recommended the electric chair, testified at the hearing. Gerry had kept a low profile during the controversy, busy with his duties as commodore of the New York Yacht Club. He had been in Newport when the hearings began. At first he declined an offer to participate in the hearings and showed up only after a subpoena had been issued by Becker.

He testified about the procedures and findings of his commission but caused a stir in the hearing room when he stated publicly for the first time that he thought poisoning was preferable to electrocution as a means of capital punishment. The problem with poisoning, he said, was that it would be difficult to administer without the presence of a doctor, and most doctors would refuse to participate for ethical reasons.

Following Gerry on the witness stand was Dr. Landon Carter Gray, professor of nervous and mental diseases at the New York Polyclinic Medical School, who testified that no electric current, no matter how strong, would be able to cause instantaneous death in all cases. He based this opinion on the contradictory evidence of animal experiments and the effects of lightning. Because human beings have such a variable resistance to electricity, he said, the voltage required would vary from person to person.

He discussed the results of studies made in Germany that showed that the electrical resistance of human bodies varied from 555,000 ohms to 1,500 ohms. Every day as part of their practice, he said, doctors administer low doses of electricity, and the result is beneficial rather than deadly. Under the procedures being planned by the state, he said, it was likely that the flesh of the victim would be burned because even the weak current used by doctors as part of their therapy sometimes caused burns.

Most interesting of all, however, were studies he attributed to a Dr. D'Aronval of France, who used a strong electrical current to stop the hearts and breathing of dogs. Then, using artificial respiration, he brought them back to life. This was a point that Cockran kept coming back to over and over during the hearings, playing on the public's fear that a felon executed by electricity would come back to life. This concern haunted the advocates of electrocution right up to the day of Kemmler's death.

Dr. Gray was one of the many witnesses who discredited Brown's experiments because he controlled the voltage but not the amperage, which had varied from as little as 5 milliamperes to as much as 145 amperes. Although he did not specifically say so, the implication was that Brown had deliberately manipulated his experiments by using a higher amperage when he used alternating current, making it seem more deadly than it really was. He reminded the panel that voltage is the pressure of the current, whereas the amperage is the actual amount of electricity.

"Electricity is just like arsenic," Dr. Gray said. "A dose of the latter that would kill one man would not be fatal to another. I do not think that either agency is a certain means of death."

The next witness, Col. Michael Kirwin, the editor of the *New York Tablet*, was one of several witnesses who described receiving massive jolts of electricity and living to tell the tale. Kirwin said he was struck by lightning while he stood under a tree during his service in the Union army in the Civil War. Three horses that were under the same tree were killed, but he survived with a partial deafness in one ear and a partially paralyzed right arm.

Henry M. Stevens, a Boston electrician, testified that in Lowell, Massachusetts, in 1883 he was examining the brush on a 1,450-volt dynamo when he slipped and fell. One hand rested on the positive terminal and the other on the negative.

"I felt that something was filling up my veins and became unconscious," he testified. "My weight pulled me to the floor, where I lay for some time. A physician, Dr. Barry, examined me and not being able to hear my heart or pulse beat or to see any signs of respiration, declared that I was dead. Sometime afterward I began to recover my senses. The pain was excruciating. I felt that I was being drowned, run over by a train and was enduring a thousand other tortures. In a few days I was almost well and had the pleasure of reading the account of my death in the newspapers."

Arthur E. Colgate of the Western Electric Company, a witness at Brown's dog and pony show at the Edison Labs in West Orange, testified that the animals' deaths were anything but painless. "The animals howled and underwent contortions as if the pain they endured was something awful," he said. "Some of them were not killed after a number of shocks were passed through them and I finally dispatched one of them with a brick to relieve him of his agony."

"And that shock was fatal!" joked Cockran in response.

Alfred West, a New York bricklayer, told of being struck by lightning in June 1880 while he stood with two companions under a tree in Fort Lee, New Jersey. He heard the thunderbolt and the next moment was lying unconscious twenty feet away. He recovered his senses just as he heard someone pronounce him dead. The bolt had struck him on the chest, and he had a burn two inches wide down his right side and leg. The jolt had also knocked off his shoe. His watch was found 25 feet away. At first his left arm was drawn up under his chin and both his legs were paralyzed, but this soon wore off and he was able to ask for and enjoy a glass of "Jersey lightning," a cup of tea and a piece of pie. He was bedridden for three weeks during treatment of his burns.

T. Carpenter Smith, an electrical engineer from Philadelphia, said that like other members of his profession he was accustomed to being shocked with high voltage electricity but that it seldom interfered with his work. He had survived shocks as high as 1,500 volts of direct current and 1,000 volts of alternating current. Being shocked felt like "all the fillings are being knocked out of your teeth" while being "pelted with a number of bricks." The only permanent injuries were some burns on his hands.

Benjamin D. Acker of the Keystone Light and Power Co. of Philadelphia told the story of a coworker named Wright, who was putting up some electric lamps in a damp location when he grabbed a live wire and took the full force of 1,000 volts of current. He fell down, dragging the wire with him, and could not be rescued until the current could be shut off, some seven or eight minutes later. By that time, Wright's face was purple, and he had stopped breathing. Everyone was sure he was dead, but shortly afterward he began to breathe again and was back to normal. Acker said he had been shocked many times without any noticeable effects.

Frank H. Mackin, a lineman for the Manhattan Electric Light Co., held up two badly burned hands as mute witnesses to the painful effects of electric shock. On the Tuesday before, he said, while working on a line, he slipped and fell onto a Fort Wayne "Jennie" dynamo, rated at 1,200 volts. "I did not lose consciousness," he said, "but felt that terrible vibration passing through my body and made up my mind that I was going to see the angels. I felt as if something inside me was going to burst, when someone turned off the switch and relieved me of my torture."

All of this testimony was reported verbatim by the New York newspapers and sent over the wires to other newspapers around the world, where readers were fascinated with the morbid details of the effects of electricity on the human body.

In its edition of July 20, 1889, a *New York Tribune* editorial criticized the hearings as too many anecdotes and too little substance. "In view of the fact that the inquiry directly involves the fate of a human being, and, incidentally the interests of large corporations ... it is somewhat remarkable that so much good nature and so laudable a desire to increase the sum of human knowledge have been displayed."

The conflicting testimony of the electric engineers, the editors said, was confusing the public rather than educating them, and many who were entirely in favor of the new law now had some doubts. "Popular distrust of electricity as a means of inflicting the death penalty has nothing to do with the specific case," the editors said, predicting that the final decision was likely to be made by the U.S. Supreme Court.

> It is entirely proper that this test should be made, and we have never seen any occasion for sneering at the proceedings now going forward. Whatever interest the people take in them is not inspired by maudlin sympathy with a convicted murderer. The law was not primarily designed to make capital punishment less painful and ignominious, but to make it sudden, certain and decent in respect to the accessories and circumstances. The welfare of the convict was not the first consideration.... Kemmler's counsel are endeavoring to show that execution by electricity would be "cruel and unusual" because that is their only means of proving the law unconstitutional, but the public is chiefly concerned in ascertaining whether or not the law certainly provides a decent and efficient method of inflicting the death penalty.

But even if the law is found to be constitutional and Kemmler's execution is successful, the editors predicted, "it would not be surprising if the people should determine to repeal it.... It was inevitable that a complete departure from all experience and tradition in the means of inflicting capital punishment should be followed by a strenuous effort to overthrow the legislation which brought it about. Such an effort is now being made. It involves questions of great general interest and importance and it is quite worth while to learn as much as possible about it instead of treating it with contempt."

On July 22 Deputy Attorney General William A. Poste opened the state's case in favor of the new law by calling as his first witness Dr. Alphonse D. Rockwell, a specialist on nervous and mental diseases and electrotherapeutics and a professor at the New York Post Graduate Medical School. In his 25 years of experience, he said, he had become familiar with the electrical resistance of human beings and disputed the view of previous witnesses that because human bodies' electrical resistance varied the amount of voltage required would also vary.

"While the resistance of persons varies greatly when a weak current is first applied," he said, "the milliampere measurement shows that it becomes approximately the same after the current has flowed for some time. The size of the electrodes and the efficacy of their contact with flesh of the subject also lessens the resistance. Some people are more susceptible to electricity than others, but this depends largely on their ability to endure pain of any kind. It would amount to little or nothing in the case of a current strong enough to be fatal."

Rockwell, who was present at Brown's experiments in West Orange, said the current caused instantaneous death in every case but one, in which a dog endured the current for a minute or two before it was killed. The problem in this case, he said, was that too much of the zinc sulfate solution had been applied to the electrodes, and it ran down the animal's side, scattering the current.

"I am convinced that a current can be generated that will cause instantaneous and painless death in every instance," he said. "Experiments have shown that the alternating current is more deadly than the continuous and I believe that 1,000 volts of the former would be fatal in every case. If 1,500 volts are used there would not be the slightest doubt in my mind. I don't know what exactly the pathological effects of the current would be, but it is known that the tissues in the interior of the body are ruptured, the blood coagulates and the action of the heat and lungs stopped. The effect of the current of course depends on the circumstances and if the execution were not conducted on scientific principles, I could not be as positive as to its result."

Rockwell also testified about the differences between natural and artificially produced electricity: "The action of static electricity on the human body affords no certain means of judging of the effects of a dynamic current. The latter, as we learn by using it in medicine, passes through the brain, while the former remains for the most part in the surface of the body. In charging a pail of water with static electricity, it is found that the charge is entirely on the surface. This explains why people are not always killed by a stroke of lightning that burns them severely and tears their clothes from their bodies. The force of the electricity is mainly spent on the periphery of the body, and little reaches the nerve centers. A dynamic current, on the other hand, is generally diffused throughout the body, following the paths of least resistance.... The skin, bones and flesh of the body are in themselves non-conductors of electricity, but when moistened with the blood become fairly good conductors. The current, therefore, follows the course of the blood vessels and hence permeates the whole body.

"If large and thoroughly moistened electrodes were used, there would be little probability that the criminal would be burnt. If death did not follow at once, however, the current would, in time, perhaps several minutes, burn the flesh, unless the electrodes were kept wet. This could be done, I suppose, by an arrangement for constantly dripping water on them."

On July 23 the state brought in its most prominent witness, the wizard of Menlo Park himself, Thomas A. Edison. The event had been publicized ahead of time, and Edison's remarks were on the front pages in

New York the next day. Edison, who had previously said he would stay out of the controversy, was persuaded by a letter that Brown wrote to Samuel Insull, Edison's private secretary, saying that Cockran had raised many points that "Edison could dispose of with a word."[11]

Before his testimony began, however, there was an interesting exchange in the hearing room that was overheard by a reporter for the *New York Tribune*. Brown, who had been attending the hearings each day, asked Edison to comment on the previous testimony of T. Carpenter Smith, the Philadelphia electrical engineer who claimed to have survived several shocks with a 1,000 volt AC current. Edison, in reply, said he would give Smith $100 if he would allow him to send a 100-volt alternating current through him. Brown said he would add his own $100 to the challenge.

This kind of behind-the-scenes banter not only showed the confrontational aspect of the hearing but demonstrated once again that Edison and Brown seemed to be coconspirators despite the claims that Brown was not, nor ever had been, an employee of Edison.

Edison began his formal testimony by introducing himself as someone who, through his experience, "knew something about electricity and dynamos." He then went on to give what reporters said was the best description yet of the difference between alternating and direct currents. He said it was helpful to think of electricity as water in a pipe. With direct current the water flows from one end of the pipe to the other. With alternating current the water flows back and forth in the pipe, switching directions many times a second. In the Westinghouse dynamos, he said, the direction was reversed about 150 times a second.

In preparation for his testimony Edison had spent the previous Saturday shocking some 250 of his own employees as an experiment to see how they reacted to various kinds of current. The most significant finding was not the variation in resistance from person to person, he said, but that the measurement seemed to depend more on the method used to attach the electrodes. When the contact was not secure, he said, the resistance increased enormously, sometimes as high as 200,000 ohms, and resulted in burns. The strength of the current seemed not to matter much, he said, although his employees tended to react negatively when he raised the voltage much above eight volts.

When asked about the design and safety of alternating current systems, Edison could not resist a little Westinghouse bashing. "I am not familiar with the Westinghouse dynamo," he said, "but I know how they are constructed. They can be made to give a higher voltage than ordinary by increasing the speed of the revolutions of their armatures. I should think that they ought to stand a threefold acceleration in the rate of their revolution without danger of the armature bursting. The Edison Company owns patents of dynamos producing the alternating current, but we don't use the machines, as we regard them as dangerous.

"I believe that an artificial current can be produced to kill instantaneously and painlessly in every case," he said. "I think the best way is to put the criminal's hands in a solution of caustic potash and then I feel sure that 1,000 volts of an alternating current, or of a frequently interrupted continuous current, would be certainly fatal. I have found that the alternating current is the most effective of the two, as some persons cannot stand eight volts of it, while they hardly feel the same amount of a continuous current."

Edison then described an experiment he conducted on a frog that had the nerve in one of its hind legs surgically exposed so that an electrode could be attached to it. Each time the current was turned on, Edison said, the leg twitched, even though only a tiny amount of current was used. With alternating current, he said, he could produce the same effect on the leg of a person.

Claiming he was not a medical expert, Edison declined to speculate about electricity's effects on the body but denied previous testimony that such a current would severely burn the body.

Cockran had told reporters that he was looking forward to cross-examining Edison, hoping to get the electrical wizard to admit some of the deadly qualities of electricity, but throughout these questions, Edison remained cool and professional. At one point, however, he complained about Cockran's questions, calling them "nonsense."

Asked why he had taken the unusual step of performing electrical experiments on his own employees, Edison said he had done it to resolve some of the questions raised at the Kemmler hearings.

Cockran questioned the accuracy of the equipment used. Wasn't the Wheatstone Bridge, the device used to measure electrical resistance, somewhat arbitrary? Edison claimed it was as accurate as a ruler. Did he take the time to measure any of the men twice to determine if the resistance changed? No, Edison said, he did not think that was necessary. Was it possible to burn a man up with 1,500 volts of electricity? Certainly, said Edison, but it would not be like a bonfire, more like a carbonization.

"With a *wicked* Westinghouse dynamo," asked Cockran, "how long would it take to burn up the body?"

"It would not be burned," insisted Edison. "The temperature would rise three or four degrees and it would be mummified in time. This would be done by the evaporation of the fluids of the body."

Referee Becker then asked about the size of the largest dynamos in existence. Edison said the largest were in England and produced 10,000 volts, or about 5,000 horsepower. He thought that two Westinghouse dynamos could be run in tandem so that they could produce a combined voltage of 2,000 volts.

The impact of Edison's testimony on the hearing shouldn't be underestimated. His credibility, even at this point, was unquestioned. The *Albany Journal* said that with Edison's testimony the hearing "at last has an expert that knows something concerning electricity. Mr. Edison is probably the best informed man in America, if not in the world, regarding electrical currents and their destructive powers."[12]

Another editorial said, "If Edison is any authority upon the subject of electricity, and it is difficult to think of another, it would seem that there will be no doubt as to the efficacy of electricity as a death-dealing agent."[13]

After Kemmler's execution, the *New York Times* said it was Edison's testimony more than any other factor, that led the courts to rule that the electric chair was neither cruel nor inhuman.[14]

Dr. Cyrus Edson, president of the state Board of Pharmacy and official physician for the State Board of Health, had assisted at Brown's experiments at Columbia and was present at the autopsies of some of the animals. He told the hearing officers that all of the organs and nerves were in their normal states, except that the heart had stopped beating. There was nothing to show how death had been caused, but he believed it to be the result of a kind of nerve paralysis. He was convinced that an apparatus that could produce a current of 600 to 1,000 volts and one fourth to one half an ampere would produce death instantaneously and painlessly and without a doubt.

"But is not the effect of a current on human life entirely experimental?" asked Cockran on cross-examination.

"No," said Edson. "It has been demonstrated that a current, properly applied, will kill one of the lower animals and from this we reason that the same would be true in the case of a man."

Dr. Rudolph A. Witthauk, professor of physics and chemistry at the University of the City of New York and at the University of Vermont, talked about the effects of electricity on the human body in such technical terms that few in the room understood him. He was not questioned at length and Cockran chose not to cross-examine him.

Schuyler S. Wheeler, an electrical expert for the New York City Board of Electrical Control who was present at Brown's Columbia experiments, said he could explain why some of the previous witnesses had apparently survived exposure to massive amounts of electricity. Because electrical wires are much better conductors than the human body, he said, when a person came into contact with such wiring only a portion of it passed through the body. Most of it continued to be carried by the wires. So a person could seem to have come into contact with high voltage but was really only exposed to a fraction of it.

Cockran asked Wheeler to explain the difference between exact science and experimental science, attempting to show that although there was some knowledge about the effects of electricity, there was still much that was in doubt. Wheeler made some attempt to answer these questions, but he admitted he was not an expert.

The state then brought in witnesses who had seen the deadly effects of electrical current.

Joseph Ocker of Brooklyn described the death of Thomas Murray, an electrical lineman who had come into contact with the wires he was working on in April 1888 in front of the Bierman, Heidelberg & Co. store at 616 Broadway, where Ocker was employed.

Bernard J. Hughes, a dynamo engineer employed by Western Lighting Company, described the death of George Schneitzer at the Harlem Lighting Company plant on 122nd Street in September 1887. Schneitzer had been standing on a damp floor when he took hold of an electric lamp, fell down and died in a few moments.

The final hearings were held in Buffalo City Hall on August 1 and 2, apparently to accommodate witnesses who found it difficult to travel all the way to New York. The first witness there was Dr. Joseph Fowler, the coroner who performed the autopsy on Smith in 1881. Fowler said the organs were normal, but the blood was thinner than normal. In attempting to trace the path of the current, he said, he found a discoloration extending across the chest from one shoulder to the other.

"There was no apparent cause of death, was there?" asked Cockran.

"No apparent cause, no sir," said Fowler.

Charles C. Weber, former superintendent of the Brush Electric Light Company, said he visited the spot where a man, referred to only as Isaac Moulton, had been shocked on Michigan Street in Buffalo. One wire had been crossed over another, he said, in a system of 1,000 volts, alternating current, designed to provide electricity for 650 lights. The voltage in this case was significant because 1,000 volts was the expected power of the generator that would be used to kill Kemmler.

Dr. George E. Fell, the Buffalo inventor who assisted Southwick in experiments using electricity to exterminate stray dogs in 1887, explained his technique. In answer to Cockran's usual question, Dr. Fell said, "My belief is that death can be produced by electricity painlessly and certainly so that respiration cannot be renewed."

"Can you tell what voltage would be sufficient to cause death in every instance?" Cockran asked.

"I don't know exactly how to answer that question," said Dr. Fell, "without experiments having been made on human beings."

Charles F. Durston, the warden of Auburn Prison, where Kemmler was being kept and the apparatus for his execution was being constructed, testified that the chair had been designed by Brown under the authorization of the superintendent of prisons. Significantly, Durston said the contract signed by the superintendent specified that alternating current was to be used. The state had purchased a dynamo, electrodes and everything that was necessary except the lamp board that was to be used as a kind of testing device and meter. It was to be attached to the wall and contain 28 lamps, indicating the amount of current flowing through the wires.

"Will you use it?" asked Cockran.

"After it has been tested," said Durston.

"What test do you propose?" asked Cockran.

Durston admitted that no test would really be sufficient until the device was tried on Kemmler. He said most of the apparatus was already in place at the prison but that the dynamos had not yet been started up.

Under the terms of the original contract between Brown and the state, he said, Brown was to actually conduct the execution, but terms of the original contract had already expired and were in the process of being extended. Brown was to be paid $1,600 by the state for his work but only after the equipment was ready for operation.

Cockran then asked him who would be the one to actually pull the switch, sending the electricity into Kemmler's body. Durston said that although the law was not specific on that point, he assumed that it would be his job, even though he had no knowledge of electricity.

After the completion of the testimony, there was a month's delay while it was being typed up for submission to the court of appeals on September 17. Meanwhile, New Yorkers had a chance to take a breath and consider all they had heard about electricity and death.

"A great deal is said about the electrical execution of Kemmler being an experiment," wrote the *New York Tribune* on August 9. "Undoubtedly it will be. So is every other execution an experiment, and many of them are comparative failures. When a man is to be hanged no one seems able to guarantee beforehand, at least in this country, when the drop will fall or that the rope will not break or stretch or slip into such a position as to prolong the victim's agony.... With all that is known of the deadly effect of the electric current, the chances are infinitely greater in favor of an immediate killing upon its first application...."

"No method of execution seems absolutely trustworthy except some which Anglo-Saxon nations hesitate about accepting. But as between hanging and the electric current the chances ought to be a hundred to one in favor of the certainty and prompt efficiency of the latter."

Park Benjamin, a professor of electrical engineering, told the *New York Herald* that the "clap-trap" apparatus being prepared at Auburn Prison was inappropriate to be used for the most solemn act that society could perform and charged that the entire process had been prostituted "to the purpose of a business advertisement."[15]

The editors of *Scientific American* said Brown had been "most unmercifully abused by some of the newspapers" during the hearings and by "the parties interested in the electrical machines," meaning Westinghouse. The editors said Westinghouse seemed more concerned about the fate of a brutal murderer than about the safety of his electrical wires.[16]

On his way back from the Buffalo hearings, Brown stopped off at Auburn on August 5 to examine the progress that had been made in getting the chair ready for Kemmler. Davis, who was already in Auburn, had hoped to conduct some tests but neither Dr. MacDonald nor Dr. Fell had been able to attend. Asked by a reporter if the chair would be able to kill Kemmler, Brown said any report that it would not do so was "rot" and that Cockran's attempts to save Kemmler were "useless."[17]

Meanwhile, just a week after the hearings concluded in Buffalo, the National Electric Light Association held its annual meeting in nearby Niagara Falls and complained bitterly that the publicity about the electric chair was having a negative impact on their industry. One speaker said "punishment of death by means of the electrical current is so cruel that legislators in New York ought to repeal their law and so cruel that the courts of New York ought to pronounce the statute unconstitutional."

Dr. Otto A. Moses, another speaker, said electrocution was the most barbarous method of killing that could be devised. He attacked Brown as someone who had brought disgrace on the profession by his activities and had deliberately pitted one system of lighting against the other because of his "personal malice." At his suggestion the convention passed a resolution asking the legislature to repeal the electric chair law.[18]

Meanwhile, Brown's fortunes took a turn for the worse on August 25 when the *New York Sun* published 45 letters to him and from him that exposed his secret negotiations with Edison and his company officials dating back to the beginning of the year. The letters were stolen from his desk in his office at 45 Wall Street. Much of what we know today about these negotiations comes from the letters, which historians have certified to be genuine. Brown later charged that they had been altered and offered a $500 reward for information leading to the conviction of the person responsible for taking them. He clearly assumed that Westinghouse was behind it, but no one was ever charged with the crime. The best guess as to who stole the letters and leaked them to the *Sun* is probably one of Cockran's Tammany Hall friends. Although it did not seem apparent at the time, this was the beginning of the end of Brown's involvement with the electric chair. From this point his credibility came into question, and his usefulness to Edison and the other advocates of the electric chair was greatly diminished.

From the time Cockran filed the legal papers that set the appellate process in motion it was clear that the case would not be decided in Cayuga County and would eventually end up before the U.S. Supreme Court. The Eighth Amendment's prohibition against "cruel and unusual punishment" language was also included in the state constitution, but legal experts thought that using electricity as a means of execution was so radical that it clearly required a high court ruling.

Becker, the referee who conducted the hearings, submitted his report to Judge Day on September 17, 1889, and oral arguments for both sides were scheduled for the same day. While he was in Auburn, Cockran went to the prison and spoke with Kemmler for about a half hour before the hearing began. Then he delivered an address to the court that lasted from 11:30 A.M. to 1:20 P.M., arguing that death by electricity was cruel and unusual and therefore unconstitutional.[19]

Of all the witnesses interviewed during the hearings, he said, there had been only one who pretended to explain how death was caused by electricity. That one, he said, was the "charlatan" Harold P. Brown, who had testified that nerves of the animals he executed had been torn to pieces while every other expert had said exactly the opposite.

The manner in which electricity caused death, said Cockran, was "a blank, impenetrable mystery" that seemed to act differently in every case. Because there was no way to determine how much voltage was necessary to kill, there was no way it could ethically be used for executions. The experiments at Edison's laboratory found that the electrical resistance of reporters was greater than members of the bar. What was one to make of that? Cockran said the Constitution's ban on cruel and unusual punishment clearly prohibited the use of Kemmler as the subject of a macabre experiment such as that being planned by the state.

In his final remarks Cockran once again denied charges that had been printed in the newspapers that he was being paid by Westinghouse or anyone else with an interest in the outcome of the case. No one other than the "miserable wretch in the basement of Auburn Prison has promised me any

Charles Tabor, the New York State attorney general, who would argue the pro–electric chair case all the way to the Supreme Court. (New York State Library)

reward for my services in this case," he said. As was revealed later, this was an outright lie.

Attorney General Charles F. Tabor argued the case in favor of electrocution himself. Speaking for about an hour, he said the scientific evidence clearly showed that electrocution brought swift and consistent death and that there was no reason the law should not be enforced as written.

On October 9, Judge Day issued his opinion in favor of the state and against Kemmler. He said the new law did not violate the Constitution and issued a warning to the judges higher up who he was certain would hear the case on appeal. If the law was ruled to be unconstitutional, he said, Kemmler would have to be set free along with every other murderer convicted since January 1.[20]

Day said he had expected that the results of the hearings conducted by Becker would be conflicting, speculative and hypothetical because the issue was such a novel one, without precedent. No one knew for sure what would happen when the switch was pulled in Auburn, he said. The question, then, was whether the new method was cruel and unusual.

"There seems to be an element of cruelty inseparable from the taking of human life as punishment for a crime," he said, "but it is clearly not against this that the Constitutional prohibition is directed."

Because the U.S. Supreme Court had ruled that neither hanging nor death by firing squad were unconstitutional, he said, it was not the infliction of death that was at issue but merely the means. "And can it be said that in this case it has been certainly and beyond doubt established that electricity as a death dealing agent is likely to prove less quick and sure in operation than the rope?" he wrote. "In my judgment these questions must be answered negatively. The most that can be justly said in

[Kemmler's] favor is that there is a diversity of opinion on the principal question."

The judicial branch of government, he said, has no business overturning an act of the legislative branch unless it has overwhelming evidence that the act is unconstitutional. A simple matter of controversy is not enough to do that.

While Bourke Cockran saw the decision as a mere setback on a long legal road, the public saw it as a sign that Kemmler's days were numbered. Most newspaper editors praised Day's ruling.

The *Albany Evening Times* said the ruling was "the right view," and that the state obviously had the right to change its method of punishment or it would still use "the pillory and the whipping post." Part of the problem, the editors said, was one of language. Although most people thought of electrocution as an "unusual" means of punishment, the word had a different legal meaning from the common use.[21]

"The term 'unusual' is moreover coupled with and preceded by the term 'cruel' and no man yet has risen who can positively testify that killing by electricity is cruel, any more than killing by the rope."

The process of electrocution as described at the hearings seemed to involve "too much manipulation of the victim" involving "several minutes of horror" that seemed to add "torture to the regular penalty," the editors said. It would probably be a lot easier to simply chloroform a prisoner in his cell, they added.

"But the new law is here and as a matter of expediency, if not constitutionality, it is best that it remain in force," they said, especially because its repeal would leave "no possible recourse in its treatment of murderers.... If there is not capital punishment by electricity now, all murderers condemned to death for crimes committed this year must go absolutely free."

Cockran immediately filed an appeal with the state's highest court, the court of appeals in Albany, which agreed to hear the case on February 25, four months after Judge Day's ruling. It was one more step on the way to the Supreme Court.

Meanwhile, the battle of the currents moved on to a different front: the pages of the *North American Review*, a respected intellectual journal. The November 1889 issue carried separate articles by Brown and Edison.

In his article Brown used the official title, "New York State Expert on Electrical Execution" and said that he had been "reluctant" to take on the job of killing the first man in the electric chair but believed it was necessary to "educate the public to handle [alternating current] with caution and thus save many lives."[22]

He insisted that death in the chair would be painless and that 1,000 volts AC would do the job adequately. The use of a higher voltage, he said, "would be dangerous to the attendants" because even insulated wires were not enough protection for this deadly force. His description of the chair at this point was quite different from that he described earlier. He said the condemned man would have his feet immersed in a liquid solution.

Also, contrary to other descriptions, he said the switch turning on the current would be pulled by a sheriff's deputy instead of the electrician. This was considerably different from Durston's description given a few months earlier. At the moment the switch is pulled, Brown said, death would come with the speed of light.

"The majesty of the law is vindicated, but no physical pain has been caused," he said. "Such is electrical execution. And yet strenuous attempts have been made to befog the public mind in order to prevent the use of the alternating current for the death penalty, lest the public should learn its deadly nature and demand that the Legislature banish it from the streets and buildings, thus ending the terrible, needless slaughter of unoffending men."

In his article in the same issue, "The Dangers of Electric Lighting," Edison took a cooler-handed approach and didn't mention the electric chair but insisted that the passage of any amount of alternating current through the body would result in "instantaneous death," whereas most people are able to survive contact with direct current.[23]

Alternating current, he said, was being used by unscrupulous companies "to reduce investment in copper wire and real estate," and the safety of the public should be put above such costcutting. The solution to the problem, he said, was to either set a limit on the voltages that power lines could carry or outlaw alternating current.

"My personal desire would be to prohibit entirely the use of alternating currents," he said. "They are as unnecessary as they are dangerous."

The next month, the *North American Review* published "A Reply to Mr. Edison" by George Westinghouse, which took Edison's argument apart section by section. He complained that "interested parties" were attempting monopolistic control of the electric light industry.[24]

"Thousands of persons have large pecuniary interests at stake," Westinghouse warned, "and, as might be expected, many of them view this great subject solely from the stand-point of self interest." He offered to tell the public "the story of this business rivalry." Many of the fatal accidents that Edison mentioned in his article, Westinghouse said, actually involved direct current.

The best argument, he said, was that in the past three years cities across the nation had been choosing alternating current systems over direct current systems. "If the opinion of these persons, who can have no interest except to purchase that which they believe to be the best, is of any value, then the alternating system has been demonstrated to be the one which can give to the public that which they so much desire—a safe, cheap, efficient and universally applicable system of incandescent electric lighting."

Nowhere in his article did he mention Brown or the electric chair, but Westinghouse was already making plans to carry the defense of Kemmler to the nation's highest court.

—7—
Cruel and Unusual Punishment

Even before Judge Edwin S. Day made his ruling on the constitutionality of the electric chair, Harold Brown, Edwin Davis and their assistants were already testing it at the three New York prisons where the chairs had been installed. The tests were witnessed by members of a commission that Austin Lathrop, the superintendent of prisons, had appointed to make sure that the chairs were working properly before they were used for their intended purpose.

The commission members were Dr. Alphonse D. Rockwell, professor of electrotherapeutics at New York Post-Graduate School; L. H. Laudy, a professor at the School of Mines at Columbia; and Dr. Carlos F. MacDonald, chairman of the State Board of Lunacy. Although they witnessed the tests and wrote the official report, the actual tests were conducted by Brown and Davis.[1]

The committee members watched as Brown and Davis put the belts onto the generators, adjusted pulleys and attached wires and meters. In their report the commissioners complained that so much time was spent adjusting the machines that little time was left for the tests. When the generators were finally running properly the voltage was tested using a Cardew voltmeter. The average voltages were measured at 1,404 at Sing Sing, 1,512 at Auburn and 1,653 at Clinton. Although these voltages were considered sufficient for the purpose, the commission recommended some further adjustments, such as balancing the pulleys and adjusting the machines so that they produced a constant voltage.

At Clinton they attached a 600-pound bull to the generator, which was run up to 900 volts for 10 seconds, "killing it instantly." At Auburn they killed a calf and a 1,000-pound horse by attaching one electrode to the head and the other to one of the hind legs and running the generator up to 1,200 volts. At this latter experiment, Dr. George E. Fell attempted to revive the calf using his Fell Motor but gave up after a half hour. The electrical contacts varied from 10 to 20 seconds. In their report to Lathrop the committee members said they "entertained no doubt as to the efficiency of the three dynamos ... to accomplish the work for which they are intended."

At Auburn the generator had been installed in such a way that it could run machines in the prison's wood and metal shops. The execution chamber itself was built in the basement of the administration building just inside the front gate. The execution chamber was 17 feet wide by 25 feet long and dimly lighted by two small iron-grated windows about four feet above the floor. Looking through the windows, a visitor could see the castle-like front entrance to the prison, which had a statue of a soldier on the front known as "Copper John." Since the soldier faced outwards, prisoners at Auburn said they looked forward to the day they could "look copper John in the face," an act that could only be accomplished from outside the gates.

Between the windows, on the east wall of the room, there was a board about 10 feet long and 3½ to 4 feet wide containing the various electrical devices for testing, measuring and controlling the current. On the far left of this board there was what was described as a "common electric push button" that was to be used to send messages to the room where the dynamo was located. The button would tell the technicians in the dynamo room when to increase or decrease the voltage.

The controls included two different kinds of voltmeters and a transformer that was apparently the final step down of the current before it went to the chair. There were also some switches that enabled the voltmeters to be switched in and out of the circuit. Later, a lamp box with 24 16-candle lightbulbs would be added to serve as yet another visual gauge of the voltage. These bulbs were wired in such a way that the number of bulbs lit indicated the force of the electricity. When all 24 bulbs were lit the dynamo was running at full power. At the end of the line were two large switches. One of them was a main "off" switch that broke the entire circuit, and the other was the switch that would hook the chair into the circuit. The Westinghouse generator, located in the north wing of the prison, was connected to the death chamber by two large black wires, about 1,000 feet long.

The only thing missing was the chair itself, which had not yet been completed, or at least had not been brought into the room. The two wires that were to be attached to the chair, one to the head and the other to the base of the spine, were, as of April 25, still dangling from the ceiling of the room. Brown had tried his hand at designing a chair, but it had been rejected as unworkable. Southwick had also drawn up plans for a chair, but it is not known if it was ever built. Several people claimed to have built the chair that was finally used at Auburn, including Davis, Mac-Donald and Rockwell.

In a February 15 letter to the *New York Times* Dr. Rockwell claimed that the public was warming up to the idea of using electricity instead of hanging and predicted that every state would follow New York's lead and switch to electricity.

"There are always opposition and friction attending changes for the better and this change has been no exception," he said. "The whole tendency of our civilization, however, is in the direction of humane methods in dealing with criminals, and that form of execution that is quickest and least repulsive should be adopted. It is a mathematical impossibility that any human being receiving in proper form an electrical current of lethal energy should appreciate even for a fraction of a second the slightest pain." The electric chair ought to "supplant everywhere the barbarous process of hanging. If the law must kill, let it kill decently."

In order for that to happen, however, the electric chair still had a number of legal challenges to face. The New York court of appeals actually heard two separate appeals on behalf of Kemmler on February 25. The first, brought by Cockran, charged that the electric chair was cruel and unusual and therefore unconstitutional. The other was brought by Charles W. Sickmon, one of Kemmler's original defense attorneys, who argued that certain statements Kemmler made to a doctor while he was in jail in Buffalo were inadmissible because they violated the doctor-patient relationship.

In most ways Sickmon's appeal was a routine one that probably would have been made in any case, even if the electric chair had not been part of the sentence. However, there seems little doubt that he was at least being encouraged by the many powerful interests that had become involved in the Kemmler case since the trial.

Sickmon's complaint was that two doctors, Dr. Phelps and Dr. Slater, should not have been called as prosecution witnesses to testify about the mental condition of their patient and that without their testimony Kemmler might have been found insane due to his heavy drinking. District Attorney George T. Quinby argued that the doctor-patient relationship had not been established in the case and that therefore the doctors were free to testify.

In his ruling on behalf of the court, Justice John C. Gray, a native of New York City who graduated from Harvard, said that even without the doctors' testimony, there was ample evidence in the case that Kemmler had been able to distinguish right from wrong and even on the morning of the murder appeared to fully realize the nature and gravity of his act.[2]

"All the facts respecting his habits of life, the conduct of his affairs, his appearance and actions before, at the time of and subsequent to the commission of the criminal act, were before the jury and we cannot say that there was any absolute, or positive, or preponderant evidence of unsoundness, or enfeeblement of mind to warrant our interfering with the verdict," Judge Gray ruled.

The physicians had been sent to the jail by the district attorney to examine Kemmler, Gray ruled, and did not testify about any conversations with Kemmler but gave their expert opinions based on their observation of him.

Although he was not ruling on the use of the electric chair, Judge Gray felt justified in addressing it. In his opinion, "punishment by death, in a general sense, is cruel; but as it is authorized and justified by a law, adopted by the People as a means to the end of the better security of society, it is not cruel within the sense and meaning of the Constitution.... In my judgment, we should assume that the enactment of the legislature was based upon some investigation of facts, and, where the declared purpose and end of the law are the infliction of death upon the offender, we may not say, upon a ground work of possibilities and guess work, that it is, in any sense, an unconstitutional act, because a new mode is adopted to bring about death."

In other words death penalties are pretty much equal in the eyes of the law, and if the legislature approved it, the courts have no reason to question their motives. Later, more activist courts were to take a much different view on this point. They were to see their role as protecting the people from the legislature, especially the rights of the underprivileged, exactly the kind of people who were to become the electric chair's victims.

The main decision on the electric chair, however, the one that directly addressed the constitutional issues, was on a separate appeal made by Cockran and opposed by Tabor, the state attorney general.

Using electricity in such a way, Cockran argued, was a form of torture and therefore "cruel," and its use was, certainly by any definition, "unusual." He used a long list of legal citations on the history and interpretation of this wording in both constitutions. Unless the electric chair produced immediate death it would torture the victim. Nothing that came out during the hearings proved that the devices purchased by the state would produce immediate death.

"It being conceded that the infliction of the penalty will expose [Kemmler] to the risk of torture," said Cockran, "the sentence is in violation of the Constitution and therefore void. The act is unconstitutional because upon its face it provides for the infliction of an unusual penalty."

Tabor argued that historically the ban on "cruel and unusual punishments" was made to limit the power of the judiciary to impose sentences and was never intended to limit the powers of the legislative branch, which passed the law. The courts, he argued, had no right to impose their interpretation upon that of the legislature in such a matter. He also argued that experts had certified that the apparatus the state intended to use would produce instant and painless death.

The state could not go back to hanging as a form of capital punishment, Tabor said. That law had been repealed. If the electric chair was thrown out, the state would have to free all the murderers in the state convicted since January 1 of the previous year. If the state ruled the electric chair law unconstitutional it must also rule that the repeal of the old law was also null and void or all those convicts would be set free.

Justice Denis O'Brien, who wrote the unanimous opinion in the case, was a native of Ogdensburg, a former mayor of Watertown, a member of the Democratic State Committee and a former attorney general. He traced the origins of the "cruel and unusual" terminology to the reign of William and Mary in England, where it was part of the English Bill of Rights.

"It is not very clear whether the provision as it stands in our Constitution was intended as an admonition to the legislature and the judiciary or as a restraint upon legislation inflicting punishment for criminal offenses," he wrote. Originally, he said, it was probably intended more as a declaration of rights of the subjects and had no immediate impact on any existing laws or in criminal sentencing. The intent of those who wrote the words into the New York Constitution of 1846 was to give the courts the power to overturn an act of the state proscribing punishment in criminal cases. While the legislature clearly has the power to proscribe the method of capital punishment, he said, the sentence itself is not the issue. The punishment now, as before, is death. The only issue is the means of causing that death.

"The infliction of the death penalty," he said, "in any manner must necessarily be accompanied with what might be considered in this age, some degree of cruelty, and it is to be resorted to only because it is deemed necessary for the protection of society."

The question to be decided was whether the new method of execution "subjects the person convicted to the possible risk of torture and unnecessary pain. This argument would apply with equal force to any untried method of execution, and when carried to its logical results, would prohibit the enforcement of the death penalty at all."

Instead of taking into account the tens of thousands of words of testimony collected by the Cayuga County Court from the hearings, O'Brien ruled that the constitutionality of the law had to stand or fall on the wording of the statute itself.

"If the act upon its face is not in conflict with the Constitution," he wrote, "then extraneous proof can not be used to condemn it." The question of whether the new method of execution is better or more humane than the old method, he said was up to the legislature and not the courts. Citing the formation of the Gerry Commission in 1887, he said, the legislature seemed to have performed its duty to determine "the most humane and practical method known to modern science of carrying into effect the sentence of death in capital punishment cases."

The legislature had debated and discussed the proposed changes in the law "with care and caution and unusual deliberation." It would be "a strange result indeed," he continued, "if it could now be held that its efforts to devise a more humane method of carrying out the sentence of death in capital punishment cases have culminated in the enactment of a law in conflict with the provisions of the Constitution prohibiting cruel and unusual punishments."

Since the legislature had more information on which to make that decision, he said, there was no reason for the court of appeals to think it could make a better determination of the same issue. The testimony taken at the hearings by the referee, he said, may have produced "a valuable collection of facts and opinions" about using electricity to produce death, "but nothing more."

O'Brien said the court examined all of this testimony "and can find but little in it to warrant the belief that this new mode of execution is cruel, within the meaning of the Constitution, though it is certainly unusual. On the contrary, we agree with the court below that it removed every reasonable doubt that the application of electricity to the vital parts of the human body, under such conditions, and in the manner contemplated by the statute, must result in instantaneous and consequently in painless death."

The law, he said, does not violate any part of the state Constitution and the appeal must be denied.

This was the end of the line as far as New York courts were concerned, and a new date was set for Kemmler's execution at a resentencing on April 1. The proponents of the new law, including people like Southwick, Governor Hill and the attorney general breathed a sigh of relief.

H. D. Hamilton, chief clerk of the Gerry Commission, told the *New York Times* that the court of appeals decision was a gratifying one because the question of the constitutionality of the new law had finally been determined, and there could be no further legal procedure in the case. Facts were soon to prove him far from accurate.[3]

Just hours after the court ruled in the Kemmler case, a New York City judge sentenced James J. Slocum, a former professional baseball player, to be the electric chair's next occupant after Kemmler. He was convicted of beating his wife to death with a baseball bat on New Year's night.[4]

Cockran, who was in Washington when the court of appeals ruling was released, did not comment on it immediately but indicated that he felt there were still ways the law could be fought. In a letter to Charles F. Hatch on April 2 Cockran discussed other points that could be raised. For example, he said, the law took away from the county sheriff his traditional responsibility for inflicting capital punishment and gave it to the prison warden, who is not an elected official. Recent court rulings seemed to reinforce the point that a power traditionally given to an elected official cannot be transferred to an appointed official. Hatch tried to file a new writ based on this issue, but the court denied it, saying it had no merit.

Cockran then wrote to Governor Hill, using the same argument to ask for a stay of Kemmler's execution. Hill turned this down, saying in an April 25 letter to Cockran that he found the argument about the powers of the sheriff unconvincing and refused to interfere in the case.

Three days later, prisoners at the Auburn Prison wood shop were said to be putting the final touches on Kemmler's pine coffin while Kemmler, still in solitary confinement in a room adjacent to the death chamber, made out his will, doling out his few possessions for valuable souvenirs. He was reported to have spent much of this time signing his name over and over again for the hundreds of autograph seekers who wanted to add his name to their collections. He directed that an illustrated Bible he had been using be given to Daniel MacNaughton, one of his keepers. One of the prison chaplains, the Rev. Dr. Houghton, was given his "pigs in the clover" jigsaw puzzle. To the head chaplain he gave a slate chalkboard covered with copies of his autograph and to the warden's wife he gave a deck of cards with his autograph on every card. Kemmler was close enough to the death chamber to hear the construction work that was going on there.[5]

The ruling of the court of appeals against Kemmler also seems to have been the signal for Harold P. Brown, who had been associated with the electrical execution process from the very beginning, to finally bow out, but the reason for that is unclear. Perhaps, now that the final legal obstacle was out of the way, Edison and the others who were pulling the strings behind the scenes thought he was no longer needed. Or, perhaps, he felt that he did not want to become Kemmler's executioner, a role that everyone up until that point had expected him to play. Or, perhaps, the exposure of his ties to Edison as shown by the publication of his letters made him less useful to Edison than before.

In any case his role as chief electrician and erstwhile executioner in the process was taken over by his "assistant," Edwin F. Davis, a man who remains an enigma to this day. His name had been barely mentioned in the newspapers before April 28, when he was suddenly described as the man in charge of the final preparations in Auburn. Davis, who was to become the official state executioner in New York and several adjoining states, was fated to pull the switch on over 300 prisoners before he retired in 1914. He also filed a number of patents for improvements he made to the design of the electric chair.

In late April the witnesses who had been invited to the execution began to arrive in Auburn, a signal that the execution was expected within days. When Southwick arrived on April 28, he was already being called "the father of the electric chair" and was given a tour of the death chamber by the warden. District Attorney Quinby and members of the press also went along, with Davis explaining how the apparatus was to be used.

The chair, described by the reporters as being stored in a room next to the death chamber, was much different than the one Brown had described in his original drawings. The reporters described it this way: "It is large, with a high back and comfortable seat and has a footrest, which may or may not be used. An adjustable bar of wood projects from the back over the head of the occupant, and there is a rest for the head which can also be regulated. But for the broad straps which are attached to the sides of the chair, its purpose would hardly be suspected."[6]

The electrodes were to be attached to a metal cap in the top of the chair and through a circular hole in the seat of the chair, where the spinal electrode was to be placed. Both electrodes contained a sponge that was to be soaked in saline solution to ensure a good electrical contact. The head electrode was spring loaded and the spinal electrode was to be held in place by a belt.

Dr. Daniels, one of the official witnesses from Buffalo, bravely sat down in the chair and allowed himself to be strapped in as part of the demonstration. Davis adjusted the straps and the leather chin piece, which was designed to push the head up into the spring in the head electrode.[7]

Southwick was clearly annoyed that it took Davis so long to make all the necessary adjustments to the chair. "I am opposed to so much para-phernalia," he told Davis, "but the present arrangement will have to do, because we cannot afford to suffer failure. The whole world is watching the result of this experiment and if we neglected any precautions there might be a slip and the system would therefore be condemned."

The public's mood, reflected in newspaper editorials, was a great sigh of relief that the long debate seemed finally to be over. "It is much to the advantage of public order and tranquillity that a decisive conclu-sion of this long controversy has finally been reached," the editors of the *New York Tribune* proclaimed on March 22, because the public had feared that a reversal of the law could result in the release of Kemmler and other murderers. The editors felt that the hearings and the court rulings were time well spent in considering such an important matter.

"A new mode of capital punishment, departing radically from the customs of the past and depending for its results upon a mysterious agency, of whose nature and operation those who know most confess that they know little, is not a trivial matter."

The editors traced the problem back to the 1888 Gerry Commission, which they said should have included some electrical experts. That fail-ure allowed "witnesses with private interests at stake," meaning Brown and Westinghouse, to cloud the issue. Now all the objections seemed to have been put to rest.

The *New York Times*, in its March 22 editorial, called the whole legal procedure "scandalous" because Cockran had been arguing that Kemm-ler should be set free rather than sent to the electric chair.

"If the Legislature was not competent to prescribe the substitute it did provide," the editors wrote, "then its action amounted to an abolition of capital punishment until a new act was passed.... This result nobody except murderers can have contemplated with any satisfaction."

The editors then went on to blame Westinghouse, referred to as "the corporation," for trying to show that the electrical apparatus purchased by the state was not deadly enough when the real probability of Kemm-ler's death was "simply overwhelming."

The real scandal, the editors said, was "that the time of the courts was taken up trying to persuade the public of the harmlessness of their machine. The culprit under sentence was used merely to enable the cor-poration to get a standing in court and the issue of life or death for him was a mere incident of the litigation."

The real appellant in the case, the *Times* said, was not Kemmler, a "poor and friendless murderer" but "a rich corporation amply able to retain expensive counsel and expert witnesses."

Despite this, the editors said, the court had rightly found "once for all" that execution by electricity was neither cruel nor unusual punishment.

The decision that electricity was the most certain and humane means of executing criminals had been made much earlier by the Gerry Commission, the editors said, and they were more qualified to make that determination than "the interested opinion of a corporation which makes homicidal machines or of the experts retained by that corporation," and the court's ruling "leaves the corporation which has spent so much of its own money and of the time of the courts in resisting the execution of the law in a worse position than if it had made no efforts for obstruction and had left the condemned murderer to his own devices."

With the chair ready, the witnesses standing by in the Osborne House Hotel and all the legal roadblocks apparently cleared up, everyone expected Kemmler to die soon. On the morning of April 29 Warden Durston quietly passed the word to the witnesses that they should be prepared to spend the coming evening at the prison, taken as a sure sign that the execution was to be held early the next morning.

Newspapers around the country had their stories about Kemmler's death in print, waiting for the word to set the presses rolling with an extra edition. In fact a newspaper in Port Arthur, Ontario, jumped the gun and actually printed the story of his death on May 2 under the headline "Painless Death of Murderer Kemmler." The article said Kemmler died painlessly while saying the Lord's Prayer when 7,000 volts were sent through his body."[8]

The first sign that this was not to be the case was spotted by a reporter from the *New York Times*, who recognized Henry Gayley when he registered at the Osborne House. Gayley was chief clerk of the law firm of Carter, Hughes and Cravath of New York, who were the official attorneys for the Westinghouse Electric Company. Gayley refused to answer reporters' questions about why he was there, but a rumor began to circulate that someone was attempting to stop the execution. After these rumors began, Gayley suddenly disappeared.

At about 11 A.M. Durtston arrived at the Osborne House and gathered the witnesses into a private conference room. When they came out, the witnesses refused to say anything to reporters, but hinted strongly that there had been "an important development" in the case. When Durston returned to the prison he met with James W. Hogan, a deputy attorney general, who had been summoned to discuss this complication.

During this meeting with Hogan, Roger M. Sherman, a former federal attorney and one of the most prominent lawyers in New York City, arrived with a legal document containing the signatures of federal Judge William J. Wallace, of the Northern District of New York and Melville Fuller, the Chief Justice of the U.S. Supreme Court. The order, issued in the name of the president of the United States, ordered Durston to bring Kemmler to federal court in Canandaigua at 10 A.M. on the third Tuesday in June. The execution was, therefore, postponed.

Sherman's great-grandfather was a brother of the Roger Sherman who was one of the signers of the Declaration of Independence. A Republican and a native of Albany, he was a graduate of Columbia Law School and had previously served as pardon clerk to President Grant and was a partner in the firm of Darlington, Sherman & Jenkins with offices at 206 Broadway in New York City.

Although they both denied it until after Kemmler's execution, Sherman had been hired by Westinghouse to take Kemmler's case to the Supreme Court. Why Westinghouse dumped Cockran at this point is not clear. Perhaps he was unhappy with the way the case had been handled. Perhaps he thought a Republican was a better choice than a Democrat. Although he was a prominent attorney, Sherman was nowhere near as well known as Cockran, so price may have been a factor as well. It was estimated at the time that it had cost $100,000 to fight the battle for Kemmler in the courts.

Sherman asked to be able to see Kemmler, but Durston turned him down, saying he had no proof that Sherman represented him. Sherman then returned with a court order to see Kemmler, but then, suddenly and mysteriously, Sherman left Auburn on the 3:05 train for Syracuse.

After dinner, the witnesses, angry that they had come to Auburn only to have the execution postponed, paid their hotel bills and made a last visit to the prison before boarding the train for home. The general consensus was that the latest development was nothing but an annoying delay and that Kemmler's appointment with the electric chair would not be far off.

Judge Day, who had ruled on the first appeal in the Kemmler case and had been invited to witness the execution, said he was sure that the federal courts would follow his lead and throw out the appeal. "I am confident that this case will not be reviewed by the United States court," he told reporters, "because there are a number of decisions by the United States Supreme Court which hold that the section of the Constitution in question applies entirely to national laws and not to state law."[9]

Southwick, another of the witnesses, did not hide his disgust. "Electricity is bound to be used to kill murderers and the enemies of the present law will soon use up their available ammunition," he said.

The reporters described Durston as wearing a look of "extreme impertinence that he knows so well how to assume." He admitted to reporters that the delay was something of a mixed blessing because he had many misgivings about being in charge of an execution. When he became warden of a state prison, he said, performing executions had not been part of his assigned duties. Another calf had been executed in the chair just that morning as a further test. About 1,200 volts had been used and the animal had been killed instantly. Doctors then attempted to revive it without success. For Kemmler, he said, the voltage would be increased to 1,600 volts.

Harold P. Brown, who was at the meeting with Durston, said he had been in the dynamo room that morning with electrician C. R. Barnes of Rochester while they were testing the chair on the calf. Asked what his duties would be during the Kemmler execution, Brown indicated that he was no longer in charge and that Barnes and Davis had taken over that role.

"My contract with the state simply called for the furnishing and the setting up of three machines. These machines have been furnished and the state has approved and accepted them. My representative, Mr. Davis, of the firm of Noel & Davis of New York, has been here several days and has finished the work of adjusting the apparatus. A test I have just made has demonstrated to me that Kemmler could be killed instantly if placed in the chair. This writ of habeas corpus releases me from further connection with electrical executions. My contract provided that I was to personally superintend the dynamos and electrical executions that were to occur prior to May 1. There will be no such execution within that limit now, and you may rest assured that I am glad to be relieved of the unpleasant responsibility."

Can this be the same Harold P. Brown who had been one of the main advocates of electrocution and had taken such delight in the killing of dozens of animals? What was behind this sudden and last-minute bit of cold feet? There seems to have been a major dispute behind the scenes over who was actually assigned to pull the final switch, over who was to become the modern equivalent of the hangman, the executioner. Durston had insisted that he did not want to perform that task and thought it beyond his responsibilities because he knew nothing about electricity. It seems unlikely that Brown, who had pulled many such switches, would have any problem with executing Kemmler. What seems more likely is that he was called off by Edison or someone else from the Edison companies. His excuse that his contract had expired was a weak one. All he would have had to do was ask and it would have been renewed. Davis, as became clear later, had been brought in for the sole purpose of replacing Brown and becoming the state's official executioner.

Durston told reporters he had not informed Kemmler about the delay until most of the outside world had been told. When he went into his cell, he told him, "Well, Kemmler, you've got a reprieve."

"All right," replied Kemmler without a hint of emotion.

"It saves us a good deal of trouble," said Durston.

"It makes me feel a little easier," said Kemmler, as he returned to pacing the floor of his cell.

While everyone assumed that Westinghouse was behind the latest delay, the newspaper reporters were busy during the next few days looking for the proof. A reporter for the *New York Times* cornered Sherman on a train between Syracuse and Utica and put the question to him directly.

"Is Kemmler your only client in this matter?" asked the reporter.

"Kemmler is the only client whose name I am permitted to mention," said Sherman.

"Are the Westinghouse people or any other electrical company responsible for your action in the matter?"

"No, emphatically, no," said Sherman. "I cannot tell you by whom I am employed, but I can say that the Westinghouse Company has nothing to do with it."

He then explained that the court of appeals had merely been interpreting the state constitution, and even though the U. S. Constitution contained the same words, "cruel and unusual punishment," the two courts had different standards for what those words meant. The court of appeals had not really decided if electrical executions were cruel or not and had merely sidestepped the issue.

Sherman's law partner told the *New York Tribune* on April 30 that there were still some serious questions to be answered about the law. The fact that the date of execution was vague and included an entire week, he said, "opens the way to all kinds of bribery" and could have some bearing on matters of inheritance. Also, he said, the provision that the execution had to be performed in secret seemed somewhat cruel.

The main speculation, however, centered on who had hired Sherman. His law partner said he had been sworn to secrecy because it was "a matter which concerns him and them," but the *Tribune* said it was the "general belief" that Sherman had been retained by Westinghouse, which had the most to gain from a ban on the use of the electric chair. The *Times* even more bluntly blamed Westinghouse for the delay.

Westinghouse denied this the same day, saying he had initially opposed the use of Westinghouse dynamos for the purpose but had given up his opposition and was now totally indifferent to the issue. As subsequent events showed, this was entirely untrue, and Westinghouse was not only watching the Kemmler case carefully but was doing everything he could to keep Kemmler alive, including spending thousands of dollars in legal fees. Westinghouse had learned how to play the game the same way Edison did: use your money, power and influence from behind the scenes while seeming aloof and unconcerned about the issue in person.[10]

Paul D. Cravath, the general counsel for the Westinghouse Company, admitted that a member of his firm had been in Auburn the Tuesday before the writ was filed but claimed that he was there on other business. He said that if it had wanted to, the company could have filed a lawsuit claiming New York's use of the dynamos was an infringement of Westinghouse patents but that the company had decided against that route.

Cockran, contacted by reporters about this new development, said he was surprised to hear about it but declined to make any comments. The newspapers, however, found it to be too much of a coincidence that Sherman's involvement in the case, on April 25 or 26, seemed to coincide with Hill's final denial of Cockran's request for a stay of execution.

Judge Wallace, a graduate of Hamilton College and Syracuse University and a former mayor of Syracuse, said he granted Sherman's request for a writ because he considered it a case of great emergency.

"I declined at first to grant it and told Mr. Sherman that he must make application to the United States Supreme Court," he said. "He showed me, however, that Kemmler might be killed before an application could be made. If a judge refuses to grant a writ of habeas corpus when there is the slightest possible reason for doing so, he makes himself liable to criminal prosecution. I therefore consented on condition that Mr. Sherman would make an application as soon as possible to the Supreme Court in Washington to support the writ. Otherwise, I said I would cancel it. I can't say what action the Supreme Court will take. It may grant it, or it may decline to grant it. In the latter case the execution will probably take place. The case may be tried in the Circuit Courts or it may be tried at once by the Supreme Court."

The newspapers were quick to condemn this latest legal procedure as an unnecessary delay and an unwarranted federal interference in state affairs. They pinned the blame squarely on Westinghouse.

"Here was a man convicted of chopping a human being to pieces," the *New York Tribune* wrote about Kemmler.

> He now makes no denial of his guilt. The State of New York says he shall forfeit his life in accordance with the law. He appeals again and

again but finally abandons the fight, says his fate is only just, expresses contrition at the crime he has committed and gets himself ready for the grave. At this point a lawyer steps in and without any authority whatever from this convict, without any petition, but simply by personal representations to a federal judge obtains a writ commanding the State of New York to stay its hand. This may be lawful, but it does not look either lawful or becoming.

One of two facts is indisputable. Either a bumptious, egotistical attorney is employing Judge Wallace's court to obtain notoriety or a dynamo corporation is employing it to serve a supposed business interest. In either case the state of New York is being molested in its sovereign right and the wretch in Auburn Prison is being tortured with a succession of empty hopes.

The *Tribune* editors said they had determined that the dates on the court papers had been falsified, with Kemmler signing them only after the writ had been granted by the judge. Although Kemmler's signature was dated April 28, according to prison officials, it was not given to him to sign until about 2 P.M. on April 29, after the stay of execution had been served on the warden.

"There may be an explanation of this queer business," the *Tribune* editors wrote, "but it does not look right. To be frank it looks like a piece of impertinence on the part of the lawyer Sherman and like an irregular proceeding on the part of the judge."[11]

The editorial writer for the *Times* called Sherman "a mere busybody" who was obviously motivated by his not-so-secret "client and paymaster" in Pittsburgh and then went on to include Durston in the plot. "It seems quite plain," the *Times* said, "that the Warden of Auburn Prison has been acting in collusion with the person who has applied for the stay." Since the stay did not arrive until the second day of the week in which Kemmler was to die, the editors said, it was clear that Durston had been notified beforehand to expect it and to therefore delay the execution.[12]

There seems to be no basis for this charge other than Durston's acknowledged reluctance to take on the role of executioner, but the *Times* editors were clearly seeing conspiracies everywhere.

The *Times* editors also criticized Durston for allowing Dr. Fell to be in the execution chamber with his device to attempt to resuscitate Kemmler after the electric chair was used. Fell had said he wanted to do this to make certain that Kemmler was dead and not merely stunned. This was, in part, in answer to the concerns raised by Cockran that Kemmler might not be killed and end up being buried alive.

"It is his business to put a man to death and not to revive him, nor to allow anybody to attempt his revival," the editors said of Durston. "A nice position the warden would have been in if he had electrified Kemmler into a state of suspended animation and the resuscitating process, being promptly applied, had worked!"

The *Albany Law Journal* said there was clearly no reason for the federal courts to become involved in the case but that Judge Wallace was put in a difficult situation. If he refused Sherman's request and Kemmler died, there would be no second chance to consider the matter. "We think the judge did right in granting the writ, in spite of the mysterious and culpable neglect of the attorneys in delaying the application until the prisoner was at the very point of death. But it seems to us that he was wrong in postponing the hearing for two months.... It is very serious that a single judge of the inferior Federal court should have the power *ex parte* to postpone the execution of a state sentence, ratified by the highest court of the state, for two months or even for two days.... If this precedent is to stand, we shall hereafter have this new phase of delay introduced in every capital case in which the ingenuity of counsel can invent a question or suggest a doubt."[13]

That concern, of course, turned out to be quite prophetic in the next century when appeals in federal courts held up executions for decades at a time.

On May 5 Kemmler's case finally reached the highest court in the nation when Sherman came to Washington to defend his petition for a stay of execution. There had been some talk that the Court might throw it out before he had a chance to argue it. He said the writ had been prepared in a hasty manner because it had been something of an emergency.[14]

"You say there are special circumstances, which make this case an emergency," interrupted Associate Justice David J. Brewer, the newest member of the court. "Has not this man been under sentence of death more than a year?"

Sherman explained he had only recently taken on the case and the previous attorney had not taken the federal route. He then explained the basis of his case, that he considered the use of the electric chair to be cruel and unusual punishment.

"If it is instantaneous, it cannot be cruel," remarked Associate Justice Stephen Field, a former state legislator from California who had been appointed by President Lincoln.

"That is an assumption of fact," said Sherman, who added that because the electric chair had never been used on a person, there was no guarantee it would not result in "prolonged torture."

The Court granted the stay of execution and agreed to hear the case on May 10.

While the public's attention was focused on the Supreme Court in Washington, the New York Assembly suddenly stole it back in another of the strange incidents that revolve around the electric chair story. With some obvious behind-the-scenes help from Westinghouse, the New York legislature threatened to do away with capital punishment all together.

Hardly anyone had noticed when Assemblyman Newton M. Curtis of St. Lawrence County, the state's foremost opponent of capital punishment, introduced at the beginning of the 1890 session a bill to abolish capital punishment. He had done exactly the same thing every year since he was first elected in 1883. Every year he gave a lengthy speech in favor of abolishing capital punishment and introduced his law only to see it die in committee without ever coming to a vote.[15]

The Assembly put up with this annual ritual out of respect for Curtis, who had been awarded the Medal of Honor for his heroic exploits as a general in the Union army during the Civil War. He had been wounded many times in battle. With his long, dark beard and six-foot, six-inch frame, he was a remarkable figure in the Albany Assembly chambers, and he had devoted much of his career to humanitarian issues, such as establishing special hospitals for the mentally ill.

So it came as a surprise to everyone on May 1 when his bill suddenly attracted dozens of enthusiastic supporters who gave speech after speech in the Assembly supporting it. The newspapers were quick to attribute this support to Westinghouse's interference, although it is hard to understand how this would have helped Kemmler. Changing the law at that point would not have helped a felon who had already been sentenced.

"Are there any bounds to the ambition of the Westinghouse Electric Light Company?" asked the *New York Tribune* in a front-page editorial on May 2.

In the era of Tammany Hall political bosses, these kinds of political turnarounds were not that unusual in Albany, where most legislation was crafted at backroom political meetings and the actual vote was little more than a formality. Charges of bribery and corruption were so common as to be taken for granted. Jobs, franchises and contracts were sold openly. It would be absurd to think that dozens of legislators suddenly changed their minds about capital punishment. The passage of the bill was certainly nothing more than an unusual political maneuver, and it is difficult to think of anyone who would profit from it besides Westinghouse.

At first Curtis's bill was headed nowhere, and no one was paying much attention as he gave it its routine second reading on the floor of the Assembly. His fellow assemblymen, who had, of course, heard his speeches many times, and often joked about how unlikely it was that his bill would ever be approved, took the occasion to retire to the smoking room.

No one thought that Curtis had any serious plans to pass the bill, and no one paid any attention when he asked, and the Assembly consented to, a third reading. Curtis then arranged with two Albany newspapers, the *Albany Argus* and the *Albany Express,* to print his speeches verbatim on four columns of the front pages. Curtis said he had arranged this by agreeing to buy a certain number of copies of the papers.

Word began to circulate that Westinghouse had endorsed his bill, but Curtis denied this, saying he knew nothing about it and that it was merely a coincidence that the bill was being read at the same time that Kemmler's appeal had been turned down by the court of appeals.

A powerful swing vote was that of Assemblyman Galen R. Hitt of Albany, a Democrat who was closely associated with the Tammany bosses. Asked by reporters why he had suddenly become a powerful enemy of capital punishment, he said he had been "impressed with the rhetorical beauty" of Curtis's speech.

So while the Assembly was busy with the many tasks necessary before adjournment, Curtis suddenly called up his bill for a vote, and Hitt made a fervent speech in favor of it. "I trust that this bill will pass," said Hitt, "because I think that capital punishment ought to be abolished. Humanity calls for it and is revolted at executions. I am glad to say that at present there are only two classes of the community who yet favor capital punishment and these are clergymen and prosecuting attorneys. I have had a large experience in defending murderers and I have come to the opinion … that capital punishment should be abolished."

No one replied to this speech, apparently because none of the advocates of capital punishment thought it had any chance of passing. But for mysterious reasons, which the newspapers charged were orchestrated by Westinghouse, a significant number of votes had changed sides since the last time a vote had been taken on Curtis's bill. As more and more assemblymen began to speak in favor of the bill, death penalty proponents finally became alarmed.

Assemblyman Tompkins said there was no stronger argument opposing capital punishment than the newspaper articles that had been written about the Kemmler case. Assemblyman Blumenthal said he had only recently made up his mind about how to vote on the bill, "but I have at last concluded that the worst cause to which you can put a man is to kill him and I shall therefore vote yea."

The astonishing result was that the bill passed by the huge majority of 74 to 29. The Assembly's clerk, in recording the vote, was quoted by the *New York Tribune* as remarking that "the bill has been passed by the money of the Westinghouse Electric Company."

At first the bill seemed to be headed toward a similarly rapid passage in the Senate. Sen. Charles T. Saxton of Wayne County, who had been one of the main supporters of the electric chair bill when he was head of the Assembly Judiciary Committee, was one of many who seemed to have changed his mind. He moved that the abolition bill be given a third reading on May 2, the day after it passed the Assembly. The third reading was the final step before calling a vote. Newspapers charged that Saxton seemed to have compromised his integrity by bowing to the Westinghouse interests.

Senator Cantor of New York City objected to Saxton's motion for a third reading, sending it to the Judiciary Committee. The chairman of that committee, Senator Robertson, said, "I rather favor the bill for the abolition of capital punishment."

"Apparently the most powerful of influences are at work to pass the measure in the Senate," the *New York Tribune* reported. "But will the Legislature of New York act in this hasty and inconsiderate manner on this bill of such unusual importance?"

The *Tribune* editors continued to blame Westinghouse. In an editorial published on May 3, it said the Assembly bill had been passed "by the exercise of some force which is not thoroughly understood.... [U]ntil some better explanation is offered, most people will believe that it was generated by a dynamo.... [I]t is extraordinary how many strange coincidences have occurred this week," including the "sudden and dazzling success" of the heretofore unsuccessful attempts to abolish capital punishment and the sudden conversion of Senator Saxton to the cause." The editors said they felt it likely that the bill would die in the Senate Judiciary Committee because there was little time left in the session to consider "a measure of such immense importance."

"No sensible man denies that strong arguments can be arrayed against capital punishment," the *Tribune* editors said. "An ideal society might find a better use for murderers than the execution of them, except for the fact that an ideal society would have no murderers to deal with.... Humanity is revolted by executions, says Mr. Hitt. If that be granted, the fact remains that humanity is still more revolted at premeditated murder, and that society will continue to regard its own welfare of more importance than the welfare of a criminal."

The editors suggested that a popular referendum on the issue might be one way to determine the public's will.

"But there is absolutely no defense of an attempt, in the closing hours of a legislative session, to enact a change of law so radical, so visibly sustained by invisible influences and so destitute of support; a change on which the people have never expressed an opinion, and to which the institutions of the State have never been adapted."

The next day the *Tribune* published Westinghouse's response to the charges in a letter to the editor. Westinghouse denied that he had anything to do with the new appeal filed by Roger Sherman or with the passage of Curtis's abolition bill in the Assembly. "I therefore desire to say," wrote Westinghouse, "in the most emphatic manner possible, that neither I, nor the Westinghouse Electric Company, nor any person associated with me, has any connection, direct or indirect, with the habeas corpus proceedings instituted by Mr. Sherman in the Kemmler case, or with the effort to abolish capital punishment in this State by legislative enactment."

Westinghouse went on to suggest that if there were any electrical companies involved in the strange events, "it is more likely to be those electrical companies, who, in hope of injuring the businesses of a rival, caused electric lightning dynamos of a particular manufacture to be adopted by the State for execution purposes, and now find that the agitation which they have instituted and kept alive is reacting against themselves."

This charge, that Edison was somehow behind the appeal and the abolition efforts, seems highly unlikely. Despite his protestations, Westinghouse later admitted that he had hired Sherman, and he was likely involved in the passage of the abolition bill as well. After a slow start in the marketing campaign initiated by Edison, by the spring of 1889 Westinghouse was sparing no expense or effort in his counterattack.

General Curtis also objected to the way he had been portrayed in the press. He said his bill had been introduced as early as February 4 and made its way through several stages before its passage. This was not, he said, hasty and unconsidered legislation but carefully considered legislation. The *Tribune* editors, after printing Curtis's complaints, repeated their charges that the sudden and unexpected support of his bill astonished the voters of the state and "has been condemned with gratifying emphasis and unanimity since the public became aware of its existence."

On May 6, just before the Senate was set to adjourn, the Judiciary Committee held a hearing to consider the abolition bill. Curtis rounded up a group of witnesses that he said represented the bench, the bar, the Church and philanthropy in general. They included the editor of the *Albany Law Journal*, a Quaker minister and a former judge. They testified about the worldwide humanitarian effort to abolish the death penalty and documented cases in which a prisoner had been put to death before evidence was produced that clearly showed he was not guilty. There were no witnesses called to testify on the other side, but the committee voted 7 to 2 to "report the bill unfavorably"; that is they killed it, bringing this most unusual sideshow to a close.

In a May 24 editorial, the *New York Times* called the whole affair "the most disgraceful exhibition ever made of itself by a legislative body in a civilized country." The vote in the Assembly had nothing to do with the merits of capital punishment, the editors said, and showed that they were as unfit for office as if they had "been shown by proof that every one of them took a bribe for his vote."

The *Albany Law Journal* said there was no reason to attribute corrupt motives to the episode because the legislators involved had unquestionable integrity. Instead, they attributed it to general dissatisfaction with the way the Kemmler case was being handled. "The result undoubtedly came about from a disgust felt at the outrageous course pursued by counsel in Kemmler's case, in which there never was a shadow of a doubt nor a decent pretense for debate, but in which, as nearly everybody believes, some powerful citizens or corporations have undertaken to defeat the laws of this state lest their business should be hurt. We should like to see capital punishment abolished, but we do not care to have our wish granted so rashly and from such apparent motives."[16]

In the same issue Matthew Hale, the legal expert on the Gerry Commission, wrote a lengthy commentary on the Kemmler case as it had developed. He concluded that it was within the federal court's power to issue the writ, even though it set the precedent of the federal government's issuing what amounted to a reprieve of a state's death sentence. He argued that the Eighth Amendment prohibition of "cruel and unusual punishment" applied to the federal government only and not to state governments.

"It matters little whether this wretched murderer shall live or die," wrote Hale, "but it is of importance that the laws of the state be executed, and it is unfortunate that where a murderer has been convicted and the penalty imposed by law has been adjudged against him, the ingenuity of counsel upon pretexts so flimsy and unfounded should be able to prevail upon a federal judge to interfere with the due course of justice and to introduce a new element of uncertainty in the administration of criminal law." He said such trivial procedures "bring contempt upon the administration of justice and thereby encourage crime."

On May 10, the court of appeals found that it had to deal with yet another appeal on Kemmler's behalf, this one brought by Charles S. Hatch, one of Kemmler's original lawyers in Buffalo, along with Cockran. This was the issue, first raised by Cockran in a letter to Hatch, that it was unconstitutional for anyone other than a county sheriff to conduct an execution. Because a sheriff was an elected official, his legal standing was somewhat different from a prison warden's, who was appointed. The legislature, according to the appeal, had no power to make this change. Cockran argued that executions had been part of the duties of sheriffs "since time immemorial." The court of appeals listened for only 10 minutes before postponing the issue until June, apparently to wait until the Supreme Court had ruled on the constitutionality of the law.

In a letter dated May 7 and released after Kemmler's execution, Westinghouse wrote to Sherman, who was preparing his brief for the Supreme Court. Westinghouse told him the generator being used in Auburn had not been designed to kill anyone and has "a hundred times the power required for the purpose."

"The machine has to run at an abnormal and dangerous speed to obtain the pressure required," Westinghouse wrote, "which gives a greatly increased current and a proportionally increased liability of failure." He suggested that it would make more sense for New York to use a storage battery for executions.

On May 20 William Kemmler's appeal finally reached the U.S. Supreme Court. Roger Sherman, the former federal prosecutor, presented his case first, taking the line that Cockran had used all along in the New York courts, that electrical execution was cruel and unusual and therefore a violation of the Eighth and Fourteenth Amendments. He also attacked the section of the law that allowed the exact date of the execution to be set by the prison warden.[17]

Because prison wardens had not been trained in the use of electrical instruments, he said, they could make mistakes in the process that could result in "terrible torture." He then went on to give many of the arguments that had been raised at the hearings the previous year: that human beings had differing electrical resistances, that alternating current produced a series of blows.

One of the oldest members of the court, Associate Justice Samuel F. Miller (who would die before the year was out), interrupted him at one point to ask if he thought the New York Law was "an ex post facto law," that is, if it had been passed to have an impact on a case tried before it was enacted.

"There is no contention of that sort," said Sherman.

Then Tabor argued the state's side, saying that the state had gone to great lengths to find the most humane means of capital punishment and that the law was the result of "the thoughts of eminent humanists." The law had the backing of the legislature, the governor and the courts of the state. He insisted there were no federal questions involved in the case.

"Has this court any power or right to review the decision of the highest court in New York?" he asked. "The good people of New York were beginning to be a little fearful that there was not enough vitality left in the State of New York to execute its criminals."

Associate Justice John Harlan, a former attorney general of Kentucky, insisted that the Supreme Court does have a right to ensure that state laws comply with the federal Constitution. For example, he said, the Fifth Amendment prevents a defendant from being tried for the same crime twice. If a state passed a law that permitted that, the court would have a right to rule on that law. Tabor agreed with that opinion. Then the court adjourned, promising a decision in two days.

On May 23, as promised, Chief Justice Fuller delivered the court's opinion. After giving a lengthy history of the case and quoting from the many legal decisions, Fuller ruled that the electrical execution law did not violate any section of the Constitution. Fuller wrote that although some punishments, such as burning at the stake, disemboweling or hanging in chains could be considered "cruel and unusual," electrocution did not fall into that category. "Punishments are cruel because they involve torture or a lingering death," he wrote, "but the punishment of death is not cruel within the meaning of that word as used in the Constitution. It implies something inhuman and barbarous, something more than the mere causing of dissolution." The obvious intention of the law, he wrote, was to find the most humane method of execution, not to find a more cruel or more unusual method.

The Court also disagreed with Sherman's argument that Kemmler had been denied "due process of law" as outlined in the Fourteenth Amendment. Fuller said he could find nothing in the law that seemed to violate that provision. For the Supreme Court to overturn a decision by the New York court of appeals would require a finding that the state had committed "an error so gross as to amount in law to a denial by the State of due process of law to one accused of a crime. We have no hesitation in saying that this we cannot do upon the record before us."

Technically, the Supreme Court's denial of Sherman's writ merely sent the case back to Judge Wallace, the federal judge in New York, for a final decision, but everyone understood that Wallace had been given pretty strict direction about how to handle the case.

Wallace refused to comment on the decision for reporters, saying he had been misquoted by some of the New York papers about his positions. This involved some question about the dating of the papers and the fact

Melville Fuller, the chief justice of the U.S. Supreme Court who wrote the opinion approving the first use of the electric chair. (New York State Library)

that they were missing the necessary seals. Some of the newspapers interpreted this as evidence that he was in league with Westinghouse to keep Kemmler alive. "One of the papers absurdly enough hinted that I was favoring corporations and attributed motives to me that were far from the truth," he said. He hinted, however, that he was not surprised by the Supreme Court ruling and had in fact expected it. When the case came back to him, he said, it would be quickly disposed of.[18]

The newspaper editors had long since tired of the legal processes keeping Kemmler alive and were quick to criticize the process. The *Tribune* called Sherman "a legal busybody" and his appeal "frivolous…. The only results of it have been a vast amount of trouble and annoyance to the officials of New York, the erection of false hopes for Kemmler and the reaffirmation of ancient doctrines that every schoolboy is familiar with."[19]

The *Times* compared Sherman's argument that the execution law was "cruel and unusual" to a character in a Charles Dickens novel who produced an article on Chinese metaphysics by combing encyclopedia articles on China under *C* and metaphysics under *M*. The same arguments, the editors said, could be made about any execution that had ever been held.

It called the whole process to spare Kemmler "a conspicuous example of frivolousness" and suggested that some way should be found to keep the courts from being abused in this way, suggesting that lawyers like Sherman should be held in contempt of court for bringing up such "silly questions."

The real blame, the editors said, should fall on Sherman's clients, who are "apparently willing to incur any expense to avoid the execution of Kemmler by electricity. From any point of view their action does not seem sensible. Even if they could protract their case until Kemmler died of disease, or old age, there would be other criminals condemned under the law."

The process seems to have cast the state court in a bad light, the editors said, by showing that justice could be delayed by persons who had no real standing in the cases involved. "If Kemmler were a millionaire he could not have commanded more persistent or unscrupulous efforts to get him free of punishment than have been made at the instigation and expense of persons who do not care a straw whether he lives or dies, and would not give a dollar to save his life from being taken by another agency than that which has been chosen for this purpose under the law." It was "monstrous" the editors said, that the courts had been used in this way by "a commercial interest," meaning Westinghouse.[20]

Finally, on June 11 Judge Wallace formally dismissed the federal suit, leaving only one remaining case before the court of appeals on the question of whether a prison warden could assume the execution duties of a sheriff. Cockran and Tabor argued against each other one last time. Tabor had barely begun to present his case when Chief Justice Ruger interrupted him by saying that further argument was unnecessary because the court was ready to issue its opinion. His brief ruling was that the legislature had the power to make the changes in the law and that there was no reason to overturn the lower court's ruling.

The newspapers were a bit more hesitant this time in declaring that Kemmler's fate was finally sealed. By now there were five other murderers who had been sentenced under the new law and the end of the appeals process also sealed their fates. Since Kemmler was to be the first, however, there was a chance that if his execution proved to be remarkably gruesome, an appeal might still be brought to save the others.

There was also some speculation that Westinghouse might attempt to seize the dynamos purchased by the state to prevent their being used in the executions. A spokesman for the Westinghouse Electric Company told the *New York Times* on June 24 that he knew of no effort to do that, but by now Westinghouse denials of anything were not taken very seriously.

With the long appeals process at an end, the *Albany Law Journal,* in its July 5 edition, took the opportunity to criticize the entire legal battle. "If Mr. Bourke Cockran had really been sincere in his pseudo-philanthropic efforts on behalf of 'poor Kemmler' he might better have evinced it by offering himself to be experimented on by the dynamo. A person of his adamantine composition would have stood in no possible danger from any number of volts.... A lawyer of average sensibility would have felt chagrined by the implied censure of Chief Judge Ruger's remarks on defeating the last device and exposing the last trick in this shamelessly contested case."[21]

With the courts finally finished with him, Kemmler was now in the hands of the electrical engineers who were performing the final tests of the Westinghouse dynamo, the electrical circuits and the wooden chair that stood at one end of a plain room in the basement of Auburn Prison.

—8—
The Human Experiment

W hen the state and federal appeals process came to an end in June 1890, the focus of attention shifted back to Auburn Prison, where Kemmler had been in confinement for 14 months. The chair and the other electrical apparatus had been installed in the basement of the administration building near Kemmler's cell and had been tested numerous times. Now it seemed there was nothing in the way of the execution.[1]

Kemmler was taken to Buffalo on July 4 so that he could be sentenced once again to die in the electric chair. Each time an appeal delayed the process the warrant for his execution expired and he had to be resentenced by Judge Childs. This was to be his third and final sentencing, with the execution date set for the first week of August.

One issue that still remained to be settled was the section of the law that prohibited newspaper coverage of the execution. This change had been recommended by the Gerry Commission as a way of hiding some of the more morbid aspects of executions from public exposure. The intention was similar to the law passed earlier in the century outlawing public executions, a change that significantly reduced the public's opposition to capital punishment.

The *New York Tribune* had argued that this kind of censorship was unnecessary and even dangerous. "Respectable newspapers do not make a practice of printing detailed and sensational accounts of executions," the editors said in a March 22 editorial. "Our readers are certainly aware that *The Tribune* is above criticism in that respect. But there are occasions of this nature when not simply a legitimate curiosity but the best welfare of society requires a complete disclosure of the attendant incidents and circumstances. That the first execution by electricity will be such an occasion we feel bound to declare in the most emphatic manner. The public ought to be, and is, profoundly interested in ascertaining promptly and fully how well the new process is adapted to its purpose, and in ascertaining this from disinterested and independent observers unconnected with the execution of the law."

The editors argued that newspapers are the only means of providing the public with an unbiased account of exactly what was to happen when the switch was pulled with Kemmler in the chair. While an official report would be presented to the legislature, this would take too long, the editors argued, and "this is not the way in which in this age of the world, the people like to get important news."

The editors then went on to give the worst case scenario: "There is a possibility—we trust it is extremely remote—that the execution of Kemmler will be a horrifying spectacle of inadaptability on the part of the machinery and of incapacity on the part of those in charge of it," and the citizens of the state deserved to have an unbiased account independent of "the men officially responsible for its success or failure."

Although an army of reporters at the execution was unnecessary, the editors said, one reporter from each of the national wire services seemed a reasonable compromise. Warden Durston and officials at the Department of Prisons in Albany must have read this editorial because it is similar to the policy they eventually adopted for Kemmler's execution.

The *Times* editors took a similar tack in an editorial on April 12. They thought the intent of the law was a good one. Publication of long and detailed accounts of executions, they said, served only the "morbid" interests of newspaper readers and tended to transform criminals into "popular heroes of a kind." Young and impressionable readers sometimes have trouble distinguishing between notoriety and celebrity, they said, and publication of these kinds of accounts was an affront to public decency.

On the other hand, the editors said, passing a law prohibiting coverage of executions was something else entirely. Newspapers that resorted to sensationalism, or "flash papers" as they called them, had poor reputations anyway, and intelligent readers avoided them. "People who are careful about the quality of their own reading or of that of their families refuse to take it and leave it to those to whom its contents are congenial." The state's prohibition, the editors said, was a step toward official censorship of the press.

Although there were few substantial reasons to print detailed reports about executions, the editors said, the Kemmler case in particular would provide details that were an important part of the public's genuine concern about whether this new form of execution was a good idea or not. "Questions have been raised and argued elaborately and at length as to the lawfulness, the certainty and the humanity of the proposed mode of capital punishment," the editors said. "These questions were dismissed by the courts but enough of a doubt was raised to make it very desirable that a detailed statement of the working of electricity in the first case in which it has been applied with the intention of causing death, should be given to the public. To limit the report in this case to the official requirements would be a public injury."

On the day before the execution, the *Times* editors added that the law was an unconstitutional restriction of the freedom of the press and was nothing more than censorship. Editors across the country would choose to ignore it, they predicted.

A bill, backed by the state's newspaper editors, was introduced in the Assembly to repeal the portion of the law that restricted press coverage, but it never came to a vote. At the time of the aborted execution of Kemmler in April, the one that had been postponed at the last minute, there were no reporters among the list of witnesses to be present in the execution chamber.

Southwick, who had helped write the law that outlawed reports of the execution, had changed his mind about it, telling reporters he thought it was essential that the details be published as widely as possible. There had been many questions raised about electrocution and the public deserved to know the answers, he said.

During the summer a deal was apparently worked out between the state and the newspapers that kept most of the press outside the prison but permitted two wire service reporters to attend the execution as witnesses, with the understanding that their reports would be sent out over the wires and used by the other reporters. This seemed a reasonable compromise at the time, similar to the "press pool" system used a century later. The plan failed, however, as we shall see, and led to wildly conflicting reports about what happened during the actual execution.

During most of the long appeals process, Kemmler remained silent. From time to time word leaked out that he was alternately hopeful or disappointed about the process, but his confinement in solitary left him little contact with the outside world. That began to change in late July, when stories about him, apparently smuggled out of the prison by guards at the urging of reporters, began to be printed.

On July 23 the *Auburn Advertiser* printed that Kemmler's attitude toward death was beginning to change. For most of the 14 months he had been at Auburn he had been quiet, with a remarkably stolid demeanor, accepting and even welcoming his coming execution. Now he seemed to be changing in significant ways. The chaplains at the prison suggested this was a result of their work, such as reading Bible stories to him. Lately, the paper said, Kemmler had expressed "a wholesome dread of the coming execution. He no longer retains his ruddy complexion. His features are pallid and wan. His appearance is unkempt. His appetite no longer craves the delicacies that he formerly obtained from the prison kitchen."

Deputy Warden Daniel MacNaughton, who seems to have been the source for this story, was quoted as saying this change had come over Kemmler quite suddenly the Saturday before, when Kemmler requested the presence of the warden's wife.

Mrs. Durston, who lived inside the prison, was ready to retire for the evening when she was told that Kemmler wanted to see her, and she came to his cell immediately. Kemmler said he wanted to talk with someone who could soothe his nervousness and talk in sympathetic tones. He complained of a headache, and she ordered him some tea. Then she urged him to bear up until he regained some of his previous composure. He then tried to sleep but was reported to be disturbed by strange dreams.

A few days later the *Advertiser* reported that Kemmler avoided the company of his spiritual adviser, the Rev. Dr. W. E. Houghton, pastor of the First Methodist Church in Auburn. "All hope has fled," the newspaper said, "and with it all the bravado, stoicism, stolidity, stupidity, fortitude or whatever it was that has characterized his eventful stay in Auburn Prison. Kemmler is visibly and unmistakably weakening."

By the beginning of August the world's attention was focused on Auburn and the historical event that was about to take place there. The *Saturday Globe* said there was as much attention focused on Auburn as there was during a presidential election. Much of this attention came from those with a legitimate interest in what would happen, such as electrical engineers, doctors, legal scholars and the legislatures of other states that had passed or were considering electric chair laws of their own. The general public, which had been following the story for two years now, also had a morbid curiosity about the outcome of the experiment.

According to Kemmler's third sentence, the execution could have taken place any time between August 3 and August 9. Reporters from across the nation gathered in Auburn beginning on August 3, waiting for something to happen and wiring back every detail of the preparations.

Many of the reporters were the same ones who had covered the aborted execution in April, and there was some speculation that Westinghouse still had an ace up his sleeve that could lead to a last-minute delay. Governor Hill denied that there had been any attempt by an electric company to seek a stay of execution for Kemmler. The reporter for the *New York Tribune* wrote that Kemmler had given up all hope that the courts or Governor Hill would interfere to help him.

"If he were a man of sufficient intellectuality to understand that the sooner the electric current does its work the quicker his earthly miseries will cease, he would beg the warden to do his duty immediately."

MacNaughton, the elderly deputy warden who befriended Kemmler and whom Kemmler called "the good Daniel," was the one who told him on August 3 that the end could come any day now. Kemmler's reaction was to utter something under his breath that sounded like an oath.

Kemmler, of course, had been through all of this the previous April and was now said to be listening to every sound from the execution chamber, which was right next door to his cell in the prison basement. He had been told that the chair was in place and connected to the machinery. Although the prison had conducted a new test of the chair, Kemmler was not told about the results, apparently to spare him the details. However, MacNaughton told reporters that Kemmler's greatest fear was that there would be some kind of malfunction that would result in something less than an instant and painless end, the very concern that all the hearings and court procedures had dealt with.

After building up something of a rapport with Warden Durston, Kemmler was said to be disappointed that the warden had not visited him for two days and that their friendship had apparently cooled off. Kemmler was now reported to be saying he thought Durston was looking forward to killing him. Durston had made it clear that he would have done anything in his power to avoid his new responsibility and was more likely avoiding Kemmler because he was busy with the machinery and the last-minute preparations. There is also the possibility that Durston did not want to look his victim in the face too often before the final hour. He left the prison on the Friday before the week designated for the execution and spent two days to New York. There was speculation that he was making a last minute appeal to the governor to get someone else put in charge of the execution because he had no stomach for it. There were also rumors that during the most recent test one of the voltmeters was not working and looked like it had been tampered with and that Durston went to New York to obtain a replacement. The truth, as Durston explained when he returned, was that he had gone driving along the New Jersey coast with a friend from Illinois.

While he was gone there had been some wild rumors reported in the press that Kemmler had lost his mind while waiting to be executed. When he returned, Durston's frustration with such stories was apparent. "These reports are wearisome and annoying," he said. "Kemmler is no more crazy than I am. He is an odd piece of humanity, to be sure, but is, as far as I can see, in about the same condition now as he was a year ago."

Charles T. Hatch, one of the two lawyers who defended Kemmler at his original murder trial, sent a farewell letter that arrived on August 3. Kemmler could not read, so one of the guards read it to him, but it had no visible effect.

The prison officials, the reporters and members of the Auburn community spent the next few days speculating about the hour and day when the end would come. The visitors and members of the press were taking bets that yet another last minute court order would arrive to save Kemmler. The reporters speculated that the execution could not take place on Monday because none of the witnesses had yet arrived.

Beginning on Monday, August 3, hundreds of people crowded around the main gates of the prison, staring at the ivy-covered wall. The convicts sweeping the front lawn and tending the flower beds regarded them curiously but understood why they were there. Each person who left the prison had to run the press gauntlet, answering as many questions as they liked. Not surprisingly the information was conflicting. Whereas some said Kemmler was passing the time quietly, others said he was dancing and singing to his cellmate Frank Fish's banjo playing.

Prison physician Sawyer told the press that Kemmler was in excellent health and that any reports that he had been ill were false. "I have not had to visit him professionally for fourteen months," he said.

Haughton, who said he had been warned by Durston not to talk to the press, said Kemmler was "calm and brave and hopeful" and that he had "shown spiritual growth since he first came under my observation. I feel much encouraged."

The next day, Tuesday, August 4, there was a brief flutter of concern after a test of the electric chair showed that the electrode that attached to the skull plate was not making sufficient electrical contact and needed several hours of last-minute adjustments.

Even at this late date there was uncertainty about who would pull the switch. During the original discussion of the operations of the electric chair it had been assumed that Brown would be the one to do so after Durston gave the order. With Brown no longer part of the execution team, it was unclear who would perform that duty. Durston had said that he did not want to do it, and many of the electricians who had been called in to test and adjust the chair also said they would prefer not to.

Charles R. Barnes of Rochester, quoted in the wire service stories printed on August 3, said he didn't want the job either and was growing increasingly weary of the entire business.

"My duty is to regulate the current at one switch," he said. "Another person will close a second switch, which will send the current that I have regulated to the chair.... I hope that the Westinghouse people will secure an injunction and prevent the execution from taking place. I am sick of the whole business."

The next day it was confirmed that Barnes would be in charge of the dynamo room. Davis would be in charge in the control room and the third electrician, Charles. R. Huntley of Buffalo, would be mostly an observer.

Also at this time a change was made in the configuration of the death chamber. A wall was built dividing it into two rooms, one with the electric chair and another with all of the controls, switches and meters. Durston said later this change was made so that Kemmler and the witnesses would not see the person who threw the switch that sent the power to the chair. This was apparently part of the last-minute arrangements over who would become the official executioner.

Although there had still been no announcement of the date or time of the execution, the witnesses had been told to report to the prison by 7 P.M. on August 5, virtually assuring that the execution had been scheduled for the morning of the sixth. The reporters, ready to report any rumor that came out of the prison, were told by the guards that there would need to be a final adjustment to the Westinghouse dynamo, which was also used to supply electricity to the prison machine shop while it was waiting for its intended purpose. The dynamo would have to be switched out of the machine shop circuit and into the electric chair circuit, the guards said, and that would probably not be done until just before the execution.

According to the terms of the law and the procedures established by the state Department of Prisons, there had to be at least 5 witnesses to the execution, and as many as 21, to be chosen by the warden. Among those who were required to be present were the judge who passed the sentence, the district attorney in the case, the sheriff of the county in which the crime took place and two physicians.

On the evening of August 4, Durston made public a list of witnesses he had invited:

Dr. H. E. Allison, Superintendent of the Asylum for the Criminally Insane

Dr. Carlos F. MacDonald, director of the State Commission on Lunacy

Dr. George F. Shrady, editor of the *Medical Record*

Dr. A. P. Southwick, the Buffalo dentist and father of the electric chair

Dr. E. C. Spitzka, a New York brain expert

Dr. George E. Fell of Buffalo, who conducted the Buffalo experiments and helped design the chair

Dr. C. M. Daniels of Buffalo, who testified at Kemmler's original trial

Dr. Charles Fowler of Buffalo

Deputy Coroner William T. Jenkins of New York City

Dr. Louis Balch of Albany, secretary of the State Board of Health

Dr. W. J. Nellis, of Albany

Dr. Henry A. Argue of Corning

John D. Stanchfield, district attorney of Chemung County

Tracy Becker, the Buffalo attorney who acted as referee during the court hearings

Robert Dunlap of New York, president of Dunlap Cable News Company, a personal friend of Superintendent of Prisons Austin Lathrop

George T. Quinby, the Buffalo district attorney who prosecuted Kemmler

Oliver A. Jenkins, sheriff of Erie County

C. R. Huntley, an electrician from Buffalo

Frank W. Mack, a reporter from the New York office of the Associated Press

George Grantham Bain, a reporter from the Washington office of the United Press

Because the electrical execution law outlawed reporting on executions, Durston was careful to point out that Mack and Bain had not been invited as reporters but as citizens of the state.

In his formal report on the execution to the Department of Prisons, Durston said he was overwhelmed by the number of people who had requested to attend the execution. "Ordinarily there would not be much responsibility in selecting such witnesses," he said, "but this being the first execution of the kind that was to occur, applications were made by men versed in all the learned and scientific professions from all parts of this and many other states. It was impossible to comply with all the requests that were made, as my aim was to select men who would treat the facts and circumstances of the execution frankly and fairly, and without any bias or prejudice. Subsequent events would seem to indicate that some of the witnesses were actuated by ulterior motives and used their position as eyewitnesses to further the interest of those who were engaged in the effort to nullify the law, and making the carrying out of its provisions odious and unpopular."[2]

Asked which of the doctors would perform the autopsy, Durston said he would leave it up to them. There was some speculation that Kemmler's family had taken some steps to prevent an autopsy from being conducted. Kemmler's brother had reportedly sent a registered letter requesting this, but Durston said he would not divulge what had been in the letter. There was even some speculation that Westinghouse had paid Kemmler's brother to make this objection, hoping it would delay the execution.

The doctors contacted by reporters said there had never been a chance to conduct an autopsy immediately after someone had been electrocuted, so Kemmler's death was an opportunity to further the advancement of science. The only autopsies conducted in such cases were performed many hours after death. It was hoped, they said, that the autopsy would show once and for all, whether death from electricity was painful or not.

Meanwhile, Kemmler continued to sit on his cot, gazing into space, lost in meditation and waiting for the sign that meant the end of his life. The guards posted a suicide watch on his cell even though he had never shown the slightest interest in killing himself. There had never been a condemned prisoner at Auburn before, because executions had been conducted in the county jails, and the guards seemed more than willing to supply the reporters waiting outside with news about their most famous guest.

When Kemmler ate his meals the guards watched him carefully, ready to take his knife and fork away from him if he tried to injure himself. When the guards asked him questions he answered them with brief replies. After he read the letter from his brother, however, his mood seemed to improve. He smiled and engaged in some brief talk with his guards and with Mac-Naughton. But within an hour or so his old sullen mood returned, the guards said. For 24 hours he had been tortured with the idea that his death could occur at any minute.

At 1 A.M. on the morning of Wednesday, August 5, Chaplain Yates and the Rev. Houghton woke Kemmler up to tell him that the time of his execution had been set for 6 A.M. the following morning. He is said to have taken this notice calmly and then went back to sleep. Meanwhile, outside the prison gates, the curious onlookers and newspaper reporters kept an all-night vigil. All the Auburn hotels were full. In Albany Governor Hill denied rumors that he had received an application for a stay of execution. There were reported to be a thousand people waiting outside the prison gates.

Although Auburn residents had taken little interest in the case up until then, the pressure of being on the front pages of newspapers all over the country was taking its toll. Instead of discussing baseball scores and the races in Saratoga, the usual topics in August, they began to gather outside the prison gates, staring at what they assumed to be Kemmler's cell window.

Inside the prison Durston was doing his best to maintain the regular routine, despite the crowds outside the gates and the pressure from so many people who had a personal interest in the outcome of the execution. The prisoners marched to their breakfasts and went to their work posts as usual, not knowing if the execution was being carried out at that exact moment.

In Durston's office, however, things were far from ordinary. Reporters were desperate to pry out of him the exact time of the execution, not just so they could report it but so they could tell editors all over the country when to plan for the news to arrive. Would it be on the morning or evening cycle? Would it meet the regular deadlines, or would it require an "extra edition"? Durston refused to tell them anything.

Robert Dunlap, the wire service executive from New York City who had been invited as a witness, arrived on the afternoon of the fifth. He was a personal friend of Lathrop and many reporters complained about this special access to Kemmler. After meeting with Durston, he went to Kemmler's cell for a brief interview and described him as "cheerful." The guards, however, said that this mood was only temporary and that immediately after the interview Kemmler fell back into his sullen and morose mood. Others said he was so nervous and fretful that drugs were given to him in an attempt to make him relax.

That afternoon, his cellmate, Frank Fish, a convicted murderer from Canandaigua, was taken out of the cell they shared and moved to another part of the prison. The two were allowed to shake hands and say their farewells. Kemmler knew that this change meant the end was near.

"Keep your courage up," Fish told Kemmler. "It will all be over soon."

Later that afternoon, the Rev. Dr. Houghton and Chaplain Yates administered the last rites to Kemmler. They described him as weak and penitent and anxious for the end to come as quickly as possible. The guards said that after the ministers left, Kemmler threw himself on his cot with a snarl that reminded them of a "wild beast at bay knowing there was no escape." He spent these last hours listening to the tolling of the prison bell as it ticked off the hours of the day. He also spent some of his time writing his name on little scraps of paper, souvenir autographs for the many people, both inside and outside the prison, who had asked for them.

Later that afternoon he was visited by a trio of men from Buffalo who all had a personal stake in the experiment. Dr. C. M. Daniels was accompanied by Quinby, the district attorney who had prosecuted Kemmler's case. Quinby, who had read some of the newspaper stories, had voiced some misgivings about Kemmler's sanity. To some degree this concern was legal rather than compassionate. The law prohibited the execution of an insane man, but Quinby also expressed an uneasy conscience of his own, saying he would never rest easy if Kemmler was really insane. After meeting Kemmler, Daniels assured him that Kemmler was perfectly sane.

Southwick told reporters he was opposed to strapping Kemmler into the chair because it might make him nervous and cause trouble. For him it was the end of a long process that had begun nearly a decade before, and he obviously had an interest in making sure that nothing got in the way of the final stage of the experiment. He said it was important that the first execution be performed flawlessly because it would set an important precedent. He predicted that electrocution would become the universal means of capital punishment and planned to attend a meeting in Paris where it would be explained to representatives from a number of nations.

Later that afternoon a thunderstorm rolled across Auburn; the sky filled with the lightning bolts that some of the reporters said were prophetic of what was about to happen. The flashes were followed by a steady downpour that lasted into the early evening. The guards said that Kemmler jumped with every lightning flash and every peal of thunder. Just before sunset, however, the clouds parted and the prison was bathed in a golden glow of the setting sun. The dark clouds were purple and red, creating a beautiful sunset.

Kemmler, who could not see the sunset from his window because it faced in the wrong direction, did manage to catch a glimpse of one of the purple clouds. He watched this until it was dark. Then, still without saying a word, he returned to his cot. MacNaughton stayed in the cell until midnight, speaking with Kemmler about Bible stories and other things.

At 7 P.M. Durston called a meeting in his office with the medical and electrical experts to go over the final plans for the execution. Because it had been written about so frequently in the medical journals, the execution had attracted much attention from doctors, and Durston had been overwhelmed with requests to perform the official autopsy. Durston insisted that he would retain control over the autopsy and refused to delegate this to any of the doctors. Among those attending this meeting were most of the official witnesses to the execution.

Later the doctors met at the Osborne House Hotel and discussed the situation with reporters. They agreed that the autopsy should not take place until at least three hours after the execution. The reason, they said, was the concern raised by Cockran that the condemned man might come back to life after being stunned by the current. If they performed the autopsy too soon, they said, they might be accused of killing Kemmler with their scalpels rather than with electricity. Southwick was said to be the most adamant about this waiting period. He said he and Dr. Daniels would not take part in the autopsy if it was made before the end of this waiting period. This waiting period was to become common at electrocutions but not for this reason. Doctors found that the body was too hot to touch when it was removed from the chair and had to be allowed several hours to cool down.

The doctors also agreed to make public, in great detail, the results of their findings, again because of the many issues that had been raised during the long debate. They wanted to make sure the public understood exactly how Kemmler died.

It was agreed that Daniels and Jenkins would be in charge of the autopsy, assisted by Shrady, MacDonald and Spitzka. Dr. Fell told reporters he had brought with him a Fell Motor that he planned to use on Kemmler during the three-hour waiting period. He was never granted permission to use it, however.

As soon as the doctors were finished with their meeting another took place, apparently in the same room. Durston met with Barnes, Davis and Huntley to go over last-minute plans for the use of the apparatus. Although this meeting was said to have begun with much excitement and shouting, Durston and Barnes finally reconciled their differences, and all four went to the prison to make a last-minute inspection of the apparatus.

The final version of the electrical system installed at Auburn reflected many of the concerns raised by Durston throughout the year. Although the basic system was quite simple—an electrical dynamo connected by wires to electrodes attached to the prisoner—the circuit had been complicated by a number of switches, meters and indicators to establish more control on the part of the operators. Durston apparently wanted a way to monitor the current and had insisted that all of the equipment be kept in a separate room, out of Kemmler's view.

The Westinghouse dynamo was located in the northwest wing of the prison, 800 to 1,000 feet from the chamber in which the chair was located. It was turned by a steam engine in the basement of the prison. The wires ran out of the window of the dynamo room to the roof and then along the roof line to a point directly over the death chamber, in the southern wing of the prison. This wire was connected to the electrode in a metal cap, with sponges inside, which was to be connected to the prisoner's head. The other electrode was connected to the back of the chair, also with a sponge connector, but came to the chair through the control room.

There were also two smaller wires running between the death chamber to the engine room and the dynamo room. These wires were the communications link between the switchboard room next to the death chamber and bells in the other two rooms. A coded system was devised. One bell was the signal to turn on or shut off the dynamo. Two meant to increase the current. Three meant to reduce the current. Five bells were the signal to get ready for the execution and six bells meant that the entire process was finished.

The switchboard, located in a small room adjacent to the execution chamber, was five feet long by three and a half feet wide and included a voltmeter, a lamp board with two rows of electric lights that acted as a kind of meter, a regulating switch, an ammeter to measure the quality of electricity and a large knife switch, 18 inches long, that switched the chair into the circuit. One of the main current wires was directly connected to the chair. The other ran through the switchboard and the switch.

The execution chamber itself was a square room, lighted by two windows about seven feet from the floor. It had once been used as a prisoner reception room, and it still contained a small sink and washtub that had been used to wash incoming prisoners. The windows looked out of the front of the prison across to the railroad station. Strangely, there were no electric lights in the room. Instead, it was illuminated by two gas jets with double arms, one on each side of the room. The walls had been painted a quiet gray color. The floor was of regular boards.

On the eve of the execution it was decided that Barnes would remain in the dynamo room and be in charge of its operation, and Davis would be stationed at the switchboard, where he could hear instructions from Durston. Although the execution would be under Durston's direction, it would be Davis who actually controlled the switches, including the one that would execute Kemmler. MacDonald and Daniel stayed in the prison's medical center, where the autopsy was to be performed, until 2 A.M. to make sure that all their equipment was ready for the task.

At 5 A.M. on August 6 the two ministers, Houghton and Yates, were the first of many visitors admitted into the prison. Spectators began to gather at the gate long before dawn, and the numbers increased throughout the morning. Besides the merely curious were throngs of reporters waiting for the news. Although two reporters had been included in the list of official visitors, hundreds of others were forced to wait outside in a pack, just across the road in front of the gate where they had set up a makeshift telegraph office in the dimly lighted freight room of the New York Central Railroad. Some reporters had climbed trees and were standing on rooftops, 20 feet above the ground, attempting to see over the prison walls.

Among the press corps was a reporter for the *Albany Evening Journal*, who wrote that there was a row of telegraph operators at little tables that had been specially set up by the Western Union Telegraph Company so reporters could send out their stories. "The fingers of the operators hung trembling over the keys," he wrote. "The first click from the sounder meant to the man at the other end of the line that the tragedy had been enacted."[3]

Kemmler awoke just before dawn from a troubled sleep at the first sound of steps outside his cell. He hastily threw on the new suit that had been specially prepared for this day: a sack coat, vest and trousers of a dark gray material, a white shirt and a bow tie with a black-and-white check pattern. In the dim light of a gas jet he saw the people who had come for him: Durston, Houghton, Yates and Joseph Velling, a deputy sheriff from Erie County. Kemmler quietly bowed his head as Durston read the death warrant to him one last time.

"All right, I am ready," said Kemmler in an offhand way. Then, turning to Joseph Velling, a jail attendant he had known in Buffalo, he added, "Joe, I want you to stay right through this thing. Don't let them experiment [on] me more than they ought to do."

Velling then cut a slit in Kemmler's trousers at the base of the spine to make a space for the electrode to be attached. Then he cut Kemmler's hair off, including the little forehead curl that had been one of his distinguishing characteristics. The preparations were completed by shaving a spot in the center of Kemmler's head. At 6 A.M. breakfast was sent in, and Kemmler and Velling ate together in the cell. When they were finished the two ministers said some prayers to which Kemmler added the appropriate "amens."

August 6 was a clear day in Auburn. The ivy on the walls outside the prison administration building were filled with twittering sparrows. The armed prison guards took their places in the prison towers.

Meanwhile, the witnesses ate a light breakfast at the Osborne House and set off for the prison, passing through the large crowd that was gathered there. They were then treated to coffee and sandwiches, served by prisoners in white caps and aprons, in Durston's private dining room on the second floor of the prison. The autopsy bags and Fell's resuscitation machine attracted considerable interest from the crowd when they were brought through the gates. When all of the scheduled witnesses had entered the prison, a hush passed over the crowd, which knew that the end could now not be far off.

Kemmler was led from his cell at exactly 6:32. One witness said he looked like a schoolboy who must speak his piece and has determined to do it as well as possible. Another said Kemmler was "spruce looking, a broad-shouldered little man, full-bearded, with carefully arranged hair." When he entered the execution room he found the physicians and other witnesses grouped around the death chair in the form of a horseshoe or semicircle.

"Gentlemen," said Durston in a matter-of-fact tone as Kemmler entered the room, "This is Mr. Kemmler." Witnesses said Kemmler was the coolest man in the room. He hesitated at the door as it was closed behind him and locked by a guard. Sunshine was streaming in through the windows. The electric chair was located just to the right of the main door to the room through which the visitors entered.

Many of the witnesses had never seen the chair before or had seen earlier versions of it. Witnesses described it as a square, high-backed easy chair with a seat of perforated wood. The arms were about two inches wide. Across the back were three wooden braces, to the upper two of which was fastened a hard rubber cushion. The lower electrode was attached by a cotton band to the back of the chair and ended in a round rubber cup, which contained the electrode. The upper electrode was inside a metal cap and a wire from it ran towards the ceiling.

"Give me a chair," was Durston's next command. This baffled the witnesses, who thought Durston was referring to the electric chair and that his command was part of some prearranged ritual. One of the guards pushed forward an ordinary kitchen chair and Kemmler sat down on it. The witnesses said Durston looked extremely nervous, with his hands and voice both trembling. Kemmler sat down as ordered, facing the witnesses, and showed no signs of emotion. He looked, witnesses said, as through he was rather pleased to be the center of so much interest.

"I have warned him that he has got to die and if he has anything to say, he will say it," said Durston.

"Well, gentlemen, I wish everyone good luck in this world," Kemmler said. "And I think I am going to a good place and the papers have been saying a lot of stuff that isn't so. That's all I have to say."

At a sign from Durston, Kemmler rose and the kitchen chair was taken away. The guards removed his coat and handed it to the warden. For the first time the witnesses got to see the slit that had been cut in his trousers. Kemmler started to unbutton his vest as well but Durston told him it was not necessary. However, since a portion of Kemmler's shirt was protruding from the hole in his pants he asked one of the guards to cut the material away to make sure that the contact would not be obstructed. Kemmler adjusted his tie and was escorted a few feet to the electric chair. Witnesses said he stepped into it with as much coolness as if he were going to have his shoes polished. Durston and Velling then attached the straps that held Kemmler to the back and arms of the chair. Durston's hands were trembling to much that he could barely get the straps into the buckles.

"My God, warden, can't you keep cool?" said Kemmler. "Take your time. Don't be in a hurry. Be sure that everything is all right."

When the straps were secure, the headpiece that continued the electrode was adjusted. It was connected to the back of the chair by a long arm that was adjusted by a clamp called a "figure four" on the back of the chair. Inside this metal cap was a rubber insert and a moistened sponge. The straps attached around Kemmler's chin, forcing his head into the spring-loaded electrode in the head piece. The warden assisted by holding Kemmler's head while the deputies made the adjustments. Kemmler thought the straps were still too loose, so he asked Velling to tighten them more securely.

"Press that down," insisted Kemmler.

The headpiece was a kind of muzzle of broad leather straps which went across the forehead and the chin. The top strap pressed down along his nose, flattening it slightly against his face.

While this was being done, Dr. Spitzka, who was standing nearby, said, "God bless you, Kemmler," and Kemmler answered softly, "Thank you."

The second electrode was then connected to Kemmler's spine through the back of the chair with some more straps. His legs were strapped to the legs of the chair.

The door leading into the control room was partly open. There was a man in the doorway and two others inside, although they were not identified to the witnesses. One of the ones inside was Edwin F. Davis. The reporters asked Durston which of the men would actually throw the switch, but the warden insisted that was to remain a secret. Through conversations with the control room it was determined that the dynamo was running and producing enough volts for its purpose.

"Do the doctors say it is all right?" asked Durston.

Dr. Fell stepped forward with a long syringe in his hand and applied a wet solution of salt water to the electrodes. Then Dr. Spitzka replied with a crisp, "all right." The other doctors and the technicians then echoed that remark.

"God bless you, Kemmler," Dr. Spitzka said.

"Thank you," said Kemmler through his mask.

Durston walked over to the doorway of the adjoining room, where Davis and the switchboard were located. As Velling stepped back from

William Kemmler in the electric chair at Auburn Prison. This newspaper illustration erroneously shows the switch in the execution chamber. It was actually located in a separate room off the main room. (*New York Herald*)

the chair, Durston said, "Ready," and then, speaking into the control room said, "Everything is ready."

"Good-bye, William," Durston said as he rapped twice on the door.

Within the room, Davis sent the two-bell signal to the dynamo room. The voltage was increased, lighting the lamps on the control panel. Then Davis pulled down the switch that placed the electric chair into the circuit. The switch made a noise that could be heard in the execution chamber. Kemmler stiffened in the chair. The plan had been to leave the current on for a full 20 seconds.

Dr. Spitzka, who had stationed himself next to Kemmler in the room, watched Kemmler's face and hands. At first they turned deadly pale but quickly changed to a dark red color. The fingers of the hand seemed to grasp the chair. The index finger of Kemmler's right hand doubled up with such strength that the nail cut through the palm. There was a sudden convulsion as Kemmler strained against the straps and his face twitched slightly, but there was no sound from Kemmler's lips.

Dr. Spitzka held a stopwatch before him and counted the seconds while examining Kemmler. After just ten seconds had passed he shouted "Stop!" which was echoed by other people in the room. Durston gave the order to the control room, and Davis pulled the lever back, switching the chair out of the circuit. The current had been on for just 17 seconds.

Kemmler's body, which had been straining against the straps, relaxed slightly when the current was turned off.

"He's dead," said Spitzka to Durston as the witnesses who surrounded the chair congratulated each other.

"Oh, he's dead," echoed Dr. MacDonald, as the other witnesses nodded in agreement. Spitzka asked the other doctors to note the condition of Kemmler's nose, which had changed to a bright red color. He then asked the attendants to loosen the face harness so he could examine the nose more closely. He then ordered that the body be taken to the hospital.

"There is the culmination of ten years' work and study," exclaimed Southwick. "We live in a higher civilization from this day!"

Durston, however, insisted that the body was not to be moved until the doctors signed the certificate of death.

Dr. Balch, who was bending over the body looking at the skin, noticed a rupture on the right index finger of Kemmler's right hand, where it had bent back into the base of his thumb, causing a small cut, which was dripping blood.

"Dr. MacDonald," said Balch, "see that rupture?"

Spitzka then gave the order, "Turn on the current! Turn on the current, instantly. This man is not dead!"

Faces turned white, and the doctors fell back from the chair. Durston, who had been next to the chair, sprang back to the doorway and echoed Spitzka's order to "turn on the current."

"Keep it on! Keep it on!" Durston ordered Davis.

This was not as easy as it might have been. When he had been given the stop order, Davis had sent the message to the control room to turn off the dynamo. The voltmeter on the control panel was almost back to zero. Davis sent the two-bell signal to the dynamo room and waited for the current to build up again.

The group of witnesses stood by horror-stricken, their eyes focused on Kemmler, as a frothy liquid began to drip from his mouth. Then his chest began to heave and a heavy sound like a groan came from his lips. Witnesses described it as "a heavy sound," as if Kemmler was struggling to breathe. It continued at a regular interval, a wheezing sound that escaped Kemmler's tightly clenched lips.

Durston continued to shout to the control room to turn on the current as some of the witnesses turned away from the chair, unable to bear the sight of Kemmler. Quinby was so sickened by the sight that he ran from the room. Another, unidentified, witness lay down on the floor.

Then, just two minutes after it had been turned off, the dynamo was up to full speed again. The voltmeter read 2,000 volts, and Davis switched the chair back into the circuit. It was a repeat of the first shock, with Kemmler's body straining against the straps. The moaning sound ended immediately as the body became rigid, but the frothy foam continued to drip down from his mouth onto his gray vest.

The estimates of how long the current was on this second time vary from witness to witness. Some estimated it to be as long as four and a half minutes. Others said it was more like two. The official report was that it stayed on for 70 seconds. No one was anxious to give the order to stop this time. Smoke was seen coming from the top of Kemmler's head, and the room was filled with the stench of burning flesh. There was a sizzling sound. The reason for this was that the electrode that was attached to Kemmler's head had been loosened at Spitzka's order after the first application of power. It was therefore not in close contact with Kemmler's skin and had created a spark that had burned his head.

Again there were cries to turn off the current. Durston gave the order, and Davis pulled the switch. Kemmler's body sank once again into the chair. At 6:40 the current was shut off for the second and last time. After years of debate, the final event was quite brief. Kemmler had been in the chamber for only eight minutes.

Dr. Fell turned to G. G. Bain, the United Press reporter who was next to him, and said, "Well, there is no doubt about one thing. The man never suffered an iota of pain."

The other physicians in the room were quick to agree, but they openly disagreed about what Kemmler's state had been after the first jolt of the current. Those with the greatest stake in the outcome of the experiment, Spitzka, Southwick and Daniels, insisted that the sounds coming from Kemmler's mouth were not evidence of suffering. They were merely involuntary actions caused by chest muscles. Southwick said the first jolt had killed Kemmler but thought it probably should have been left on longer. Other witnesses told Bain they were certain that Kemmler had been on the verge of regaining consciousness.

Kemmler's body was unstrapped from the chair and carried to a table on the other end of the room where the autopsy was to be performed. Durston, meanwhile, asked each of the witnesses to sign the official certificate of death.

Outside the prison there was no visible sign to the crowd that the execution had been completed. About a dozen prison workers, their lunch boxes in hand, waited outside the gates because the huge iron doors had been locked during the execution, and no one was allowed in. When the gates were reopened at 6:48 it was the signal to the crowd that the execution was over. The gate opened with a bell that was also the signal to the reporters to send out the bulletin that Kemmler was dead.

A few minutes later Quinby walked slowly out the prison gate, the first person to tell the crowd that Kemmler was dead. In answer to reporters' questions, he said Kemmler died like a child but admitted that he had not witnessed the final moment. At the last second he was overcome and ran from the death chamber into the corridor where he fell, almost fainting. When he revived he returned to the cell and saw Kemmler lying dead in the death chair.

Three hours later Daniels and Jenkins performed the autopsy in the prison's hospital. The report, prepared the same day, was given out to the press. In many ways the autopsy was more important than Kemmler's death because it was hoped that it would finally answer the question of whether electrocution was more humane than hanging. The results of the autopsy, like those of the execution, were inconclusive.

The doctors found a discoloration of Kemmler's forehead and chin caused by the leather straps. There was also a crescent-shaped burn on the top of his head, an inch and a half long and half an inch wide, which scorched his hair at the point where the top electrode was attached. Later, when the scalp was removed, the burned area was found to be much larger, about four inches by four inches. Parts of his brain had been burned. The doctors also noticed that three hours after the electrocution, while the other parts of Kemmler's body were quite cold, his brain was still hot, measured at 97 degrees. Kemmler was found to have ejaculated during the execution, but the spermatozoa were found to be dead.

There was another black circular burn on the base of his spine where the other electrode had been attached. Below this, the doctors found that the spinal muscles were "cooked throughout their entire thickness" but that there seemed to be no damage to the spinal cord. Parts of Kemmler's brain and spinal cord were reserved for further research, as were containers of his blood. The doctors ruled that Kemmler died as a result of a "sudden destructive change in the molecular elements of the brain centers and blood" and that his heart had stopped beating when the electricity was applied.[4]

The next day Kemmler's body was buried without ceremony between 4 A.M. and 5 A.M. in an unmarked section of state land adjacent to Fort Hill Cemetery on Fitch Avenue about a mile from the prison. The unusual hour was chosen because reporters had heard about the plans and had gathered at the cemetery earlier in the day.

The body, wrapped only in a blanket, was taken out of the prison in a wagon through the back door. There was no ceremony. No friends or relatives attended. The body was unceremoniously dumped into a hole in the ground. Quicklime was poured into the grave to consume his body as quickly as possible. The grave had been dug by a prisoner known only by the name of King.

Sometime after the news of the execution reached the world, at least one amateur poet was moved to record the historic event in verse. Although the author's name has not survived, his work seems typical of the reactions of the public.

> August Sixth, that fateful day,
> when New York burned her soul away,
> The nation's pride was deep in shame,
> for hell had won the wicked game;
>
> This greatest state, mid din and strife
> has stopped to take a human life,
> And not by hanging, as the rule,
> but by some new electric tool.
>
> They turned the switch at break of dawn,
> and soon the victim's soul was gone;
> Without a curse or word of hate,
> bowed his head and left the state.
>
> The State that said he'd feel no shock,
> when current caused his frame to rock,
> For they had fixed a fancy rig,
> to kill this human guinea pig.
>
> Too bad before he took the heat,
> he did not offer them his seat;
> Too bad they did not have the pluck,
> to wish, for him, the best of luck.
>
> But now that it is done and past,
> we pray the first one is the last;
> No more we want our state to thrill,
> about this easy way to kill.[5]

—9—
The Reaction:
"A Thrill of Indignation"

Within seconds of Kemmler's death on the morning of August 6, the news was flashed by telegraph from Auburn to newspaper offices throughout the world, where it was published in "extra" editions. The *Saturday Globe* said, "In London, Paris, Berlin and Vienna, the populace awaited the meager details of the execution and in our own country it attained importance almost rivaling the result of a presidential election." Under headlines such as "The End of Kemmler" and "The Terrible Death of Kemmler" newspapers printed thousands of words about every detail of the execution. In some cases the stories went on for many pages.[1]

The details of the botched execution were ghastly enough, but many of the newspapers, because their reporters were not able to be present, invented even more terrible accounts—that Kemmler's body caught fire, that flames erupted from his mouth, that he had cried out in pain when the current was turned on. Accounts of the execution varied considerably from paper to paper, with the most responsible papers, such as the *Times*, the *Herald* and the *Tribune*, using accounts based on the reporting of the Associated Press and United Press reporters who actually attended the execution. The more sensational papers, such as the *World* and the *Sun* felt free to use stories based on rumor and their own imaginations.

The *New York Evening Post,* one of the few papers that conformed with the state's censorship of news about the execution, limited its coverage to one paragraph giving the time and duration of the shock that killed Kemmler. In an editorial the next day the *New York Times* editors, who were opposed to censorship, could not resist pointing out that even the few words printed by the *Post* violated the law and that the *Post* editors were guilty of a misdemeanor.

Because of the conflicting news about what exactly had taken place in the basement of Auburn Prison, the public policy debate about whether the experiment with electricity had been a success was clouded by a lack of solid information. Had there been a mistake? Did the equipment work properly? Had Westinghouse managed to sabotage the process at the last minute? Had Kemmler been tortured to death?

Even the accounts of eyewitnesses varied considerably. Southwick declared the execution a total success, but others described the smell of burning flesh, the sounds Kemmler made after the first attempt and the smoke rising from his body. Several witnesses called it the most horrible event they had ever witnessed. Although it is certain that there was some smoke during the second application of the current and that Kemmler's body had been burned, the extent of the damage was not immediately clear. Some of the less reputable newspapers' stories about flames shooting from Kemmler's body created a legend that persisted for over a century. It was repeated on National Public Radio in 1995 in a story about New York switching its execution method to lethal injection. The truth is that not one of the witnesses to the execution ever claimed to have seen flames, only smoke.

With a lack of clear information about what had happened, it wasn't surprising that the debate that followed was confused as well. Important and powerful people had staked their reputations on the results of the experiment. Southwick and many of the doctors, such as Carlos Mac-Donald and Edward Spitzka, were on record insisting that electrocution was humanitarian, painless and instantaneous. The New York legislature and Governor Hill, who had taken a bold stand on the experiment, were watching closely for any political fallout from the botched execution. The legal establishment all the way up to the Supreme Court had come down squarely on the side of electrocution. But perhaps the most interested of all were the owners of electric utilities, especially Edison and Westinghouse, who had millions of dollars worth of contracts at stake.

There is no doubt that Kemmler's execution was botched. The current was cut off too soon and then, on the second application, left on so long that it burned his body. Whether he was killed by the first jolt or was still alive at the second one is a matter for conjecture. It is clear that the head electrode was loose during the second application of electricity, causing the burning that was noticed by the witnesses. It is not known for certain what voltage was used on either the first or second applications. The witnesses' accounts vary considerably. It is also not known if, as was charged later, some of the switches were set improperly so that some of the current was sent through the bank of lightbulbs that had been installed as a measuring device. These bulbs were supposed to be taken out of the circuit when the chair was used, but some accounts said they were left on, draining away some of the voltage that was supposed to go to the chair.

One of the early scapegoats of the botch was Dr. Edward Spitzka, who gave the order to turn off the current too soon and then ordered it turned back on. Others blamed Durston, the nervous warden who held the ultimate control that day and gave many of the orders before and during the execution. The decision to hide the voltmeters in the control room, for example, was cited as a factor in the confusion after the first application of electricity.

The finger pointing and face saving efforts started before Kemmler's body was cold. Some of the doctors in the execution chamber made a point of telling the wire service reporters that Kemmler had died without pain. Many of the doctors present also took part in the autopsy and therefore influenced the official record of what happened to Kemmler.

Southwick, the father of the electric chair, insisted that Kemmler felt no pain. The burning of the flesh on the head, he said, was because the current was left on too long, burning out the caustic soda in the metal cap that was used to make the contact there.

"There will be hundreds more executions by electricity," Southwick predicted, "for the experiment of yesterday morning was a success. I don't care what anybody says, science has proved that Kemmler died an absolutely painless death. Ladies could have been in that room and not known what was going on, so silent was the process. Not a cry from the subject. Not a sound. Kemmler died without knowing anything about it."[2]

His only regret, he said, was that he had not interfered to keep the current from being turned off too soon. "I think Dr. Spitzka got rattled," he said. "Electrocution is the humane way to inflict the death penalty and is a complete success…. It is the grandest success of the age."

Southwick was also busy denying that the execution was anything other than perfect. "The fact is there has been a great deal of senseless, sentimental talk about the execution. For instance, the big story in regard to the sickening spectacle of froth, saliva, etc., coming from Kemmler's mouth is ridiculous. It was a perfectly natural thing and was caused by the muscular contractions of the stomach. It was nothing unusual at all…. The burning of the flesh was also exaggerated. That was caused simply by the fact that [the] sponge under the electrode was too small. A light current was passing through there and the sponge having dried out the electrode just touched the skin."

Dr. Fell also insisted that the execution was a success. "Those who say that it was not," he said, "are the natural enemies of the system. Death was instantaneous. The apparent gasps for breath were nothing more than a mechanical action of the muscles caused by the relaxation of the current.... A hen with her head cut off flops for some time, while amputated frogs' legs can be made to walk."[3]

Those reports differ considerably from those of witnesses like District Attorney Quinby, who admitted that he fainted during the execution, even though he had been brave enough to sit in the chair before the execution. Others who managed to stay to the end were disgusted with what they saw.

"I am thankful it is over," said Sheriff Oliver A. Jenkins, who some reporters said was crying when he came out of the prison. "The smell of that burning flesh haunts me still. It was not a nice scene to assist at.... I never want to see another such sight as that was. It was terrible. When the current was removed, Kemmler doubled up, his thumbs tightened around the arms of the chair. His entire body seemed to be convulsed and he acted as though he was making a terrible struggle for life. The muscles of the face quivered and he seemed to be in an apoplectic fit. In a second or two he appeared to be breathing and froth and foam came from his mouth and nostrils."[4]

The newspaper reporters said Deputy Coroner Jenkins of New York was "shaking like a leaf" when he spoke with them a few minutes after the execution. He thought that he saw pain on Kemmler's face and that Kemmler seemed to be struggling to get away from the current. Although he had seen many executions, he said none of them was as terrible as Kemmler's death.

Dr. George F. Shrady, editor of the *New York Medical Journal* and the doctor in charge of the autopsy, was a well-known opponent of capital punishment. Shrady, a graduate of Yale Medical School, was a surgeon during the Civil War and later served on the staff of President Ulysses S. Grant. He said he had seen many hangings, but the electrocution of Kemmler was much more terrible.

"I am inclined to think that if the current had been stronger it would have been better. I do not think any autopsy has ever been made which equals this in interest and importance, unless it was that of the body of General Garfield. This autopsy took from three to four hours and it was hard work all of the time. We learned this much, that electricity, if applied with sufficient force, will produce instantaneous death. I think the difficulty here was that the machine was not properly arranged. I am personally opposed to this business of murdering life by a mysterious death."[5]

Charles Huntley, the manager of the Brush Electric Light Company in Buffalo and the only electrician who was listed as an official witness, was horrified by what he saw. He later wrote an article for the *Telegraphic Journal and Electrical Review* called "Kemmler's Execution as Seen by an Electrician," in which he condemned the electric chair as legal torture.

"Oh, it was horrible!" he told a reporter after the execution. "It was one of the most horrifying sights I have ever witnessed or ever expect to witness. There is no money that would tempt me to go through the experience again."[6]

Other electricians were willing to comment based on reading the press reports. These included Harold P. Brown, who was contacted by reporters in Louisville. He said that from everything he had read and what he knew about the process Kemmler died with the first jolt of electricity. "Kemmler was killed instantly and painlessly within the first second," he said.[7]

Westinghouse, contacted at his home in Pittsburgh, was also horrified. "It has been a brutal affair, " he said. "They could have done better with an ax. My predictions have been verified. The public will lay the blame where it belongs and it will not be on us. I regard the manner of the killing as a complete vindication of all our claims."[8]

Thomas Edison, interviewed by the *New York Times* at his home in Llewellyn Park, New Jersey, said he preferred "not to discuss the circumstances" because he had not had time to read any of the reports.

"Kemmler was undoubtedly killed at the first unless some big mistake was made," Edison said. "Undoubtedly all those present were greatly excited. I should have been excited myself at such a time. In that excitement there may have been some bungling. I think when the next man is placed in the chair to suffer the death penalty, that death will be accomplished instantly and without the scene at Auburn today."[9]

Edison laid the blame on bumbling doctors who insisted on connecting the electrodes to the head and spine, instead of connecting at the hands as Edison had suggested in the past. "The better way is to place the hands in jars of water," he said, "in which there is a little potash to eliminate all grease from the hands, and let the current be turned on there."

Eugene T. Lynch, Jr., former general manager of the United States Electric Lighting Company in New York, told a reporter from the *New York Tribune* that it was a mistake to use a commercial dynamo, especially one associated with a particular company, when it would have been easier to build one specifically for the project. The Westinghouse dynamo was designed to generate 1,100 volts but could be run at a higher speed than designed to generate 1,600 volts. What was really needed, he said, was the kind of dynamo used in England, which could generate 10,000 volts. "They could have obviated all difficulties and made the execution absolutely safe and certain by using a higher voltage machine. I think, however, that if the connections were properly applied Kemmler died after the first shock. If he suffered it was probably due to poor connections."

F. S. Hastings, treasurer of the Edison General Electric Company, said he thought that Kemmler felt nothing after the first shock and that any movement was the result of involuntary muscle contractions. "It is the pressure of electricity that kills and not the quantity," he said, and when the current is left on too long it only results in burning of the body, as seems to have happened with Kemmler.[10]

Paul D. Craventh, attorney for the Westinghouse company, told the *New York Tribune,* "As a humanitarian I hope that it has now been proven that killing a man by electricity is the height of cruelty. Some less brutal manner of carrying out [the] death sentence will be adopted.

"The trouble is that it is impossible to measure electricity accurately. So long as the meter works all right the exact power can be ascertained, but it is of the most delicate construction and the least thing will throw it out of order and render it worthless. Even five minutes after an experiment it may be utterly unreliable. Hence it will be readily seen that electricity is not the thing to kill a man by due process of law."

Henry Hine, a district manager for Westinghouse, said the state of New York should have put the contract for the Auburn generator out to bid and should not have hired Brown because he was "anxious to use the fact that criminals were to be executed by electricity" as a marketing advantage for a company he was affiliated with.

H. C. Townsend, attorney for the Thomson-Houston Electric Company, told the *New York Tribune*, "If there was any trouble the electrical machinery must have been defective.... The doubt about this electrical execution may be the reason for doing away with the whole thing.

"From a scientific point of view," he said, "the Kemmler execution was a failure. Beyond doubt he suffered intense torture."

George E. Redman, superintendent of the Brush Electric Light Company in New York and an opponent of capital punishment, said it was clear to him that the voltage had been too low. Future executions should use at least 4,000 volts, he said.

There were immediate calls for the repeal of the law from a number of state legislators and others. State senator Donald McNaughton, for example, announced that he was in favor of returning to the old method of execution.

"I suggest a new office, that of state executioner, be created and that he have one or two assistants and that the mode of punishment he hanging," he said.

Alarmed by the newspaper reports that the execution had been botched and that Kemmler had suffered a horrible death, Governor Hill ordered Dr. MacDonald to prepare an official report. He denied that there was any serious interest in repealing the law.

Warden Brush of Sing Sing Prison, where four men were slated to die in that prison's electric chair, said he thought the law should be repealed. "I am convinced that none of the four men in my care awaiting their doom by electricity will ever be executed in the electric chair," he said. "I think that the law will be repealed either by an extra session or at the next session of the legislature. I don't like the job of killing a man."[11]

Gunning S. Bedford, the acting district attorney in New York City, also called for the law to be repealed: "The guilty have their rights as well as the innocent. When a man is convicted and sentenced he is still entitled to have the sentence executed in a proper manner," he said. "When the legislature assembles I will myself urge that the manner in which the death penalty be inflicted be changed. Instead of making the mode of punishment better, it seems to be worse than before."

W. Bourke Cockran, who had pleaded Kemmler's case in the New York courts, said, "It is a sort of ghastly triumph for me. The experts against me on the trial figured it all out that such a shocking thing was impossible and yet it has just happened…. After Kemmler's awful punishment no other state will adopt the electrical execution law."[12]

A number of lawyers said they were concerned about the impact Kemmler's death would have on the criminal justice system in the state. W. F. Howe of the Howe and Hummel legal firm in New York City, told the *New York Herald* that any juryman who read the Kemmler stories would never find a murderer guilty. "It will be exceedingly hard to get any convictions for murder in the first degree," he said. "In fact, I believe that the recent attempt at electrocution in Auburn has practically abolished the death penalty for some time to come." The legislature should probably abolish the law, he said, but if it did so every convicted murderer then in prison would have to be set free

With the crowds no longer blocking the gates of Auburn Prison, Warden Durston was free to take his lunch at the Osborne House, where the reporters found him quite angry with the way he had been portrayed in the newspapers. One reporter said he had "fire in his eyes" and he insisted that he had called Kemmler "William" and not "Bill" during the preparations for the execution, contrary to some newspaper reports. He denied that any of the electricians used in the execution were "Westinghouse men" as a newspaper had reported.

"The execution was a great success, as the official reports will show," he said. "The public, upon sober second thought, will feel that this is the better mode of carrying out legal executions."

The first newspaper editorials, reflecting the confusion about the facts of the execution, were divided in their opinions. Some were critical of the procedure that had been followed while others demanded an investigation or asked that the new method be given a fair chance before it was abandoned.[13]

The *New York Tribune* said that as bad as the execution seemed to have been, it was still better than hanging.

> There are only the two possible methods that our civilization will sanction—electricity and the rope. It is only because we are so familiar with hanging that its utterly brutal conditions are tolerated. One only need to reflect upon the infernal tortures that are involved in a suspension by the neck with a tightened rope cutting into the flesh to satisfy himself that no suffering could be profounder or more exquisite than that endured by a hanged man.... It is probable that the spectacle of Kemmler's death was equally dreadful, but it is also probable the sensation fled at the first approach of the electric current. This execution cannot be regarded as anything more than an experiment, and as an experiment it was not a complete success. The current was not steady and neither were the nerves of those who applied it....
>
> Unquestionably there were serious defects in Warden Durston's mechanical arrangements.... That there will now be a loud outcry against the new law is to be expected, and probably all sorts of expedients will be resorted to prevent another application of it. Such expedients ought not to succeed. While we cannot consider it settled that the law should endure, further tests of its desirability should be had. These will be in the interest of mercy and civilization. Kemmler's sufferings, whatever they may have been, were certainly no greater than he would have had to endure had he been choked to death, and they were probably infinitely less.

The *New York Herald* took a more balanced view:

> In one respect at least the execution of Kemmler was a dismal and unfortunate failure. It will fail to end the unparalleled controversy that has been waged over the substitution of the dynamo for the gallows. On the contrary it must revive the controversy and give to it a vigor which it never had before.
>
> While yesterday's experiment was a failure in the sense we have mentioned, it does not show that this mode of inflicting the death penalty is not a success. The failure was due not to the system but the bungling inefficient way in which the execution was managed. The fault was with the doctors and the electricians. But no backward step should be taken hastily. So great a reform is not to be abandoned without a good rea-

son.... It does not warrant a return to the barbarity of the gallows. Had the execution been properly and efficiently managed it would have proved the success of the new system beyond all dispute. An electric light concern should not be allowed to take advantage of the failure to further its own private interests.

The *New York Times* said, "It is unfortunate for the cause of execution by electricity that its first trial was badly bungled. It was intended to be a merciful method of putting condemned murderers to death, painless and instantaneous ... but yesterday at Auburn Prison it was evidently not successful."

That failure, the editors said, would be used by opponents of the electric chair and opponents of capital punishment to "work up a popular sentiment against the law.

"It would be absurd to talk of abandoning the law and going back to the barbarism of hanging," the editorial said, "and it would be as puerile to propose to abolish capital punishment because the new mode of execution was botched in its first application."

The *Times* editors went so far as to suggest that the failure was a result of a conspiracy between Durston and Westinghouse and that the last-minute adjustments to the chair "have given a suspicious appearance to the final preparations."

The *New York Star* took a middle-of-the-road approach: "The execution yesterday was not smoothly successful. It is not at all certain, however, that it was of so horrible a character as the reports have generally made it out to be or that the result absolutely discredits the electrical method of capital punishment. There was blundering, but there have been blunders in executions by hanging. One instance of this kind does not establish the inutility of electricity any more than accidents on the gallows heretofore are conclusive arguments against the rope.... It seems that the alternating current that was used in this instance is capable of destroying life surely. That when properly applied it can be made to accomplish that result quickly and painlessly will be generally believed."

But many editorial writers were horrified by the reports from Auburn and demanded an immediate end to execution by electricity.

The *Utica Saturday Globe* called it "the first and perhaps the last electrocution," saying that "it is not improbable that the first will prove the last.... Manufactured lightning to take the place of the hangman's rope for the dispatching of condemned murderers cannot be said to be satisfactory.... The men who witnessed the horrible scene Wednesday morning in the death chamber of Auburn Prison never wish to be present at another exhibition.… Electricity having failed to meet the expectations of its advocates, the probability is that no more executions will occur until it is demonstrated that it is less brutal than the old way of ridding us of malefactors. It is more humane to hang a culprit than it is to subject him to the pangs Kemmler underwent until the vital spark was crushed out of him."

"The first duty of the next legislature will be to repeal the electrical execution law and to restore the old method of administering the death sentence by hanging," wrote the editors of the *New York Sun,* who had printed the letters stolen from Brown's desk and were generally skeptical about the whole idea of the electric chair.

"Scientific curiosity has been gratified sufficiently by its one awful experiment. The present generation is not likely to hear of another such scene of horrible uncertainty, unknown torture, and heartsickening circumstances as was witnessed yesterday morning by the assistants at the judicial experiment upon the body of William Kemmler.… It may be taken for granted that public sentiment in New York will tolerate no further essays in this new experimental science of man killing by electricity, pending the time when the law can be repealed in the name of the state's dignity and of the enlightened humanity of the nineteenth century."

The *New York Chronicle*'s editorial said, "Seldom has a narrative more repulsive and horrible shocked public opinion. The guillotine and the hangman's rope do not compare in point of cold blooded barbarism with this achievement of modern science."

The *Utica Daily Press* said, "It is safe to say that popular sentiment does not seem to favor the new method.… [A] majority of the people of this state are opposed to it."

The *Albany Evening Union* said the execution "will live in the memory of those who saw it as the fearful descriptions of Zola's fresh-born atrocities haunt the mind and appeal to the second sense for months and even years."

The *New York World* said, "Kemmler is dead, aye and the fair, sweet mercy of electric death should die with him. Better, infinitely better, the one quick wrench of the neck encircling hemp than this passage through the tortures of hell to the relief of death."

The *Rochester Herald* said, "We hope in the name of humanity and for the sake of the morals as well as the sensibilities of the people of this state that Kemmler's death will be the last, as it was the first."

European newspapers were also revolted by the news.

The *London Standard* said, "The execution will send a thrill of indignation throughout the civilized world. The scene may be described as a disgrace to our common humanity. We cannot believe that Americans will allow the electrical execution act to stand."

The *London Chronicle* said the scene in Auburn was "worthy of the darkest chambers of the Inquisition."

The *London Times* said, "It is impossible to imagine a more revolting exhibition. We fail to see that electrical execution holds out a prospect of definite gain in the direction of humanity."

In Paris, *Le Soleil* questioned the humanity and sanity of Americans "who shed oceans of tears whenever a rabbit or guinea pig is immolated on the altar of science" but seem unmoved by "this rash experiment with a human being."

With those kinds of charges being leveled, reflecting public opinion in the streets, barbershops and taverns, newspaper reporters hounded those who had been in charge of the execution in an attempt to find out who was responsible for the blunders. Had the electricians set up the machinery improperly? Had the doctors ordered the current shut off too soon? Was Westinghouse somehow involved? Did Warden Durston commit an error in the way he handled the process? While the electricians backed each other up in insisting that the machinery worked properly, the doctors pointed fingers at each other.

The feud between the Buffalo and New York City doctors began even before the execution when they argued over who was to perform the autopsy. From the moment the execution was over they began slinging hard accusations against each other about who was responsible for the failure. The Buffalo doctors laid the blame squarely on Spitzka, saying he was the one responsible for shutting off the current too soon. The New York doctors backed Spitzka and complained that the Buffalo doctors were incompetent and should not have attended the execution at all.

Dr. Spitzka, who was one of the nation's leading experts on forensic medicine, told reporters after the autopsy that he still thought the guillotine was the best means of execution, with hanging second and electrocution third. "What I have seen today impressed me greatly," he said,

> not with horror, but rather with doubt and wonder. I have seen hangings which were far more brutal than was this execution, but I have never seen anything more awe inspiring. The execution was a success, for the man is dead. But the method is not a success, for it has not performed what was promised for it. That was to rid the execution of the feature of barbarity and cruelty. The experiment has shown that under other conditions, which might exist but which did not exist today, executions might be fearful. There were conditions here today for which the advo-

cates of the system were not responsible, and one of these was the extreme coolness of Kemmler. He was as easy to handle as a child. He took the thing coolly.

Supposing the prisoner had been ugly? Imagine the difficulty in placing him in the chair. On the other hand, supposing he broke down entirely. He would have to be carried to the chair and strapped in. All this goes to show that the new method will not take from capital punishment the barbarous features of an execution.... Kemmler showed signs of animation and made certain gurgling sounds after the current had first been taken off and it was on this account that the current was turned on again. In my opinion, however, he was dead within five seconds after the current had been turned on. I said then, and I believe still, that in that time he was beyond resuscitation. In fifteen seconds he was dead and what occurred after that was only muscular movement.

This apparent breathing was not a sufficient cause for the statement that there was still life in Kemmler's body. It was better that the current was turned on again to make death sure. The dynamo and apparatus were not what they should have been. They did not furnish enough power and the voltage varied between 700 and 1,300 volts. There might have been a corrupt reason for this. The interest of the company which manufactures the dynamos would be advanced by defects in the machinery. The company was beaten in the courts, but the courts were not its last resort. Its ends would have been served as well if the execution turned out to be a botch, resulting in public disapproval....

William Kemmler was dead one hundredth of a second after the current was turned on. Five seconds after the current had been turned on I noticed the death pallor on his cheeks. It was the same peculiar shade as that which follows death by apoplexy. The execution was not a failure, but the experiment of today, and the report which will probably be made, will not likely induce other states to adopt the electrical system of execution.[14]

Dr. MacDonald, who would later submit the official report on the execution to the state, agreed that there had been serious problems but was generally more optimistic about the future of electrocution. He also seemed to be confused about who the "executioner" was. This title eventually fell on Edwin Davis, the man who pulled the switch in the control room. Here Dr. MacDonald seems to be referring to Durston, the man who gave the order, as the executioner.

"The causes of the partial failure are easily explained," he said

> The room in which the execution took place was away from the rooms in which the men in charge of the dynamos and meters were and the executioner could not tell how much voltage the meters registered. While the execution was not all together a success, it demonstrated to my mind that this method is infinitely better than hanging as regards the certainty

and suddenness of death. But it was the first experiment. Those who took part were more or less nervous. Death was, in my judgment, absolutely painless. I think that machines for this purpose should be specially constructed by the state in order to insure certainty and also so relieve any of the companies of the opprobrium that might rest upon them. The switch board should be in the room where the execution takes place in order that those in charge of the execution may be sure that the machinery is working all right.

I want to add that the execution satisfies me that the system is the best now known. But the experiment of today proves that dynamos should be built capable of producing a voltage of from 1,200 to 1,500 volts and the contact with the body should be maintained for from 15 to 30 seconds.[15]

The doctors from Buffalo, however, had a markedly different opinion about what had happened during those frantic minutes in the execution chamber, laying the blame for the botch directly on Dr. Spitzka.

"The execution of Kemmler would have been a complete success had it not been for Dr. Spitzka," said Dr. Clayton Daniels, the doctor who had testified at Kemmler's trial in Buffalo.

> According to my stopwatch the current was turned on only 15 seconds. Then Dr. Spitzka said that Kemmler was dead. When the current was turned off, the muscles relaxed and Kemmler began to choke and gasp for breath. After a little delay the current was turned on again… One of the electrodes began to burn the flesh and hair and the current was shut off again. I am satisfied that Kemmler was not dead when the current was first turned off, but was unconscious. He could not have had the least sensation of pain, notwithstanding the convulsions of the body.
>
> The experiment was not altogether satisfactory. The public will hold the apparatus responsible when the blame does not rest there. After the execution we found that the volt meter did not register 1,300 volts when we thought it would register at least 1,800 to 2,000 volts. A current of 1,300 volts is strong enough, if left on long enough, and I am sure that if Dr. Spitzka had allowed the current to remain on thirty seconds, no such scene as we witnessed would have taken place.[16]

Adding further fuel to the fire, the *Herald* called Dr. Spitzka "the executioner in chief" at Auburn because he seemed to be the one who decided when to turn on the current.

Dr. Fell said Spitzka showed "mistaken judgment" during the execution, and Southwick added his weight to the attack on Spitzka, saying he showed bad judgment in ordering the current cut off too soon.

"He didn't know what the voltage was," Southwick said. "The voltmeter was in the other room, where he could not have seen it."

Spitzka, who was later to devote his life's work to studying the bodies of electric chair victims and collected their brains in jars at his clinic in Philadelphia, lashed back at Daniels the next day. "Were it not for his insignificance I should be tempted to go to Buffalo and have him expelled from the medical society, " Spitzka told a reporter for the *New York Herald.*

> I do not care, however, to enter into a controversy with such a man.... If the scoundrel had dared to make any such statements while I was in Auburn I really believe I would have killed him and had a chance to sit in the fatal chair myself.
>
> I had nothing whatever to do with stopping the first current of electricity. That was all arranged beforehand. I feel annoyed over the discussion as a matter of course. He makes me out the Lord High Executioner. The truth is that I went there upon the solicitation of Warden Durston. I should not have been at Auburn had it not been for his invitation. I was opposed to execution by electricity before I went to Auburn and I am opposed to it now.
>
> Dr. Daniels has perverted the facts in the case. The only explanation of his course is spite at Dr. MacDonald and myself. The district attorney had tried to force the man upon us to perform the autopsy. We decided to give him no standing. We had decided that Dr. Jenkins was the proper physician to conduct the autopsy and we were determined that he should do it. It is due to the courtesy of Dr. Jenkins that he was consulted at all. One great trouble in this whole thing is that we were compelled to associate with some men who were not what they might have been professionally.

Spitzka insisted that it had been agreed before the execution that the current would be shut off after just 15 seconds. He took responsibility for ordering that the current be turned back on after he noticed the signs of life from Kemmler. Although he was certain that Kemmler died the instant the current was turned on the first time, he said, the current was turned back on out of sympathy for Kemmler and as an additional precaution to make sure he was dead.

"We expected to see a man of brutal appearance," he said, "full of bravado and repulsive. But he was not such a man at all. His gentle behavior, his pathetic manner and speech excited our human sympathy and the emotional side of our nature."

Kemmler's life, he said, "did not last a second," after the current was turned on the first time. "The dividing line between life and death is, of course, difficult to place or draw exactly. The heaving of the chest and abdomen are explained by the relaxation of the muscles and the consequent expulsion of air. It is absurd to say that he was not dead."

Dr. Jenkins, the deputy coroner from New York, continued to disagree, insisting once again that the first shock had not killed Kemmler and that he could have been brought back to life were it not for the second shock.

Dr. Daniels, on being shown a copy of Spitzka's remarks, said he was "surprised by the lack of professional courtesy.... I supposed until now that Dr. Spitzka was a gentleman." The problem, he said, seemed to be that Spitzka was taking a lot of criticism from the New York press and wanted to divert some of it to someone else. "I understand the New York papers have been giving him a roasting for his action at the Kemmler autopsy," he said, "and he naturally feels mad about it, though why he should try to get even by abusing me is more than I can understand."[17]

Daniels, in turn, laid the blame for the blunders on Durston.

"I don't wish to criticize," he told reporters, "but I believe Mr. Durston had very poor advisers, both as to the construction and placing of the machinery and the time during which the current was applied. It should have been kept on at least ten seconds more, and, moreover, the voltage was insufficient. A 2,500 voltage applied one second would have been sufficient."

After the initial reaction to the execution died down, there was time for more thoughtful reflection on what had happened to Kemmler and whether the experiment had been successful or not.

In an editorial he wrote for the *Medical Record of New York*, Dr. Shrady said that although Kemmler's death was instantaneous and without pain, it was hardly a scientific milestone.

> Heretofore the proudest claim of science has been to save, or at least to prolong human life, and insure for its possessor the greatest enjoyment of its many bounties. In this instance it has been plainly diverted from its course under a paradoxical plea of high humanity. And yet men of science have lent their best efforts in this direction to humor the whim of a few cranks and "world betterers" who imagined they could make legal murder a fine art and enforce into it an element of sentimentality which might rob it of its atrocity. While we allow that electricity has been a success as far as the killing is concerned, we must also admit that we have gained little, if anything, over the ordinary method of execution by hanging. Experiences in the Kemmler case, in spite of all the precautions taken, have shown many difficulties in the way of a general adoption of the method.

The electric chair, he said, might yet become the pulpit from which the doctrine of the abolition of capital punishment will be preached.[18]

Dr. B. W. Richardson, in an article for the *Asclepiad* which was republished in *Scientific American,* said the methods used to kill Kemmler were primitive and unscientific: "The man was really killed by a clumsy stun," he said, "for which a dexterous blow from a pole ax would have been an expeditious substitute." He condemned the "degradation and rank immorality which has been committed in the name of science" but said Kemmler probably suffered no pain.

He went on to suggest that members of the medical profession refuse to participate in any further executions. "Ought the members of the great profession of medicine, who live to prevent pain, disease, death—ought they to lend themselves, under any circumstances, to the loathsome act of playing the part of public executioner? I, for one, answer emphatically no. On the contrary, we ought one and all to strike at these barbarities, and show the world that whatever insanity it might perform, we are no parties to it."[19]

The *Electrical Review* complained that "such a use of electricity will degrade the profession" and suggested that New York try to "kill men by steam or running railroad trains over them."

Dr. MacDonald's official report, containing the autopsy results and his own observations during Kemmler's execution, was delivered to the governor on September 20. Despite all the press reports, he said, the execution "will be regarded as a successful experiment" and predicted that "in the not too distant future" it would be "regarded as a step in the direction of a higher civilization."[20]

He then went on to admit that there had been "certain defects of a minor character" but that Kemmler's death had been instant and painless. The current should have been left on for the full 20 seconds, as previously arranged.

"In the excitement and confusion of the moment," MacDonald said, "occasioned by suspicion that death was not complete, the second application of the current was maintained too long, nearly one and a half minutes."

Since the voltmeters were not located in the room, none of the witnesses could monitor how much electricity was being used.

"Compared with hanging ... execution by electricity is infinitely preferable, both as regards the suddenness with which death is effected and the expedition with which all the immediate details may be arranged," he said.

MacDonald made some recommendations for future executions. The state should build an execution chamber in the central part of the state where all convicts would be executed. This facility would contain all the necessary equipment and be operated by an accredited electrician. The engine and dynamo should be built especially for this purpose and not purchased from a private company to ensure the proper voltage and "cause no injustice to any electrical lighting company."

The voltmeter should be located in the execution room, he said, and a competent person should take readings. The voltage should be between 1,500 and 2,000 volts and should be entered into the official record. Finally, MacDonald suggested that an official report be submitted to the governor after each execution.

Perhaps the most startling development of all in the days immediately after the execution was the admission by Westinghouse that he had indeed been supplying the money and incentive for Kemmler's appeal. Although this was an open secret for nearly a year, Westinghouse had previously insisted that he had nothing to do with Kemmler and was not even interested in what happened to him.

On August 8, two days after the execution, Westinghouse released a series of letters that had been exchanged between him and Roger Sherman, the attorney who brought Kemmler's case to the federal courts and ultimately to the Supreme Court. Westinghouse's reasons for releasing these letters can only be construed as a kind of "I told you so" to those who would not listen to arguments that his generator was not the proper engine for an execution.

In an editorial in its August 10 editions, the *New York Herald* said there was no reason to repeal the law and that electrocution seemed to have worked reasonably well during its first experiment. It then went on to blame the reporters from competing newspapers for making up most of the issues that had inflamed public opinion.

"They were a disgrace to journalism," the editors wrote, "and a gross abuse of public confidence, and their effect, as no doubt in many cases it was intended to do, is highly prejudicial to a fair test of the new law and to its orderly enforcement hereafter. We look upon this as most unfortunate and we urge good citizens to stand up strongly against it."

Although no one will ever know if Kemmler suffered any pain, the editors continued, there was no evidence that Kemmler felt anything other than numbness. Mistakes were made during the execution, but this was to be expected when such a revolutionary process was being used for the first time. These mistakes can easily be prevented in the future. Whatever suffering Kemmler endured, the editors said, "was as a prick of a needle compared to the dreadful torture of a remorseless, slowly choking rope."

The exaggerated reports of the offending newspapers, the editors continued, were designed for "working up a gruesome sensation.... A vast outcry is pouring itself forth from all sorts of people calling upon Governor Hill to reprieve all condemned murderers until the new law can be repealed. One wild-eyed legislator demands an extra session, so that he, with the grateful eyes of his murderous countrymen upon him, may save them all from this hideous death. Governor Hill will be doing an act that is worse then silly if he listens to any such nonsense.... The new law appears to be far better than the old one. It is in the interest of mercy and civilization to give it a full and candid test."

The *Albany Law Journal* attacked the press for "publishing the most sensational and false accounts" and "filling the whole country and foreign lands with horror and selling large editions of their lying and lawless prints." Even though Kemmler's execution had been bungled, it seemed to them that he had either died instantly or was rendered unconscious as soon as the current was turned on. The calls for a repeal of the law seemed to be coming from electric companies and were unlikely to be successful.

The only possible benefit of the whole incident, the editors said, was that reports of Kemmler's death seemed to be convincing more people that there was no form of capital punishment that could be considered humane.

"We shall be perfectly reconciled to see the state go out of the butchering business," the editors wrote. "There can be no doubt that popular sentiment is strongly tending in that direction and if any new experiment is to be tried, we would recommend the experiment of ceasing to kill men because they have killed others."[21]

Although many newspaper editors, doctors and electrical engineers, including many who had actually attended Kemmler's execution, predicted that the public would never tolerate another use of the electric chair, there were too many people who had staked their professional reputations on the experiment and were determined to try again. Among them were the original proponents like Southwick, MacDonald and Rockwell. Political careers were also at stake. Gov. David Hill had endorsed the electric chair all the way back to 1885, and it would have been a terrible embarrassment to his career if it was shown that he had been in error about it. The Department of Prisons had invested tens of thousands of dollars in the equipment and construction of special facilities in three of its prisons. In 1891 the electric chair was the only legal method for the state to enforce the death penalty.

Once the initial reaction to Kemmler's death died down, MacDonald, Davis, Rockwell and others made some changes to the electric chair in an attempt to make it operate more acceptably. The generator at Sing Sing was modified so that it could provide a steady 2,000 volts of current.

Thicker wires were substituted and the decision was made to connect the lower electrode to the calf of the convict's leg rather than to the base of the spine, as it had been in Kemmler's case.

The biggest change the state made, however, was to restrict information about executions. Governor Hill and Austin Lathrop, the superintendent of prisons, ordered wardens to strictly enforce the rules prohibiting press coverage of executions and to carefully select the witnesses to make sure that no opponents of electrocution were allowed into the death chambers. Finally they required that each witness to the execution sign a sworn statement not to talk to any newspaper reporters about executions. It was not the electric chair that had been the problem, the state decided, but the way the press had covered it.

In the spring of 1891 there were four convicts in the brick death house at Sing Sing Prison that had been built in the prison yard about 150 feet from the dynamo room, where the generator was located. The building, 30 feet square and one-story high, had been built by convicts and had four cells on one side and a large open space with a raised platform where the chair was located. There was space in the other side of the room for the witnesses to sit.

Other than the fact that they were all brutal murderers, the four were about as different as possible. James J. Slocum was a professional baseball player from Manhattan before he became a drunk. On New Year's night in 1889, the year that the electrical execution law went into effect, he killed his wife with an ax in their Cherry Street tenement. Although his crime was committed before Kemmler's his sentence came a month later, so he became the second instead of the first victim of the electric chair.

Harris A. Smiler had at one point been a lieutenant in the Salvation Army, preaching the evils of rum, before he fell victim to the vice himself. The newspapers called him a "west side tough" who had been married three times without bothering to divorce his wives in between. One of these wives, Maggie Drainy, threatened to leave him because of his abusive habits, so he shot her on April 13, 1889, in her room at 284 Seventh Avenue.

Schichiok Jugigo, who the newspapers insisted on calling "the Jap," was a Japanese sailor who stabbed a woman named Mura Cannt during a quarrel in a James Street boardinghouse. At well over 200 pounds and described as being muscular, Jugigo practiced the Shinto religion and refused every effort of the Sing Sing chaplains to save his soul. Roger Sherman, the attorney who had fought for Kemmler before the Supreme Court, appealed Jugigo's case several times, taking advantages of loopholes in the law. Jugigo understood little English, and because no interpreter had been found for him there was some doubt that he even understood what has happening to him. He was a violent prisoner who attacked the guards so often he had to be chained each time he was moved.

Joseph Wood, the first black man to die in the electric chair, was convicted of shooting a man named Charles Ruffian in a grocery store along the aqueduct where both of them worked. After his conviction and right up until the hour of execution, his lawyer, R. J. Haire, insisted that new evidence had been found that showed Wood was innocent, and the newspapers said that many prison officials were convinced that Wood was not guilty. The courts, however, refused to hear Haire's evidence, denying his request for a stay of execution on the merest of technicalities: Haire had not paid his $1 fee that allowed his name to be included on the list of lawyers permitted to practice in the federal courts in the Southern District of New York.

On July 6, the day before the executions, reporters who gathered outside the gates of Sing Sing, despite the state's announcement that no press coverage would be permitted, found every evidence that the newly appointed warden, W. R. Brown, was serious about the state's gag order. A patrol of blue-uniformed guards armed with repeating rifles had been stationed outside the gates and threatened to shoot any reporter who crossed the "dead line" that had been set up around the prison.

"These executions are surrounded by an air of mystery and secrecy deeper than is warranted by any transaction that is legal," the *New York Times* reporter who covered the executions wrote. "It looks on the face of things as if the queer coterie of influential cranks, scientific men and politicians who created the electrical execution law are bound to have these executions go off to suit themselves. A repetition of the Kemmler affair, they know, would knock their pet measure into a cocked hat. These executions must go before the public as successful in every way, so as to vindicate the law under which they are held. Gov. Hill, one of the first exponents of electrical execution, has said so."[22]

Forced off the prison grounds by the guards, about 50 reporters gathered on the state highway in front of the prison, but Brown came out and ordered them even further away, saying that unless they crossed to the other side of the highway he would order his men to "fill them full of cold lead." When the reporters complained that the highway was public property and that they had a right to be there, James Maher, one of the guards, told them to "Git back, git out of the road. You can't stay there while this gun is loaded." With that the reporters gave up and crossed over to the other side of the road. Then the prison turned loose a pack of bloodhounds that gathered on the prison side of the road, barking and snapping a warning to any journalist who might get too close. The reporters then walked over to a nearby bluff over the Hudson and made their headquarters there.

"There are about 50 reporters here from New York papers," the *Times* reporter wrote. "If they were Sioux Indians who had invaded a Government military post with war paint on and tomahawks they might have expected exactly the treatment which Mr. Brown has given them."

Meanwhile, the Westinghouse Electric Company was also monitoring what the state of New York was doing with its generator. N. B. Nostrand, the manager of the Westinghouse electric system in nearby Peekskill, had asked to be a witness at the executions but had been turned down by Brown. He told reporters the only possible reason for this was that the state was afraid that one of the executions would be botched.

"I am thoroughly familiar with the apparatus prepared there," he told the *Times* reporter. "It is as perfect as it can be. If it fails it will doom electrical execution, or it should…. I claim, and I believe, that these executions will prove that a shock of electricity cannot be depended upon to take life instantly…. I do not believe it is possible to get a perfect contact between bare human flesh and an electrode…. [A] reliable contact will never be had with the aid of a wet sponge placed in an electrode on bare flesh. Two thousand volts will dry up such a sponge in no time. Just wait and see if these executions do not prove my words to be true."

The reporters spent the entire night outside on the bluff, enjoying a clear sky full of stars and warm temperatures. Sometime during the night a message was sent from Warden Brown explaining an elaborate procedure for letting them know when each of the convicts had been executed. Each of the four had been assigned a different color flag, which would be flown from the flagpole at the top of the cupola to show when each had been executed. Slocum's flag was white, Jugigo's red, Smiler's blue and Woods's black, which, the warden said, "was good enough for a 'coon.'"

At sunrise the reporters could hear the cannons being fired from the Peekskill army base 10 miles up the river.

"It was a beautiful morning," the *Times* reporter wrote. "A strong breeze was blowing down the broad valley of the Hudson. Every eye among people outside was kept pretty steadily upon the flagstaff to catch the first glimpse of the flag."

Just as the Peekskill cannon was fired, as if it were the signal, the white flag was seen coming up the flagpole at 4:41 A.M. "Slocum is dead!" the reporters yelled at each other. The blue flag was next at 5:12, followed by the black flag at 5:38 and the red one 26 minutes later.

Although all the official witnesses had been sworn to secrecy and the reporters were forced off the grounds, they were quite successful in convincing people to talk. Many of their sources were guards and the chaplains, who were not required to take the oath. The reporters realized, however, that unlike the Kemmler execution, there would be no experts who were entirely unbiased. Every official witness insisted that the executions went off perfectly without the slightest problem.

The four convicts had been strapped into the chair and were not given an opportunity to make a last statement. They had been dressed in new black suits, white shirts and black ties. As soon as they were strapped in and the electrodes were attached Brown dropped his handkerchief, which was the signal to Davis, who was partially concealed in a nearby closet, to throw the switch that put the chair into the circuit. It was all done very quickly, without much hesitation, the witnesses said. As each one was killed he was taken into a nearby autopsy room, where eventually all four of them were stacked.

When the guards had come for Jugigo they found him sitting on the floor, meditating. Although the guards expected him to resist, he cooperated and went to the chair calmly and with an air of dignity they had not expected.

"I can assure you on my honor as a man and before God that these executions went off without a single hitch," Brown told the reporters after the four were dead. "Every witness in the death chamber expressed himself to me as more than satisfied at the way they had been conducted and at the results. I do not believe that the lives of four men were ever taken by the law in a more humane way."[23]

Some of the witnesses were persuaded to make a few comments as they left the prison. Southwick said he had wanted to come out during the night to make a statement but that Brown would not let anyone outside. "I was extremely well satisfied," Southwick said. "Everything passed off well. There was no mishap. I can say that these executions settle all doubt as to the practical working of the law. There can be no question of its remaining on the books."

Southwick was accompanied by Dr. Daniels, who had made the trip down with him from Buffalo. Daniels said he would never want to witness another execution because he was satisfied that the chair worked as well as it could. Asked if he thought the four executions had gone better than Kemmler's, he said, "Did you ever hear of the repetition of any great scientific experiment which did not prove to have been greatly improved? I think few objections can be made to the executions as now conducted."

Dr. MacDonald would say little to the reporters because of the gag order, but Dr. Rockwell said it was "eminently satisfactory ... so far as speedy death is concerned and the absence of revolting and disagreeable accessories, the official acts I witnessed this morning were completely successful.... My observation this morning has satisfied me that the new law ... meets all the requirements for killing decently a man sentenced to death. I am furthermore convinced that it is utterly impossible for any man to suffer pain who receives 1,500 volts of electricity."

Later that day Governor Hill took credit for the success in Ossining. "This system of electrical execution has come to stay," he said.

In his official report two years later, MacDonald said the location of the electrodes had been changed slightly to cover the victims' foreheads and temples. This time there were official voltage readings, showing that between 1,458 and 1,716 volts had passed through the victims' bodies. Each execution took only a few seconds after two or three minutes to adjust the straps. In each case the prisoner volunteered to sit in the chair without any resistance and did not make any public remarks.[24]

"Everything was done in a quiet, orderly and dignified manner," said MacDonald, "in keeping with the solemnity of the occasion."

Slocum's death required two jolts of electricity; Smiler got four; Wood and Jugigo got three each.

A few weeks later a grand jury in Manhattan indicted nine newspaper publishers, including James Gordon Bennett of the *Herald* and Joseph Pulitzer of the *World* for violating the section of the electric chair law that prohibited publishing details of executions. The nine were arrested and released on $500 bail. If they were convicted under the law they could have been fined $500 each, sentenced to a year in prison, or both.

District Attorney DeLancey Nicoll said he was personally opposed to the law and considered it censorship and was making the arrests as a test case hoping that the courts would throw out the law. The *Herald,* in particular, made the arrests into something of a public crusade, writing that its publisher had been "indicted for printing news" and that the paper would "battle for the public's right." It hired W. Bourke Cockran to defend the newspaper in court.

Cockran said the *Herald* "considers it an honor to have been chosen as the journal to vindicate the freedom of the press." The *Sun* printed a series of attacks on the law by prominent citizens.

The next legislature repealed the section of the law that restricted press coverage and acknowledged that the press had a right and responsibility to report on executions. After that, it was routine for wardens to invite the press to send reporters or editors to act as official witnesses to executions.

At the first execution after the law was amended, that of Charles E.

McElvaine, eight reporters were invited, including Arthur Brisbane, the editor of the *New York World*, William Randolph Hearst's paper. Brisbane wrote that death in the electric chair was "not as repulsive as the average hanging."

"What most repels the spectator at such an execution as that which occurred yesterday," he said, "is the sight of the number of men, who have their wives and daughters at home and decent associations generally, deliberately occupying themselves with the killing of a helpless fellow creature."

This was not the end of the electric chair, however, merely the beginning.

— 10 —
The First Era:
1892–1974

In the century after Kemmler's death more than 4,000 men, women and children as young as 17 were killed in electric chairs in 26 states. At the end of 1996 there were 1,237 inmates on death rows in the 11 states that still used the electric chair for executions.[1] The number of victims of the electric chair climbed steadily in the early part of the century, reaching a peak in the 1930s of nearly 200 per year, and then slowly declined. Then in the 1980s and 1990s it began rising again.

Many of those executions, like Kemmler's, were botched when the electrodes were not tight enough, when a sponge was allowed to dry out or even when the wires were installed incorrectly. In many of these cases the victims died a slow and agonizing death rather than the quick and efficient "electric euthanasia," the inventors of the electric chair had hoped to provide.

Law professor Deborah Denno examined dozens of independent medical reports involving electric chair victims and concluded that even when electrocutions are not botched the individuals often suffer great pain and mutilation. "Although electrocution was originally introduced as a more humane form of punishment … substantial scientific and eyewitness evidence indicates that its consequences are no less cruel than those other methods … and they may be even crueler." [2]

U.S. Supreme Court justice William Brennan also researched a number of cases of executions and wrote an article in which he described an electrocution in grisly detail.

"[T]he prisoner's eyeballs sometimes pop out and rest on his cheeks. The prisoner often defecates, urinates and vomits up blood and drool. The body turns bright red as its temperature rises and the prisoner's flesh swells and his skin stretches to the point of breaking. Sometimes the prisoner catches on fire, particularly if he perspires excessively. Witnesses hear a loud and sustained sound like bacon frying, and the sickly sweet smell of burning flesh permeates the chamber."[3]

An electrocuted corpse is hot enough to blister when touched, so autopsies have to be delayed for several hours to give the organs time to cool. Prisoners feel themselves being burned to death and suffocating because the shock causes respiratory paralysis as well as cardiac arrest. Willie Francis, who survived a botched execution in 1947, said, "My mouth tasted like cold peanut butter. I felt a burning in my head and my left leg and I jumped against the straps."[4]

Francis was the first death row inmate to claim that electrocution was "cruel and unusual punishment" since the court first ruled on the matter in William Kemmler's case in 1890. Legal historian Lonny L. Hoffman thinks that if one of the death row inmates who went to the electric chair immediately after Kemmler had appealed the case to the Supreme Court, things might have turned out very differently.

When the court ruled on Kemmler's case in 1890, electrocution was still an untried method of capital punishment. There was no scientific evidence to show what would happen when the switch was pulled. That allowed Chief Justice Fuller to rule that there was nothing "inhuman or barbarous" about the electric chair.

"It must have given the judges who assessed that evidence some pause when they read the newspaper accounts of Kemmler's terrible execution," Hoffman wrote. "Unfortunately for Kemmler the best empirical evidence against the new method came with his own death."[5]

In New York State between 1891 and 1963, when the use of the electric chair was discontinued, 694 people followed Kemmler to the chair. There were 686 men and 9 women. Seventy-seven percent of them were white. Until 1914 there were actually three electric chairs in operation, as prescribed in the original law. After 1914 all electrocutions took place at Sing Sing.

The youngest prisoners executed were only 17. They were Stanley Pluzdark of Erie County, who died in 1935, Edward Height of Westchester County in 1943 and Norman Roye of New York City in 1956. The oldest person executed was Charles Bonier of Erie County, who died in 1907 at age 75. When it finally disconnected its electric chair for good in 1963, New York had killed more people in the electric chair than any other state in the country.

All but four of the New York chair's victims were convicted murderers. Two of them were kidnappers and the other two, Julius and Ethel Rosenberg, were convicted of espionage. Ethel Rosenberg was one of the few women electrocuted, and it took five jolts of the current to kill her. Another was Ruth Snyder, whose picture at the moment of death was printed in New York newspapers after a newsman strapped a hidden camera to his leg, against prison rules, and snapped the picture.

In 1892, two years after Kemmler's execution, the battle of the currents came to an end with the merger of Edison's electric companies and the Thomson-Houston Electric Company, the company which had worked closely with Brown to buy the dynamos for New York's three prisons. The new company, called General Electric, was not so closely associated with direct current or Edison and was able to successfully compete with Westinghouse to supply alternating current equipment, which by then had become the standard. The electric chair, the strange offspring of that competition, however, took on a life of its own.

Although Southwick's association with the electric chair declined after Kemmler's death, he was still called "the father of the electric chair" in the headline of his obituary. Before he died he suffered an embarrassing professional crisis. At the annual meeting of the Dental Society of New York State in May 1893 a Brooklyn dentist objected to a motion to officially recognize the University of Buffalo's new dental school because it had awarded honorary degrees to Southwick and another dentist. The Brooklyn dentist, Dr. William Jarvie, charged that the degree had been offered to Southwick by the school as a bribe to obtain recognition from the society. The state legislature had just passed a law requiring dentists to have a professional degree to practice dentistry, and Southwick, who had learned his trade as an apprentice, had no degree. Dr. Stainton, a Buffalo dentist, confirmed that Southwick himself had told him that he wanted the degree "for use and not for honor." Southwick died in 1898.

Harold Brown went back into obscurity after Kemmler's death, operating a small electric consulting business in New York but staying out of the public eye. As far as is known he never attended an execution. Other participants in Kemmler's death, however, had their careers closely tied to the electric chair.

Dr. Edward C. Spitzka made a name for himself as an expert witness at criminal trials and was known as the world's leading expert on the criminally insane and on the central nervous system, and he published several textbooks on those topics. During this work he made use of his experience in the prison autopsy room by arguing that the brains of condemned murderers seem in no way different from normal brains. His son, Edward A. Spitzka, continued the family work by participating at the autopsy of Leon Czolgosz in 1901 while still a college student. He later went on to collect the brains of hundreds of criminals at his laboratory in Philadelphia and compared them with the brains of many brilliant scientists, which he also collected.

But it was Edwin F. Davis, the electrician who pulled the switch at Kemmler's execution, who was to have the longest and closest association with the chair. Although his official title was "state electrician," the newspapers called him the "state executioner," and a stranger life than his cannot be imagined. Between 1890 and 1918, when he retired, Davis executed more than 300 convicts in New York, Massachusetts, Ohio and New Jersey. He charged the states $150 per execution and carried his own personal set of electrodes from prison to prison in a special suitcase.

Robert G. Elliott, who was his apprentice in the early years of the century, described him as "small and wiry with piercing black eyes, high cheekbones and a drooping black mustache."

Every article written about Davis in the early part of the century describes him as being strange, reclusive and more than a little paranoid. He was terrified of having his photograph taken, for example, even by family and friends, apparently because he was afraid that the friends or relatives of one of his victims would seek him out for revenge. For the same reason he would sneak into the prison late at night in a regular prison guard's uniform and leave the next night to avoid the press and the crowds of spectators.

He refused to give anyone his address, not even the wardens of the prisons. To notify him when it was time to arrange an execution the wardens had to take out coded advertisements in certain newspapers. He changed his address in Corning frequently for fear that someone would discover where he lived. He refused to board a train at the depot, preferring to use some prearranged spot along the tracks.

Davis seems to have combined the role of the electrical scientist with the mystical qualities associated with the hangmen of England. Cornelius V. Collins, the state director of prisons during most of Davis's career, described his employee this way: "He carries it [his equipment] in a small grip [suitcase] from place to place and permits no one to examine it…. From time to time assistants have been appointed to assist Davis in this work with a view towards educating them so they could perform the duties, but not one of them have reached the point where he was willing to take charge of an execution or could explain the construction or working of the apparatus which Davis used. The consequence is that we are absolutely dependent on Davis, who is an elderly man and is very hard to find as he changes his location frequently and regardless of repeated requests, fails to keep us informed of his address. The condition is one that causes the wardens and myself much anxiety."⁶

There were hints that much of the equipment that Davis carried around with him was entirely unnecessary and an elaborate subterfuge to make the process seem much more complicated than it was, thus ensuring Davis's employment. "What value the patented and other apparatus may have or how necessary it is to the successful working of the execution," said Collins, "I am unable to learn."

Because each prison had its own chair, its own control room and its own generator, it is difficult to imagine what Davis was carrying around in his suitcase, but Collins was reluctant to take the responsibility for what would happen if they tried to conduct an execution without him.

Elliott recalled that Davis often tested the electric chairs by fastening the electrodes to a 15-pound piece of beef and turning on the current. When the meat was thoroughly cooked he refused the requests of the inmates that they be allowed to eat it and made sure it was burned up in the prison boilers.

One day when they were having dinner together in a restaurant near Times Square, Elliott made the mistake of using Davis's name. "What are you going to have, Davis?" he asked. Davis looked terrified and looked all around the room to make sure no one had heard them and then made Elliott promise never to use his name in public, despite the fact that it was a fairly common name.

In the fall of 1903 Davis offered to sell the state the "secrets" of his apparatus and the rights to his patents for $10,000. The legislature drafted a bill to seal the deal, but at the last minute Davis refused to sign the contract, saying he did not want to sell it outright but would instruct the state's assistants for a fee. The assistants were told to watch Davis carefully so they could learn his techniques, but they could make no sense of the procedures he used. After his retirement he spent his last years running a cider mill and indulging himself with his hobby, beekeeping. When he died in 1923 the headline on his obituary in the *New York Times* called him "the inventor of the electric chair."

"I feel that in putting men to death in the electric chair a humane act is being performed," he is reported to have told a prison official. "They have got to die and somebody must pull the switch that turns on the electric current. The courts that sentenced them sealed their doom, not I. And the electric chair is certainly an improvement over the crude, bumbling method of hanging."

Dr. Carlos MacDonald became the state's official medical expert on the electric chair and conducted autopsies of each of its victims until the turn of the century. He was an expert witness at the trial of Leon Czolgosz, the assassin of President McKinley, and many other famous murder cases, where he advised on the sanity of accused murderers. In his latter years he served as a visiting professor in several medical schools.

MacDonald performed autopsies on the six men who followed Kemmler to the electric chair and wrote the official reports. His obituary only mentioned his work with the electric chair in the last paragraph.

In his 1892 summary report, MacDonald indicated that he had tired of his work with electric chair victims, saying he had conducted his investigations "not from any zealous interest in the subject" but because he had been ordered by the governor to perform "what would otherwise be regarded as an undesirable task."[7]

The electric chair's fifth victim was Martin D. Loppy, a one-eyed, four-fingered deaf man who killed his wife with a pair of scissors. He was executed at Sing Sing on December 7, 1891. This was the last execution that was closed to the press. For the seventh victim, also at Sing Sing, the press was allowed to witness the execution of Charles McElvaine on February 8, 1892, using a new technique that had first been suggested by Edison. Instead of connecting the electrodes to the head and spine, as had been done in Kemmler's case, or to the head and legs, as had been done in the subsequent executions, in McElvaine's execution his hands were immersed in containers of a saline solution that were attached to the electrodes. This caused the convict to lose consciousness, but when the doctors used their stethoscopes they found a heartbeat. Then they strapped him into the regular electric chair, which was waiting nearby, attached the electrodes to his head and calf and threw the switch.

In the conclusion of his report, MacDonald said that despite the "vigorous opposition" to the electric chair from those who attempt to invest it with "an air of repulsion, brutality and horror," it had to be regarded as a success and "an important advance … in the direction of a higher civilization."

Kemmler's execution, he said, being the first, was somewhat experimental and marred by "certain minor defects," but subsequent executions had gone more smoothly as a result of the knowledge that had been acquired since then. The only problem still to be solved, he said, was that the high voltages generated too much heat, which sometimes burned the bodies of the prisoners. The sponges got so hot, he said, that the moisture in them boiled away, allowing the electrodes to burn the body.

"It is the surest, quickest, most efficient and least painful method of inflicting the death penalty that has yet been devised," he said.

Two years later, electric chair executions in New York had bec~~~

nearly routine. In his annual report for 1894, the superintendent of state prisons reported four executions at Sing Sing and two each at Auburn and Clinton. All were reported to have been performed routinely except for one in Auburn where the armature of the generator failed and a replacement had to be borrowed from an electrical company.[8]

But that report was not entirely honest. One of the executions that year had gone terribly wrong.

William G. Taylor, Auburn Prison, July 27, 1893

Taylor was already a prisoner at the time of his crime, and he was being killed for murdering a fellow inmate. At the moment that Davis pulled the switch, Taylor's legs stiffened, tearing off the front part of the chair to which the electrode had been attached. This was fixed by putting a box in front of the chair, reconnecting the electrode and trying again. After this second jolt Taylor was still breathing, so the warden ordered the current turned back on.

But when Davis pulled the switch nothing happened. He tried several times but could not get the electricity to flow. An investigation found that the old Westinghouse generator, the one that Brown had shipped to Brazil and back, had burned out.

It was a problem that no one had anticipated, and no one was quite sure what to do. Taylor was taken out of the chair and placed on a cot. The doctors gave him morphine for the pain. After working for several minutes attempting to get the generator working, the technicians finally strung electrical wires over the prison walls to connect the chair to the city's main electric lines. It took over an hour to make this connection, and meanwhile Taylor had stopped breathing and he was pronounced dead.

Just to make sure, and to comply with the letter of the law, the warden ordered his body strapped into the chair one more time and the current was turned on for a half minute. Davis told Elliott years later that the generator had broken because it had been "taxed beyond its capacity," just as Westinghouse had claimed before Kemmler's execution.

In his annual report for 1894 Collins recommended that instead of executing prisoners in each of the three prisons that a special facility be constructed. "The reformatory prisons do not seem to be the proper place for executions," the superintendent reported. "It has been found that each approaching event ... is the cause of perturbation and depression among the prison population. It is something antagonistic to the disciplinary methods of these institutions and is so obnoxious that the officers do not hesitate to condemn the practice of having such executions in the prisons."

Martha Place, Sing Sing Prison, March 20, 1899

The first woman to die in the electric chair did not cause Davis much concern. He told Elliott years later that "she was one of the coolest people I've ever executed. She didn't cause us a bit of trouble in the death chamber. We waited [and] she was in the chair before clipping the spot on her head. It was quick. I don't think she noticed at all. Her eyes were closed and I heard her say 'God save me.'"

At first, Davis said, he was worried about killing a woman, but after a while he felt that it made no difference. "Somebody has to execute her and that was my job," he said.

Place was convicted of killing her stepdaughter at their home in Brooklyn on February 7, 1898. She was a New Jersey dressmaker who abandoned her husband to live with a Brooklyn widower named James Place. Originally employed as a servant, she later married Place and lived with him and his 17-year-old daughter, Ida.

Martha and Ida took an immediate dislike to each other and Martha demanded that Mr. Place choose between them, but Mr. Place refused to get involved in their jealousies of each other. Taking matters into her own hands, Martha Place tossed a glass of sulfuric acid into Ida's face. After she sat and gloated while Ida thrashed about screaming in pain, Martha Place smothered the girl with a pillow. When Mr. Place came home, Martha attacked him with an ax, but he survived.

On the day of her execution Martha wore a black gown that she had made when she had hoped that a second trial might be held. She held a prayer book in one hand as she was strapped into the chair. A matron attached the leg electrode, drawing her skirts out between the chair and the witnesses. When Davis turned the current on, the prayerbook in her left hand twisted across her wrist, but there was no other movement.

Gov. Theodore Roosevelt had personally ordered that the matrons assist Mrs. Place at the execution. The attending physician was also a woman specially hired for the occasion. When the execution was over, the warden sent a telegram to Roosevelt: "There was no revolting feature. Mrs. Place met her fate with fortitude at 11:05 this morning."[9]

Leon Czolgosz, Auburn Prison, New York, October 29, 1901

One early execution that attracted national attention was that of anarchist Leon Czolgosz, who died in the electric chair in Auburn on Oct. 29, 1901, just six weeks after he assassinated President William McKinley at the Pan American Exposition in Buffalo. McKinley was standing in a reception line outside the Temple of Music, shaking hands with well-wishers when Czolgosz stepped up and shot him twice at close range. Many of the witnesses said the assassin had a handkerchief tied around the pistol or that he had his hand in a cast, but Czolgosz denied it, saying the pistol had been in his pocket.

The son of Russo-Polish immigrants, Czolgosz was embittered by his failure to succeed in America. He had read the news accounts of the assassination of the president of France in 1894 and asked to join the anarchists, who dismissed him as a crackpot. After the assassinations of the empress of Austria in 1898 and the king of Italy in 1900 he decided to act on his own.

Czolgosz said he killed McKinley because the president had refused to find a job for him. Although there were attempts to show a conspiracy was involved, Czolgosz insisted that he had acted alone. At his trial Dr. Carlos MacDonald testified that he had examined the assassin and found him to be sane. There were, however, serious questions about his sanity.

McKinley, 58, survived the assassination for a week, but finally died of his injuries while whispering the words to his favorite hymn, "Nearer My God to Thee."

At the time, Czolgosz's speedy trial followed by his prompt execution was seen as an excellent example of the efficiency of the criminal justice system. Cornelius Collins, the superintendent of prisons was concerned about "sensationalism" regarding his case, by which he meant he was concerned that Czolgosz would become a kind of morbid celebrity. There was some reason to be concerned. A museum "in one of the large eastern cities" had offered him $5,000 for either Czolgosz's body or his clothes. The owner of one of the earliest movie theaters offered $2,000 for permission to film the assassin entering the death chamber.

For that reason Collins was concerned about Czolgosz's family's demand that they be given the body after the execution so they could take it back to Cleveland, where the assassin lived. Collins suggested that the family might also have been offered $5,000 for the body that they might sell it to the museum. The day before the execution he held a closed-door

Leon Czolgosz, convicted of the murder of President William McKinley, died in the Auburn Prison electric chair in 1901. (New York State Archives)

meeting with the family at which he finally got them to agree to allow the body to be kept at Auburn. Just to make sure that nothing would remain to be put on display, Collins ordered that Czolgosz's clothes and possessions all be burned after the execution and even prohibited Dr. MacDonald from taking any tissue samples with him after the autopsy.

On the night before the execution several ministers attempted to see the condemned man, but he sent them away, saying, "Damn them! Send them away. And don't you have any praying over me when I'm dead. I don't want it. I don't want any of their damn religion."

Auburn no longer held its executions in the administration basement where Kemmler had been killed. A new, gray, stone building similar to the one at Sing Sing had been built in the prison yard with cells for the condemned men attached to the room that held the electric chair on a platform protected by a rubber mat. A large steel door that was only opened on execution days separated the cells from the death chamber.

Early the next morning Davis tested the chair by placing a device holding rows of electric lightbulbs on top of it, connecting it to the chair electrodes and then turning on the current. The bright glow of the lamps assured him that everything was in order. Then he shut the power down, removed the test lamps and waited for Czolgosz. He was brought in at 7:10, wearing the traditional black jacket and gray trousers that had been slit up the left leg.

He had not been asked to speak, but while he was being strapped into the chair he said, in perfect English, "I killed the president because he was an enemy of the good people, of the working people. I am not sorry for my crime," he said loudly just as the guard pushed his head back on the rubber headrest. "I'm awfully sorry I could not see my father."

Then the mask was strapped to his face and he could say nothing more. When the preparations were complete, Warden J. Warren Mean raised his hand, and Davis threw the switch, sending 1,700 volts to the chair. Czolgosz strained against the straps so hard that the witnesses could hear them creak. Then, just to make sure, he was given two more jolts of the current.

After the autopsy Czolgosz's body was placed in a coffin and taken to the prison cemetery where a grave had been prepared. To make sure no grave robbers could take away any valuable artifacts, a carboy of acid was poured on the coffin, and it was estimated the body would be destroyed in less than 12 hours.

One of the strange aftermaths of this execution was that Thomas Edison reenacted it in his new motion picture studios. *The Execution of Czolgosz* was one of the first movies ever made. Actors played the president and his assassin, and the audience got to watch the execution in a mock-up of the electric chair. It must have brought back interesting memories for Edison.[10]

Willis, Burton and Frederic Van Wormer, Clinton Prison, October 1, 1903

On Christmas Eve 1901 three brothers and their cousin, Harvey Bruce, drove 14 miles in a hired wagon to the home of their uncle, Peter A. Hallenbeck, in Greendale, Columbia County. On their way they turned their coats inside out and put on rubber masks. Hallenbeck was in the living room with his wife and mother when he heard their knock on his door. They backed him into the room, and when he tried to resist they riddled him with bullets. When his wife came to his aid they shot at her too, but she was not hit. The police were able to follow their footprints and they were all arrested nearby. The cousin testified against the three brothers.

Elliott, who was acting as Davis's assistant at Dannemora, said the three were cheerful and certain that they would somehow avoid going to the electric chair.

"They won't do anything to us," Burton Van Wormer told Elliott. "We're just up here for a nice vacation. We'll be out in no time."

On the day of the execution Davis had been held up, and as the hour of execution arrived the warden asked Elliott if he would be willing to take over. Elliott balked at the idea, saying he would not know how to do it. Finally, at the last minute, Davis arrived. Elliott, who was in the generator room during the actual execution, turned on the current as he was directed by the signal from the control room. When he finished he went home but a message was waiting from the prison asking for his immediate return.

"Get the engine going," Davis told him when he arrived. "One of the boys is alive. We've got to put him back in the chair!" So Elliott started the engine back up, but a few minutes later Davis was back telling him that he should stop the engine because the condemned man had died on his own. The 1,700 volts had not killed Fred, the youngest of the brothers, but this had not been discovered until a guard, passing by the autopsy room, saw Van Wormer's hand move and his eyes flicker. When the doctors came back they found his heart was still beating, even though he had been pronounced dead a half hour before.

Davis insisted that no one outside the prison be told about the incident, and the newspapers reported that all three had met their deaths without incident.[11]

Chester Gillette, Auburn Prison, March 30, 1908

A few years later Chester Gillette was strapped into the chair for murdering his pregnant girlfriend, Grace Brown, at Big Moose Lake two years before. Gillette's case attracted national attention because Brown's love letters to him were read at the trial. The case was used as a basis for

Theodore Dreiser's *An American Tragedy* (1926), in which the main character, Clyde Griffiths, also dies in the electric chair. Neither of the two movies made from the novel, *An American Tragedy* (1931) and *A Place in the Sun* (1951), actually show the electric chair.[12]

Chester Gillette, convicted of killing his pregnant girlfriend, Grace Brown, died in the Auburn electric chair in 1908. (*Saturday Globe*)

Mary Farmer, Auburn Prison, March 29, 1909

On April 23, 1908, Sarah Brennan a wealthy property owner, was butchered to death with an ax in her home in the tiny hamlet of Brownsville, four miles from the city of Watertown in Jefferson County. Her body was later found in a trunk. Mary

Farmer and her husband James were charged with killing their next-door neighbor in a dispute over a false bill of sale for Brennan's home that Farmer had drawn up. Mary Farmer had emigrated from Ireland nine years before and worked as a servant in Buffalo and Binghamton before coming to Watertown. Mary Farmer said later that she killed Brennan so that her son, Peter, less than a year old, would grow up rich instead of poor.

The Farmers pleaded insanity but were found guilty. Just before she was to be executed, Mary Farmer confessed to the crime, saying she had acted alone. Her husband was later released thanks to this last-minute confession.

Farmer held a crucifix in her hands as she was being strapped into the chair. She was dressed in a plain black skirt and her hair was pushed back from her face and twisted into two braids. Two or three locks of her hair were cut off just before the head electrode was pushed into place. The woman's attendants cut a slit in the left side of her skirt and through her stockings to connect the second electrode. Davis set his controls for 1,840 volts and 7.5 amps.

Her last words were "Jesus, Mary and Joseph have mercy on my soul!"

When Davis pulled the switch some of the women nurses covered their faces with their hands. The current was left on a full minute but Davis raised it and lowered it several times. After the autopsy, Farmer's brain was given to Dr. Spitzka to add to his collection.

Just before Farmer's death, Madeline Z. Doty, one of the first women lawyers in the state, wrote a letter to the *New York Times* arguing that Mrs. Farmer's life should be spared. It was poverty and concern for her child that led to the crime, she said. "She had little pleasure in her life, and when she grew to be a woman and had a baby of her own, she resolved it should have what she lacked," Doty wrote. "Can you imagine a woman, a mother nursing a small baby, deliberately taking an ax and hacking up a human body unless she had a red twist in her brain?... She is not to blame for that red twist... for no woman whose whole environment was good would murder another human being in cold blood for the sake of a few dollars, unless that woman were an atavist or insane." She was not asking that Mrs. Farmer be set free, she said, but that her sentence be commuted to life in prison.[13]

Albert Wolter, Sing Sing Prison, January 29, 1912

Wolter was a 15-year-old agent of several New York City pimps who supplied innocent young girls to them for money. His practice was to rent a cheap apartment and place an advertisement in the newspapers looking for female domestic help. When the girls arrived for an interview he would trap them, rape them and sell them into bondage. Then he would move on to another apartment. On March 24, 1910, he had rented an apartment at 222 E. 75th Street and placed an ad for a stenographer. When 15-year-old Ruth Wheeler answered the ad, she resisted Wolter, and he strangled her with a rope. Then he cut up the girl's body, pickled it in kerosene and attempted to burn it in a stove. He was caught at this when Wheeler's parents came looking for her, tracing the address in the newspaper.[14]

Charles Becker, Sing Sing Prison, July 30, 1915

The newspapers called Becker the most corrupt police officer in New York City. From the beginning of his career as a young patrolman in the 1890s he accepted bribes from criminals he came into contact with. After 1910 when he was promoted to lieutenant, he was able to expand to major shakedowns of brothels, nightclubs and gambling dens, which were required to give him 25 percent of their profits.

Finally in 1912 a casino owner named Herman Rosenthal balked at paying the protection money, so Becker raided his club, destroyed the furniture and pocketed the money he found. Rosenthal reported this in detail to the Manhattan district attorney, who had vowed to rid the city of crooked cops. Becker hired a hit man named Big Jack Zelig to kill Rosenthal in the doorway of the Cafe Metropole on West 43rd Street. The getaway car was traced, and the hit man fingered Becker as the one who had ordered the killing.

Once, many years before, Becker had sat in the Sing Sing electric chair and had his photo taken. On July 30 he sat in the chair again for his execution.[15]

After 1916 the electric chairs at Auburn and Clinton were no longer used, and all executions took place at Sing Sing. The original electric chair at Auburn, in which 55 people were killed, was put on display in a prison hallway between 1916 and 1929 when it was thought to have been destroyed in a prison fire and riot. However, during the early 1980s it was said to have turned up in the possession of an antique dealer in California. The chair from the Clinton Prison in Dannemora, which killed 26 people, is in a museum at the New York Correctional Services Training

The Auburn Prison electric chair, about 1900. (New York State Library)

Academy in Albany. The Sing Sing chair was redesigned and rebuilt in 1910 and was used until the 1960s.

By then the electric chair was in use all over the world, including such far-flung locations as China and the Philippines, but it was never used in Europe. Ohio became the second state to use it in 1896, followed by Massachusetts in 1898, New Jersey in 1907, Virginia in 1908, Pennsylvania in 1915, Kentucky in 1907, Tennessee in 1909, North Carolina in 1910, South Carolina in 1912, Arkansas in 1913, Texas in 1923, Florida and Georgia in 1924 and Alabama in 1927. By the end of the 1920s more than half of the states with death penalty laws used the electric chair.

Davis retired from the executioner's job in 1914, when New York stopped using the Auburn and Dannemora chairs and conducted all executions at Sing Sing. His replacement was one of the men who had assisted him for several years, John Hurlbert. He was a short stocky man, a resident of Auburn who was the official executioner in three states.

By the 1920s there were so many inmates being executed at Sing Sing that the old prisoner-built "death house" had to be replaced with a larger one. The new building, called "the slaughterhouse" by the inmates, cost $300,000 and was a "prison within a prison," with its own kitchen, hospital, exercise yards and visiting rooms. There were two wings with 12 cells each for the men and a separate wing for women with three cells.

There were six more cells in the hospital section and three in the special "pre-execution" chamber that the inmates dubbed "the dance hall." Condemned prisoners were taken from their regular cells to the "dance hall" on the morning of their executions. From the "dance hall" to the execution chamber prisoners walked through a green door and down a corridor that came to be known as "the last mile" even though it was only a few yards long. Next to the execution chamber was "the ice box" as the morgue was called.[16]

From their cells prisoners could see the green door and could hear the hum of the electrical generator. They could even hear the noises made by the saws and the drills the doctors used for the autopsies. These autopsies were required by a section of the law that established the electric chair. Supposedly designed for "scientific purposes" they actually had a much darker purpose, according to Dr. J. A. O'Neill, who performed one of them in 1898.

The autopsy, he said, is "part of the penalty as it reveals no cause of death and teaches nothing of interest to science; it is evident that its purpose is to complete the killing." In other words, if the electric chair failed to do its job, the doctors would make sure that the condemned man was dead. O'Neill suggested that the autopsies were not needed. "If the convict is dead," he said, "he will stay dead without the autopsy. If he is alive then the autopsy is a crime that outrages decency, a crime a thousand times more horrible than the crime for which the convict sacrifices his life.... To be rendered helpless by an electric shock and then disemboweled by doctors before the body is cold is the decree of our twentieth-century courts.... [T]he profession at large should protest vigorously against performing the legitimate functions of the hangman."[17]

Hurlbert, the second executioner, killed 120 people in the Sing Sing chair, but by the fall of 1925 he was showing signs of a nervous breakdown, throwing equipment around the room and yelling at the guards as he did his work. He had lost a lot of weight and seemed in poor health, and on one occasion he nearly collapsed as he was doing his work. Finally on January 16, 1926, he quit without warning, leaving Warden Lewis Lawes without an executioner.

When news of the resignation made the newspapers, Lawes was flooded with letters from volunteers for the job, but none of them had any experience. "I can find a lot of morbid fellows to do the work," said Lawes, "but the thing is to find a man with technical skill."

For a while it looked as if Lawes would have to pull the switch himself, but soon someone at the Department of Prisons remembered that Davis had once had another assistant, one who had left the prison system

to seek work else-
where. When he was
contacted for the job,
Robert Elliott said he
felt it was the call of
destiny. After talking it
over with his family he
volunteered and was at
the switch in a matter
of days.

While he was an
electrician at Dan-
nemora, Elliott had
once allowed himself
to be strapped into the
electric chair so that a
group of visitors could
see how it looked with
a man in it. He wit-
nessed his first electro-
cution in 1901 and had
actually pulled the
switch several times
when he was Davis's
assistant.

Robert G. Elliott, the official executioner in New York in the 1930s and 1940s. He also served as executioner in Massachusetts, New Jersey and Vermont. (New York State Library)

Hurlbert returned to Auburn, but getting away from the electric chair did not improve his health, either mental or physical. On February 22, 1929, he went down into the darkest part of the basement of his house and shot himself twice in the head with a revolver.

Elliott eventually became the state executioner in five other states as well: New Jersey, Connecticut, Massachusetts, Vermont and Pennsylvania. One of the quirks of the law was that New York, New Jersey and Connecticut all connected the lower electrode to the right leg. The other states used the left leg.

After his retirement in the late 1930s, after executing 357 people in the electric chair, he described a typical electrocution in his memoirs: "The figure in the chair pitches forward, straining against the straps. There is the whining sound of the current, and a crackling, sizzling sound. The body turns a vivid red. Sparks often shoot from the electrodes. A wisp of white or dull gray smoke may rise from the top of the head or the leg on which the electrode is attached. This is produced by the drying out of the sponge, singed hair, and, despite every effort to prevent it, sometimes burning flesh. An offensive odor is generally present."

Elliott said that although the witnesses could not see him behind his partition, he could always see the victims while he turned on the current. "Five seconds after the initial shock of 2,000 volts, I decrease the current to 1,000 volts or somewhat under. The purpose of this is to avoid sparking and needless burning. At the end of half a minute, I increase it to 1,800 or 2,000 volts, and after another few seconds cut it down again. This is repeated at half-minute intervals. As the current is increased and lowered, the body in the chair rises and sinks. Finally, after the fifth shock, I reduce the current gradually."

One of the unusual things about Elliott was that he was an opponent of capital punishment and thought the practice should be outlawed. "I do not think the death penalty is necessary to protect society," he said, "and do not believe it should be inflicted. When I first entered the work I had no particular views on the subject; but reached my conclusions after being official executioner for a number of years."

On January 6, 1927, Elliott performed the unusual feat of executing six men on the same day, three in Massachusetts and three at Sing Sing. He started the day in Boston and then took the train to New York. He had time for dinner and took his family to the movies before heading up the river to Sing Sing to kill the other three.[18]

When Texas switched from hanging to the electric chair in 1923, a death chamber with nine cells was built at the state prison in Huntsville. The new electric chair was set in concrete. The warden of the prison, Capt. R. F. Coleman, resigned the day the new law went into effect, saying, "It just can't be done boys. A warden can't be a warden and a killer too. A prison is a place to reform men, not to kill them." His successor, Walter Miller, a former sheriff who had conducted several hangings, said pulling the switch on the chair was a lot easier than sending a man to the gallows. Between 1923 and 1972, 361 convicts were executed in the chair at Huntsville.[19]

Bartolomeo Vanzetti and Nicola Sacco, Massachusetts State Prison, August 23, 1927

On April 15, 1920, F. A. Parmenter, the paymaster of a shoe factory in South Braintree, Massachusetts, and Alesandro Berardelli, the guard who was protecting him, were murdered during a $15,000 robbery. A few

Bartolomeo Vanzetti and Nicola Sacco, anarchists convicted of murder, died in the Massachusetts electric chair in 1927. (New York State Library)

weeks later, Nicola Sacco and Bartolomeo Vanzetti, two Italian anarchists who had immigrated to the United States in 1908, were arrested. Sacco was a shoemaker and Vanzetti was a fish peddler, but both were carrying guns at the time of their arrests. Neither of them had a criminal record, and no trace of the money was ever found.

Socialists and radicals protested that the men were innocent and turned the case into a cause célébre by charging that the two were being sacrificed for their political beliefs, not for their crimes. The two were tried in Dedham, Massachusetts, found guilty and sentenced to death. On November 18, 1925, a man who was already on death row confessed that he had killed the two men as part of Boston's Joe Morelli gang. The courts refused to take this new evidence into consideration, despite calls all over the world for a new trial. When Gov. Alvan T. Fuller refused to grant their request for clemency, riots broke out in cities throughout the world and bombs were thrown in New York City. The two men were widely regarded as political martyrs.

At their execution at Charlestown Prison, Elliott was stationed behind a screen that covered everything but his head. The chair was located in the center of the room, and the witnesses were seated along one of the walls.

Sacco was brought into the execution chamber at 11 minutes after midnight. He walked the 17 steps from his cell to the chair with no assistance. While he was being strapped into the chair, he shouted out in Italian, "Long live anarchy!" After the straps were in place a leather headpiece was strapped over his face. Just as the current was turned on he cried out "farewell" in English and then, in Italian, "mother."

When Vanzetti entered the execution chamber a few minutes later he stopped in front of Warden Hendry and said, "I wish to say to you that I am innocent. I have never done a crime, some sins, but never any crime.... I am an innocent man." Then he shook hands with the warden and some of the guards before taking his place in the chair. While he was being strapped in, he gently said, "I now wish to forgive some people for what they are doing to me." Then Elliott turned on the current again.

"I do not deny that I was nervous," Elliott said. "I knew that the eyes of the world were on Boston that night; that the least thing out of the ordinary or the slightest mishap in the death chamber would be inflated into a sensation that might result in serious repercussions."

Everything went smoothly, but Elliott had to be escorted through the crowds of reporters and demonstrators who had gathered outside the prison. Subsequent ballistic tests on the two guns showed that Sacco was probably guilty of the murders but that Vanzetti was probably innocent. Legal experts now agree that there should have been a second trial in the case. In 1977 Gov. Michael Dukakis issued a proclamation stating that Sacco and Vanzetti had not been treated fairly. The execution was turned into a sonnet, "Justice Denied in Massachusetts," by Edna St. Vincent Millay. Upton Sinclair wrote a novel about it, and Maxwell Anderson composed a play.

On May 18, 1928, a bomb destroyed a significant part of Elliott's home in Richmond Hill, New York. No one was ever charged with the crime, but Elliott said he was convinced that anarchist friends of Sacco and Vanzetti were responsible.[20]

During the late 1920s Lawes published a series of books about life at Sing Sing, including his own views about the electric chair. Like Elliott, he opposed capital punishment because he thought it was useless as a deterrent and simply substituted legal death for homicide. Nearly all of the condemned men were poor and illiterate, he said, and nearly all of them went to the chair bravely, without any assistance. One man threw a lighted cigar at the witnesses, hitting one of them in the face. "You're a bunch of ___ ___," he said as he died in the chair. Among the last requests were to wear a white shirt instead of the prison issue black one, a request to wear a tie and a request for a dozen roses. Lawes said he once broke the rules and smuggled in two ounces of whiskey for a condemned man who said he needed it to face the chair. When Lawes offered it to him on "the last mile," however, the prisoner refused, saying Lawes needed it more than he did.

On December 20, 1927, a vaudeville performer named Mr. Johnson, who advertised himself as an electrical genius, advertised that he would take "the hot squat" in the electric chair at the Hippodrome Theater in New York to prove that the chair could not kill him. He said he could teach the prisoners at Sing Sing how to survive the chair as well. This, of course, caught Lawes's attention, and he sent a representative named George Ogle to inspect the apparatus in the theater.

Ogle reported back that the man had admitted to being a fake after Ogle examined the electrical circuit and found that no electricity was actually running through the electrodes of the "electric chair" used in the act. There was actually a "trick connection" on the back of the chair that fed the current back to the generator, he said. Ogle said he allowed Johnson to continue his act as long as he agreed to no longer mention Sing Sing in it.[21]

By this time the electric chair had acquired its own set of slang words, invented by prisoners and newspaper reporters. The chair was called "the hot seat" and condemned men were said to take the "hot squat" or "ride the lightning," get a "permanent wave" or be "cooked, roasted, burned, toasted, fried or juiced." The Sing Sing chair acquired the name "Gruesome Gertie," but the names "Old Sparky" and "Old Smoky" apparently date back only to the early 1970s.

Ruth Snyder, Sing Sing Prison, January 12, 1928

The execution of Ruth Snyder, 34, of Queens became famous for reasons that had nothing to do with the victim or the execution. Snyder was unhappily married to Albert Snyder, the art editor of *Motor Boating* magazine when she took out insurance policies worth $95,000 and attempted to do him in. She tried at least seven times, turning on the gas while he was sleeping, locking the garage door while he was inside with the motor running, doping his whiskey with dichloride of mercury and stuffing his medicine bottles with narcotics.

Snyder, who later was said to have had at least 28 lovers, contacted one of them, Henry Judd Gray, a corset salesman, and the two of them began collecting an arsenal of weapons for the job. On March 13, 1927, they beat Albert Snyder with a pair of window sash weights, strangled him with wire and doped him with chloroform before he died. Eventually they both confessed to the murders and were sentenced to die in the chair at Sing Sing on the same day.

Counterfeit admission tickets to the courtroom were sold for $50 each, and street vendors offered miniature sash weights mounted on stick pins as souvenirs for a dime. Snyder received hundreds of marriage proposals in the mail and by telegram.

She was the first woman put to death by Elliott despite her last-minute conversion to Catholicism, which she hoped would influence Catholic Gov. Alfred E. Smith to spare her life. While waiting to be executed she wrote her life story, which was syndicated in the Hearst newspapers and later published as a pamphlet. On the day of her execution there were 3,000 people outside the gates, according to Lawes.

She went to the chair just minutes before her accomplice. She was strapped in by prison matrons, but Elliott himself attached the electrodes to her head and calf.

"Father forgive them for they know not what they do," she said while sobbing before the mask was placed over her face. Elliott, who was described by reporters as "the gray haired man," retired to his closet and at the word of Warden Lawes pulled the switch. Only one jolt was used, lasting two minutes. Elliott afterward told reporters that the multiple jolts of electricity that had been used in past electrocutions were no longer believed to be necessary.

"As the current surged through Ruth Snyder's body I thought of her mother and her little daughter Lorraine," Elliott said. "My sympathies were more with them than with the woman in the chair."

The next day the *New York Daily News* published a fuzzy photo on its front page that it claimed was Snyder at the moment of her death. Later the newspaper explained that a photographer named Thomas Howard, one of the official witnesses, had strapped a small camera to his leg and reached down to snap the photo at the exact moment. It was the first time anyone had ever photographed an execution, and prison authorities were furious.

This plot had been hatched by Harvey Duell, the *Daily News* city editor, Ted Dalton, the picture assignment editor and George Schmidt, his assistant. They practiced the technique in a hotel for several days. Because there was no way to look through a viewfinder, the focus and distance had to be worked out with blueprints of the death chamber. Howard had run

Convicted murderer Ruth Snyder at the moment of her death in the Sing Sing electric chair in 1928. The picture was taken with a hidden camera and published on the front page of the *New York Daily News*. (*New York Daily News*)

a shutter release wire up his pants leg to a bulb in his pocket. At the moment Snyder died, Howard lifted his pants leg, pressed the bulb and got the image on film, which was run with the one-word headline: DEAD!

Dr. Raymond F. C. Kieb, the state commissioner of corrections (as the commissioner of prisons was now called), asked the attorney general to prosecute the *Daily News* and the photographer who snapped the photo. "The man who took that picture … violated not only the trust placed in him by the prison officials but he violated the trust of the people," Kieb said. "It was a very serious thing to exploit a thing of this sort…. We still feel we can trust the newspaper men, but in the future we will have to be more selective."

A few weeks later Assemblyman Jacob P. Nathanson of New York introduced a bill to exclude all newspaper employees from attending executions and fine them $1,000 to $5,000 if they printed anything other than the official report of the warden. This bill failed, but for years wardens in prisons across the country required all the witnesses at executions to hold up their hands at the moment the switch was pulled. It must have been a bizarre sight, but it was the only way he could think of to prevent any more photos from hidden cameras.

Meanwhile Howard, the man who took the picture, was given a $100 bonus and transferred to the prestigious Washington bureau of the paper.[22]

Irene Schroder, Pennsylvania State Prison, February 23, 1931

Schroder and her boyfriend, Glenn Dague, lived a life of crime similar to that of Bonnie and Clyde. Dague, a former salesman and Sunday school teacher, deserted his family in West Virginia after meeting Irene Schroder. They robbed shops and stores for a time, driving around in an automobile from place to place.

They were fleeing from a grocery store holdup in Butler, Pennsylvania, when they were chased by two state policemen. Schroder wounded one of the policemen and killed the other. In the car during the chase was her four-year-old son, Donnie. Schroder and Dague got away but were tracked down in Arizona where they put up a fantastic gun battle until they ran out of ammunition, and "Iron Irene" or "the Tiger Girl" as the newspapers called her, had to surrender.

Little Donnie's remark, "My mother killed a cop like you!" was an important part of the case against his mother. "I firmly believe that Irene Schroder loved Glenn Dague with full and unfluttering devotion," said Elliott in his memoirs. "She was perfectly willing to shoulder the whole responsibility if Dague's life could be spared."

During the final trip in the prison van, he said, "the two constantly caressed each other." Just before she died she instructed the prison guards to "fry Glenn's eggs on both sides. He likes them that way."

When she came to the electric chair in her gray dress, Elliott said he noticed a smile on her face, "the most pleasant I have seen on anyone. It was not a smile of defiance or bravado, but a kindly, peaceful one ... the most fearless person I have ever put to death."[23]

On July 7, 1932, Elliott was invited to Vermont to perform the first execution in the 13 years since the state had built its electric chair. No one in the state had any idea how to do it, he said, and he had to bring a mask from Sing Sing and the electrodes from New Jersey. This execution, at the Vermont State Prison in Windsor, was the only one he performed in that state during his long career.

Joe Palmer and Raymond Hamilton, Texas State Prison, Huntsville, May 10, 1935

Palmer and Hamilton were members of the famous Bonnie and Clyde gang. They killed a prison guard on January, 16, 1934, during an escape from the Eastham Unit. They were assisted in their escape by Bonnie Parker and Clyde Barrow, who had himself been a prisoner in the Eastham Unit. They hid guns in the field where the prisoners worked and then picked up the escapees in their car.

The two were recaptured but escaped again on July 24 after smuggling a gun into the prison, forcing a guard into a cell and climbing over the wall. During this escape a guard was killed. After they were captured the third time, they were executed on May 10, 1935.[24]

Albert Fish, Sing Sing Prison, January 16, 1936

Cannibal, religious fanatic and pedophile Albert Fish was a man of "unparalleled perversity" according to the psychiatrist who testified at his trial. Although he looked like a grandfather with his blue eyes, stooped shoulders and gray mustache, Fish, 64, was eventually convicted of the murder, dismemberment and cannibalization of a 10-year-old girl. He claimed to have raped at least 100 boys, castrating them and drinking their blood.

Fish pleaded insanity at his trial, with many witnesses claiming they had heard Fish proclaim that he was Jesus Christ before sticking pins into himself. While he was sick in prison X-rays showed that he had 27 sewing needles in his abdomen and pelvis.

While he was waiting to be executed, he told guards, "What a thrill it will be if I have to die in the electric chair. It will be the supreme thrill, the only one I haven't tried."

Elliott said the story that the electric chair shorted out on the first try because of all the metal in Fish's body was not true and was made up by the newspapers.[25]

Bruno Richard Hauptmann, New Jersey State Prison, April 3, 1936

On March 1, 1932, the 20-month-old son of Charles and Anne Morrow Lindbergh was kidnapped from the second-floor nursery of their home in Hopewell, New Jersey. Left behind was a crudely worded ransom note asking for $50,000 in cash. Lindbergh, the first man to fly solo across the Atlantic, was arguably the most popular man in America. A ladder was found near the house that was believed to have been built and used by the kidnapper.

The state police and the FBI swore to find the person responsible, and the entire country was outraged by the crime. Lindbergh paid the ransom with bills marked by the FBI and was told that his son was on a boat off the coast of Massachusetts. The Coast Guard searched the area but found nothing. On May 12 the baby's body was found in the woods with a fractured skull, and police said it had probably been dead since the night of the kidnapping.

The case went unsolved for nearly three years before a man passing one of the marked bills was located at a Manhattan gas station and police arrested Bruno Richard Hauptmann. Hauptmann was a 36-year-old German born carpenter from the Bronx who was convicted largely on the evidence of handwriting experts and 15 handwritten ransom notes. Like the Sacco and Vanzetti case the "Lindbergh Baby" case remains controversial, with many still maintaining that Hauptmann was framed and that every bit of evidence against him had been fabricated or tampered with. There are even people who claim to be Lindbergh's son.

Hauptmann's date in court was called "the trial of the century," with crowds outside the courthouse in Flemington, New Jersey, and souvenir stands selling miniature 10-cent replicas of the ladder that had been used in the kidnapping. Crowds shouted "Kill Hauptmann! Kill the German!"

Bruno Hauptmann, convicted of murdering Charles Lindbergh's infant son, died in the New Jersey electric chair in 1935. (New York State Library)

during the trial. Pundit H. L. Mencken called the trial "the biggest story since the Resurrection."

While he was on death row, Hauptmann wrote, "the poor child has been kidnapped and murdered, so somebody must die for it. For is the parent not the great flyer? And if somebody does not die for the death of the child, then always the police will be monkeys. So I am the one who is picked out to die."

The New Jersey death room in Trenton had whitewashed brick walls and a scruffed linoleum floor. The heavy three-legged chair had a large metal cabinet behind it that contained the controls for the chair. There were three rows of folding chairs for the 55 witnesses. Elliott was wearing a gray suit and a brightly patterned tie that seemed to some observers a bit too festive for the occasion. The witnesses were seated behind a three-foot-high canvas curtain divider draped over a chain.

Warden Kimberling instructed the witnesses not to put their hands in their pockets. The reason for this rule was to prevent anyone from taking illegal photos of the execution and selling them to the newspapers as had happened five years earlier at the execution of Ruth Snyder.

At 8:41 Hauptmann stepped out of cell number 8 on death row wearing his bedroom slippers and sporting a shaved head. He walked right over and sat down in the chair so that the guards could attach the straps. One electrode was placed on his right calf where his khaki trousers had been slit to accept it. Elliott himself slipped the leather skullcap onto his head and tied a black mask across his face. The reporters had their pencils ready, waiting for a last statement, but there was none.

At 8:44 Warden Kimberling gave the nod to Elliott, who rotated a wheel on the control panel. The machine made a whining sound, and there was a creaking of the leather straps. A tiny wisp of smoke shot from Hauptmann's head. After a minute Elliott cut the voltage in half and held it for another minute. Then the machine was turned off and the prison doctor, Dr. Howard Wiesler examined the body before declaring him dead.

Hauptmann's final statement, written in German and given out after his execution, said "I am glad that my life in a world which has not understood me has ended. Soon I will be at home with my lord, so I am dying an innocent man."

Recently declassified FBI files cast some serious doubt on the police procedures used at the time of the arrest and trial, showing that evidence that would have helped Hauptmann's case had been suppressed.[26]

During the 1930s when the use of the electric chair reached an all time-high, it became the stuff of legends. Movie gangsters who went "up the river" to Sing Sing would take "the hot squat" or the "hot seat" or "make a date with Ol' Sparky." Murderers who were convicted knew they would "get the chair." Some electric chairs had their own special names. In Alabama, where for some reason the electric chair at Atmore was painted yellow, it was referred to as the "Yellow Mama."[27]

Martin (Bugsy) Goldstein and Harry (Pittsburgh Phil) Straus, Sing Sing Prison, June 12, 1941

These two contract killers were known as "Murder, Inc." because they carried out a number of contract hits requested by various New York underworld figures. They were known to have killed at least 83 people between 1931 to 1950, but some estimate that the total may actually have been closer to 500. They used car bombs, hanging with barbed wire, shotgun blasts, drownings, arson and ice picks.

The crime that sent them to the chair was the murder of a Manhattan bookmaker on September 4, 1939. The man was tied up, doused with gasoline and set on fire.[28]

Edward Haight, Sing Sing Prison, July 8, 1943

Haight, 17, was convicted of the abduction and murder of two girls he picked up in his car. He slashed them with his hunting knife and tossed one off a bridge and ran over the other one his car.

He was the second of three murderers executed on July 8. After he was strapped into the chair and the current was turned on, flames shot from the electrodes, and he was literally roasted to death. Greasy smoke filled the chamber and witnesses found the stench of it intolerable. By contrast, the apparatus worked perfectly on the two prisoners who were executed before and after him.[29]

Louis (Lepke) Buchalter, Sing Sing Prison, March 4, 1944

Buchalter rose from a street urchin to a crime czar in only a few years. He took over the labor racketeering activities of a crime boss after he gunned him down in 1927. At one time he had a private army of 250 professional hoodlums who committed as many as 50 murders on his orders. During the later part of his career he was involved in gambling and narcotics.

In the late 1930s the FBI and the New York district attorney's office began an all-out campaign to bring him to justice, offering a $50,000 reward. Buchalter went underground but later gave himself up to federal officials to avoid the contracts that rival gangsters had taken out on him. While he was in custody, evidence in a 1936 murder case was uncovered, and he was tried and convicted.

The poet Robert Lowell, who was in prison in 1943 as a conscientious objector, found himself in Manhattan's West Side Jail in the cell next to Buchalter, and the two had time to speak with each other at length. This conversation led Lowell to write a poem in which he said the prospect of the chair shimmered before the enfeebled gangster like a mysterious gateway back to the violent highs of his youth, "an oasis in his air / of lost connections."[30]

Willie Francis, Louisiana State Prison, May 3, 1946, and May 9, 1947

Willie Francis was one of those rare condemned men who was sent to the electric chair twice. An all-white jury in Louisiana convicted Francis, a 16-year-old black youth, of the first-degree murder of Andrew Thomas, the town druggist of St. Martinsville, Louisiana, in "Cajun" country in the southwest portion of the state on November 8, 1944.

During his trial his court-appointed lawyers did not cross-examine any of the prosecution witnesses and did not offer any evidence as part of their case, despite the fact that police lost the murder weapon and Francis's confession listed the wrong date for the murder. So there was no surprise when he was found guilty and was sentenced to die in the electric chair on March 29, 1946.

Unlike most states, Louisiana did not execute prisoners in a prison. Instead a portable wooden electric chair was delivered to the town where the crime took place. In this case it had been loaded into a pickup truck from its storage area in Angola State Prison and taken up the elevator to the second floor of the St. Martinsville jail. Then they strung wires from the generator in the pickup truck up to the windows of the jail. Several residents of the jail noticed that the two men installing the chair, one a convict and the other a prison guard, were passing a flask of whiskey between them.

Francis was strapped into the chair, and the current was turned on. He felt thousands of needles pierce his skin. He began moving involuntarily, and the chair moved with his movements. When the current was turned off he was still breathing, so they turned the current on again with more power this time.

"Take it off, take it off, let me breathe!" Francis begged.

"You're not supposed to breathe," said Captain Foster of the prison.

"I am not dying!" Francis said.

There had been some kind of malfunction. Not enough electricity was getting through to kill Francis, only enough to torture him. The guards turned the current off and waited. There was a discussion that went all the way to the governor's office about how to handle this unique situation before it was decided to give up for the day and try again in six days. Not enough current passed through the electrodes to kill him and Francis had "cheated the electric man" as the newspapers called it.[31]

Bertrand DeBlanc, a lawyer contacted by Francis's father, claimed in an appeal that to subject Francis to a second execution would be cruel and unusual. This case went all the way to the U.S. Supreme Court, the first time the court had been asked to decide whether the chair was cruel and unusual since William Kemmler's case in 1890.

Four justices agreed that strapping Francis into the chair a second time would be cruel and unusual, but the other five disagreed, saying Louisiana officials had "carried out their duties in a careful and humane manner" and that the pain Francis suffered during the botched execution was an "unforeseeable accident."

After the court decision was made, an investigation at the prison discovered that some of the cables to the electric chair had been improperly connected and that the technicians were drunk at the time. A number of human rights groups, including the NAACP, came to Willy's defense and pleaded with the Court to take another look at the case now that the reasons for the botched execution were made public. Legal experts who have studied the case think that if the reasons for the botched execution had been known to the Supreme Court it might have reversed at least one vote and spared Francis' life. The court refused to review the case again and Francis died in the electric chair more than a year after the first attempt. There was no cheating the electric man a second time.

Henry Burdette and Fred Painter, West Virginia State Prison, March 26, 1951

Some states resisted the national trend to switch from hanging to the electric chair for many years. West Virginia, for example, hanged its condemned prisoners until 1949, when it finally passed an electric chair law. On March 26, 1951, Harry Atlee Burdette, 26, and Fred Clifford Painter, 32, became the first men to die in the West Virginia chair. Their lawyers claimed they had been too intoxicated to have premeditated the murder and that they were legally insane due to drug abuse and cerebral syphilis.

Reporters were permitted to interview the two condemned men just before the execution. Burdette was strapped into the chair at 9:02 P.M. and was pronounced dead after 3 minutes and 45 seconds. Painter followed at 9:10. The first surge merely knocked him unconscious. After another jolt, Painter was pronounced dead at 9:19.

Instead of hiring an official executioner, as other states did, West Virginia used a system that included three separate buttons, two of which were dummies. Three prison officials were selected to push the buttons, but no one could be certain which button sent the current to the chair. Among the witnesses was Sen. Robert C. Byrd. During all the preparations for the first use of the chair, two prisoners escaped from the penitentiary.[32]

Julius and Ethel Rosenberg, Sing Sing Prison, June 19, 1953

In 1950 the FBI arrested Julius Rosenberg, an electrical engineer who had worked for the U.S. Army Signal Corps, and his wife, Ethel, a stenographer. They were indicted for conspiracy to transmit classified military information to the Soviet Union. At their trial in March 1951 the government charged that in 1944 and 1945 they had persuaded Ethel's brother, David Greenglass, an employee of the Los Alamos atomic bomb project, to provide them with top secret data on nuclear weapons. Greenglass himself was the main witness against them.

The Rosenbergs were the first U.S. civilians to be sentenced to death in an espionage trial. Many people claimed that the political climate — this was the time of the McCarthy hearings and the "Red scare" — made it impossible for the Rosenbergs to receive a fair trial and that the only incriminating evidence had come from a confessed spy. Others questioned the value of the information they were said to have passed to the Russians and claimed the death penalty was too severe.

Their case polarized the nation into opposing camps, one of which believed that a warning needed to be sent to those who were sympathetic to the Soviet Union and another that believed two people were being unfairly offered up as scapegoats to explain why the Soviets had acquired the atomic bomb. Part of the problem with the government's case was that the Rosenbergs simply didn't look like spies. William R. Conklin, who covered the execution for the *New York Times,* wrote, "Small and plump, Ethel Rosenberg seemed more an East Side housewife than a figure in an international spy plot. Her bespectacled, serious-looking husband likewise seemed more like the electrical engineer he was than an American contact for the Soviet spy system."

After a last-minute stay of execution ordered by Justice William O. Douglas was overruled by a majority of the court, the last appeal was to Pres. Dwight D. Eisenhower. On the night before their executions the president issued a statement blaming the Rosenbergs for starting the cold war and the threat of nuclear Armageddon: "I can only say that, by immeasurably increasing the chances of atomic war, the Rosenbergs may have condemned to death tens of millions of innocent people all over the world.

Ethel and Julius Rosenberg, convicted of treason for the sale of nuclear secrets to the Soviet Union, died in the Sing Sing electric chair in 1953. (New York State Library)

The execution of two human beings is a grave matter. But even graver is the thought of the millions of dead whose deaths may be directly attributable to what these spies have done."

As the time of their execution was moved up several hours to prevent it happening on the Jewish Sabbath, anti–American demonstrations broke out in Paris, London, Turin and Toronto. Crowds picketed the White

The execution chamber at Sing Sing Prison, showing the electric chair and the visitors seating, about 1930. (New York State Library)

House and 5,000 people gathered for a prayer rally at Union Square in New York, where they carried signs reading "We Are Innocent!"

The Rosenbergs were electrocuted within minutes of each other at Sing Sing Prison. Like the case of Sacco and Vanzetti there are many who claim that the Rosenbergs were innocent of the charges and were set up by anti–Communists who saw conspiracies under every rug. New evidence about the case came out after the fall of the Soviet Union, and it has been used to bolster the cases of those who claimed they were guilty, as well as those who said they were innocent.

State police and federal agents had sealed off a large area around the prison to prevent public demonstrations like those that had taken place during the executions of Sacco and Vanzetti 26 years before. Inside the prison, the other convicts talked about the "dance party" that was scheduled for later that day. Inside the death house, convicts number 110,510 and 110,649 were making their final preparations.

There had been a loud and strong public outcry against the executions. The Vatican and the president of France had appealed for clemency. In Washington the attorney general kept an open phone line to the prison. If the Rosenbergs confessed he had promised to commute their sentences to life in prison. Millions of Americans had written to President Eisenhower asking for mercy.

For most of their time in prison, Julius, 35, and Ethel, 37, had been in separate cells, but on this last day the warden had permitted Julius to spend his final hours in the women's wing of the prison, so the two could talk to each other through a wire mesh.

At 7:20 Julius said good-bye to his wife by touching her fingers through the wire mesh and was taken to the special execution cell, where the top of his head was shaved and his pants were slit. At precisely 8 P.M. he made his walk along the "last mile" leading to the death chamber. He was clean-shaven, no longer wearing his mustache, and dressed in a white T-shirt. At 8:02 he sat in the chair and the electrodes were attached to his head and leg and the current was sent through his body. He was taken out a few minutes later and his wife was led into the chamber at 8:08.

Ethel, five-feet tall and 100 pounds, was wearing a dark green print dress with white polka dots and cloth slippers when she entered the room. The hair at the top of her head had been cut short to ensure good contact with the head electrode. Just before she reached the chair she held out her hand to the prison matron, Helen Evans. Ethel drew her close and kissed her.

She winced when the straps were being attached and the mask adjusted over her face. Joseph Francel, who had taken over the job of state electrician from Elliott in 1939, received the nod from the prison warden and turned on the current. He turned it on three times and then stopped, but the doctors found that Ethel was still breathing so Francel turned the current on two more times before Ethel was declared dead.[33]

Charles Raymond "Little Red" Starkweather, Nebraska State Prison, June 25, 1959

Starkweather's 1958 crime spree with his 14-year-old girlfriend Caril Ann Fugate is the basis for the 1973 movie *Badlands* and a song by Bruce Springsteen. A former teenage garbage collector, Starkweather had been terrorized by fellow students because of his small size and red hair. To compensate he became an accomplished street fighter who idolized James Dean.

He committed his first murder on December 1, 1957, when he killed a gas station attendant for $108 that he used to buy gifts for Fugate. After that he killed Fugate's mother, stepfather and half-sister. On January 28 the couple set out in Starkweather's car with a pistol, a sawed-off shotgun and a hunting knife. After they killed a number of other people, including millionaire industrialist C. Lauer Ward, the state of Nebraska called out 200 members of the National Guard as protection from the 17-year-old murderer. They were finally captured after a high-speed chase in Montana.

While Starkweather was on death row, his father sought permission to raise money for legal fees by selling locks of his son's hair but was told it was not appropriate. State and federal appeals were denied. When asked the night before his execution if he would donate his eyes to an eye bank, Starkweather said, "Why should I? Nobody every gave me anything."[34]

Frederick Charles Wood, Sing Sing Prison, March 21, 1963

The next-to-last man to die at Sing Sing, Wood, 48, committed his first murder at the age of 15 and received a prison sentence. He was paroled in 1931 and committed his second murder two years later. He was paroled again in 1940 and committed his third murder a year later. He was paroled once more in 1960, despite protests from across the state.

On June 30, 1960, just weeks after his last parole, Wood slashed a man to death in a Manhattan basement apartment and bludgeoned another man with a shovel. When Wood was caught and confessed to the crime, the state's newspapers condemned the parole board for allowing Wood to kill repeatedly. When he entered the execution chamber at Sing Sing and was asked for his last words, he smiled and said, "Gentlemen, observe closely as you witness the effect of electricity on Wood."[35]

Eddie Lee Mays, Sing Sing Prison, August 15, 1963

Mays was the last man put to death in the Sing Sing electric chair, which traced its origins back to the original Westinghouse generators purchased by Brown in 1889. A native of North Carolina, Mays spent time in prison there for a previous murder before heading to New York City, where he formed a robbery ring that is said to have committed 52 robberies in a six-week period.

On March 23, 1961, they were robbing a tavern at 1402 Fifth Avenue when one of the patrons, Maria Marini did not move fast enough, so Mays placed his pistol next to her ear and fired. Although Mays was convicted of murder, there is some doubt whether the victim in the case died of a gunshot wound or medical malpractice at Bellevue Hospital in New York City.

When he was arrested five days later, Mays was in possession of the murder weapon. A last-minute plea to Gov. Nelson Rockefeller was rejected, and Mays went to the chair.[36]

Brother Cecil McKee, the chaplain at the Walls Unit at Huntsville State Prison in Texas who walked condemned prisoners along the "last mile" to the electric chair in the 1960s, said the experience was especially difficult for him because he opposed capital punishment.

"It was hard to be there, but I didn't have to see it," he said. "I closed my eyes.... You know, the flesh burns. It leaves a terrible odor. I'd go home and take my clothes off, leave 'em out, we'd go to sleep. Next day I'd have to send my clothes to the cleaners. It was just part of the job.... We have no right to demean, punish or destroy a life. If they can't be rehabilitated they should be incarcerated. But I was working in a system that says you're going to do it."[37]

The number of electric chair executions reached a peak in the 1930s and then slowly declined to zero by the middle of the 1960s. This closely reflected public opinion polls showing that support for all kinds of capital punishment was declining. By 1972 a majority of Americans said they were in favor of abolishing it. One reason was the strong pressure from human rights groups that saw the death penalty as a social ill that needed to be reformed, like poverty, racism and the Vietnam War. Studies at this time showed that blacks were much more likely to be executed than whites for committing similar crimes.

Another factor was the increasing reluctance of judges and juries to impose the death sentence. States also became more reluctant to actually perform the executions, leaving prisoners on death row for year after year. The U.S. Supreme Court became increasingly critical of the arbitrary and unfair way that capital punishment was being used. This watchful eye from the federal courts had an effect on juries, state courts and state officials. Research conducted by the NAACP Legal Defense Fund in the early 1960s showed conclusively that blacks were far more likely than whites to be sentenced to death for convictions of the same crimes.

In 1962, Richard Barrett, chairman of New York's Temporary Commission on the Revision of Penal Law, called for the electric chair to be abolished in the state that had invented it. "The electric chair is the ultimate symbol of irrationality, brutal vengeance, senseless discrimination," he said. "It is like a cancerous growth which infects the entire body of our penal system."[38]

After that the electric chair's days were numbered in the Empire State. In 1965 a bill signed by Gov. Nelson Rockefeller, who personally supported capital punishment, abolished the death penalty except for the murder of a prison guard. The Sing Sing chair was moved to Green Haven Prison but was never used there, and when New York reinstated the death penalty on March 7, 1995, it switched to lethal injection.

Between 1967 and 1977 not a single execution took place anywhere in the country. The legal challenges to the death penalty culminated in a 5–4 U.S. Supreme Court decision *Furman v. Georgia* on June 29, 1972, that struck down state and federal capital punishment laws as "arbitrary and capricious" and a violation of the Eighth Amendment's prohibition of cruel and unusual punishment.

This latter point was exactly the argument that Cockran and Sherman had made in 1889 and 1890. Two of the justices (William Brennan and Thurgood Marshall) said capital punishment was unconstitutional in all instances. Justice William O. Douglas found that the death penalty was disproportionately applied to the poor and the socially disadvantaged. The dissenters on the court argued that the courts should not challenge legislative judgments about the death penalty. This was essentially the same position the court held on Kemmler's appeal the century before.

Three of the justices, William O. Douglas, William Brennan and Thurgood Marshall, said the Eighth Amendment prohibited all forms of capital punishment. They were joined by two other justices, Potter Stewart and Byron White, who felt that the laws as they were currently implemented were not fair because judges imposed the death penalty erratically.

The death penalty is "so wantonly and so freakishly imposed," said Stewart, that those who are sentenced to death have been singled out for excessively harsh treatment. "These death sentences are cruel and unusual in the same way that being struck by lightning is cruel and unusual."

Chief Justice Warren Burger said the court's decision did not necessarily mean the end of capital punishment. States could amend their death penalty laws by making them more specific and giving justices less power to decide when the penalty would be imposed.

The dissenters on the Court said that the Eighth Amendment had been on the books for 191 years and that it had not been applied to the death penalty in all that time and that the high court was improperly interfering with the rights of the states to pass death penalty laws.

Gov. Jimmy Carter of Georgia and Gov. Preston Smith of Texas reacted to the news by saying they would push for new laws that would require life sentences without the possibility of parole as a replacement for the death penalty. Gov. Ronald Reagan of California said he would seek to amend state laws to allow the death penalty for "cold-blooded, premeditated, planned murder" if a state referendum was passed in November.

For the 600 prisoners on death row, however, the reaction was much more positive. On death row at Georgia State Prison in Reidsville, the 22 condemned prisoners greeted the news with cheers and a round of applause. At Florida State Prison, the 97 inmates on death row had just come back from a showing of the movie *Dirty Harry* when the news was announced. "I've been thinking about death for a long time. Now I can think about life," said Lucius Jackson, Jr., of Georgia.

"There wasn't a man in here who wasn't clapping and yelling like crazy," said Steve Suggs, 26, who had been on death row awaiting his turn in the electric chair for three years. "I may be here the rest of my life, but it's life, and no man wants to die."

Jack Greenberg, the attorney from the NAACP who had fought for the ruling, confidently declared that the decision was a turning point in American history. He ignored Berger's warning that the states could amend their laws and predicted that the ruling meant the end of the death penalty. "I think there will no longer be any capital punishment in America," he told the *New York Times.*

Other legal observers were not so sure. Yale Kamisar, a law professor at the University of Michigan, warned that the plug may have been pulled only temporarily. "Whenever you've got five opinions, you've got a very vulnerable precedent," he said, adding that the next justice appointed to the court could well swing the majority back again.[39]

Bills were introduced in Congress to reestablish the death penalty. President Nixon said he thought the death penalty ought to be retained for hijackings and kidnappings. Legislators in five states announced that they would introduce new death penalty laws designed to work around the objections made by the high court.

More than 600 death row inmates in the 36 states that sanctioned the death penalty had their sentences lifted. Most people thought the electric chair had finally become a museum antique from a more primitive era. Andy Warhol used a photograph of the Sing Sing electric chair as the basis for one of his series paintings during this time. However, like a vampire rising from the grave, the electric chair hadn't had a stake driven through its heart yet.

— 11 —
The Electric Chair
Reborn: 1976–1998

On July 2, 1976, two days before the two hundredth anniversary of the signing of the Declaration of Independence, the U.S. Supreme Court gave the states permission to dust off the electric chair and plug it back in again. In a 7–2 decision the high court said the revised capital punishment laws in three states, Georgia, Texas and Florida, all of which used the electric chair, met the criteria the Court had set in 1972 to make the death penalty less arbitrary.

The Court issued its ruling on the very last day of the session and, although it directly applied to only three states, the implication was that any state that modeled its law on those three could begin executions again without fear that the Court would interfere. The nine members of the Court issued a total of 24 different opinions, reflecting the lack of consensus on the death penalty that had existed since 1972.

Justices William Brennan and Thurgood Marshall said the death penalty should be banned, but the other five members of the Court ruled that it was up to the states as long as the law ensured that it would be used fairly. In its majority opinion the Court said that "capital punishment is an expression of society's moral outrage at a particularly offensive conduct. This function may be unappealing to many, but it is essential to an ordered society that asks its citizens to rely on legal procedures rather than self-help to vindicate their wrongs."

Jack Greenberg, the NAACP attorney who had led the fight to abolish the death penalty, said the ruling represented a lost battle but that the war would go on. "We intend to pursue a variety of other approaches to stop executions," he said at a press conference. "We hope that this nation's 200th year—the Bicentennial—will not after all be marked by a resumption of electrocutions, gassings, hangings and shootings."

The governors in the death penalty states were clearly overjoyed that they could start up the execution process that had been halted since the early 1960s.

"I strongly support the reinstatement of capital punishment as set forth in the Texas penal code," said Gov. Dolph Briscoe of Texas, where prison guards in Huntsville tightened security along death row, where 42 prisoners were waiting to be executed.

"We've taken very serious security precautions because we don't want a suicide, violence—we just don't want to irritate the situation," said Ron Taylor, a spokesman for the Texas Department of Corrections.

Gov. Rubin Askew of Florida said he was ready to sign the death warrants of the 72 inmates on death row there. In Georgia, Bryant Huff, the district attorney who had argued in favor of the death penalty before the high court, said he was "ecstatic" about the news.[1]

Opinion polls clearly supported the Supreme Court's new ruling. Whereas support for the death penalty had been declining since the 1940s and actually reached a minority in the 1960s, it began to rise in the 1970s, mirroring an increase in the crime rate, which had been increasing since the 1950s. The murder rate increased from 5.1 per 100,000 people in 1960 to 10.2 per 100,000 in 1980. The growth of crime resulted in an increase in the public's fear and anger. The public demanded that the lawmakers, police and judges "get tough on crime." The public demanded that state legislatures pass laws that would allow executions to continue despite the Court's objections to arbitrary sentencing.[2]

While they were revising their laws to comply with the new standards set by the high court, however, many states took a hard look at whether the electric chair was the best method of killing murderers. Some states, most notably California, had never used the electric chair, finding that the gas chamber was more efficient. Many states, when they rewrote their death penalty laws, chose lethal injection rather than the electric chair. This form of execution had been considered by the Gerry Commission in 1888 but had been rejected because doctors did not want to use hypodermic needles as agents of death. There were also ethical considerations for the doctors in using their expertise to kill. Nevertheless public opinion clearly indicated that lethal injection was much more acceptable to most people than the electric chair, which seemed to many to be a barbaric antique from another era.

Texas abandoned its electric chair in 1977 and switched to lethal injection because, in the words of Governor Briscoe as he signed the law, it would "provide some dignity with death." Oklahoma switched in 1981, and in 1983 a large group of states switched, including Massachusetts,

New Jersey, Delaware and North Carolina. By 1992 only 12 states still had electric chairs. Other states, like Florida, Alabama and Georgia, plugged in their electric chairs and put them back to work. After the court ruling, it was only a matter of time before the chair took its next victim.

Victims of the Electric Chair 1890–1966

State	Period of Use	Victims
Alabama	1927–1965	153
Arkansas	1913–1964	172
Connecticut	1937–1960	18
District of Columbia	1928–1957	51
Florida	1924–1966	197
Georgia	1924–1964	422
Illinois	1928–1962	98
Indiana	1914–1961	59
Kentucky	1911–1962	171
Louisiana	1957–1961	11
Massachusetts	1901–1947	65
Nebraska	1920–1959	12
New Jersey	1907–1963	161
New Mexico	1933–1956	7
New York	1890–1963	695
North Carolina	1910–1936	161
Ohio	1897–1963	315
Oklahoma	1915–1966	83
Pennsylvania	1915–1962	351
South Carolina	1912–1962	241
South Dakota	1947	1
Tennessee	1909–1960	134
Texas	1924–1964	361
Vermont	1919–1954	5
Virginia	1908–1962	237
West Virginia	1951–1959	9
TOTAL	**1890–1966**	**4,190**

Source: Bowers, *Legal Homicide,* 1984

John A. Spenkelink, Florida State Prison, May 25, 1979

Spenkelink, 30, was the son of an Iowa farmer who committed suicide when John was 11. The boy found his father's body and removed the hose from the exhaust pipe that fed the carbon monoxide into the family car. After that he lived the life of a loner, escaping from a prison in

California before ending up in a Tallahassee motel room with a fellow drifter, Joseph Szymankiewicz, 45. Spenkelink said he bludgeoned the man and shot him twice in self-defense after he had forced him to commit homosexual acts.

Because of the many appeals in his case the state of Florida estimated it had spent between $5 million and $7 million in legal fees trying to execute him. Two years before, he had been brought into the room with the electric chair only to have his execution postponed by a last-minute legal maneuver. Among those defending his case was the American Civil Liberties Union and Ramsey Clark, the former attorney general.

The Florida State Prison in Starke became a battleground for both pro– and anti–death penalty groups that gathered outside the gates before the execution. The abolitionist groups shouted "Thou shalt not kill" and "government murder!" while the pro–death penalty groups drove a car with a silver coffin on top and a placard urging, "Go, Sparky!"

Spenkelink told the Rev. Tom Feamster, an Episcopal minister, "Man is what he chooses to be; he chooses that for himself," before being led into the death chamber, which had been screened off by a curtain from the room in which the 32 witnesses were waiting at 10 A.M.

After he had been strapped into the chair the curtain was drawn back just seconds before two men in black hoods pulled the switch three times, sending 2,500 volts through the electrodes.

"I somehow thought he would say something," said H. G. Davis, an editorial writer for the *Gainesville Sun* who was one of the witnesses, "but what you saw was like a wax figure, something you might see on display. He was strapped so tightly as to be almost motionless, a strap along his chin held his head back, he couldn't talk, the cheeks bulging from the pressure.... The blinds were opened and there he was. Quickly, very quickly there was the first surge of electricity and it seemed as if he had been hit by a gust of wind. The hand clenched, his legs jerked and after that he was still."

State Representative Andy Johnson of Jacksonville, one of the witnesses, had introduced a bill the day before to end all executions in Florida. He called Spenkelink's death "barbaric" and "sickening" while talking with reporters in a cow pasture outside the prison walls. "We saw a man sizzle today and if you watched close you could see him sizzle again and sizzle again."[3]

During the decade in which no electric chairs were used, some of the expertise needed to repair and maintain them seems to have been lost. Until 1963 there had been a chain of apprenticeship. In New York it passed from Davis to Elliott to Francel, and a similar process was used in other states. When states passed the new laws, prison wardens had to scramble to find someone with the necessary expertise to do the job. It was not, of course, a good place for on-the-job training. Into that knowledge vacuum stepped the most recent of the unusual characters who seem to have always attached themselves to the electric chair: Fred Leuchter.

Leuchter was the president of Fred A. Leuchter Associates, a Boston firm that was the country's only legal supplier of execution equipment and training. Besides electric chairs, he also sold lethal injection machines, gas chambers and gallows. Between 1979 and 1990 he served as a consultant on executions in 27 states, including all the states that still used the electric chair. In news articles and television specials focusing on his unusual business, Leuchter came to be known as "Dr. Death."

"Fred A. Leuchter probably knows more about electric chair technology than anyone else," the *Atlantic Monthly* reported in 1990, calling him "a trained and accomplished engineer." As will be shown below, he was actually neither. Leuchter said he came about his knowledge of the chair by careful calculations of voltage, current and connections. The best system, he said, uses three electrodes, instead of the traditional two. Leuchter's innovation was to put electrodes on both ankles.[4]

When visitors and journalists came to the basement of his home to ask about the electric chair, he demonstrated by sitting in his homemade device, pulling down the metal beanie that contained the head electrode and demonstrating his innovations and insisting that tight electrical contacts "help reduce flesh burning." It was important, he said, not to use too much current.

"Current cooks, so it's important to limit the current," Leuchter said. "If you overload an individual's body with current—more than six amps— you'll cook the meat on his body. It's like meat on an overcooked chicken. If you grab the arm, the flesh will fall right off in your hands.... That doesn't mean he felt anything. It simply means that it's cosmetically not the thing to do. Presumably the state will return the remains to the person's family for burial. Returning someone who had been cooked would be in poor taste."[5]

Asked how he managed to choose his line of work, Leuchter said he "just kind of slid into it." His father had been employed in a Massachusetts Prison, he said, and when he was a boy he sat in the electric chair. "A legend developed that if you sat in the chair you'd die in it," he told an interviewer. "Well, I sat in that chair too. And I didn't get electrocuted in it later. I sat in the chair and now I make electric chairs."

He claimed to have designed navigational equipment for the Navy and to hold the patent for the first electronic sextant and an instrument used to map terrain from helicopters in Vietnam. In 1970, he said, he was called in by a New England prison warden to repair an electric chair that had been damaged in a prison riot. He did a lot of reading and talked with prison wardens around the country before going into the execution business. He found it easy to convince prison officials to let him take over as equipment supplier and trainer, and no one seems to have questioned his motives or experience. In 1990 he claimed to be on a first-name basis with every prison warden in states that had the death penalty.

In numerous articles he explained his theories about the use of the electric chair and described how his self-designed chairs and the modifications he made to existing ones used simple parts so that replacements could be purchased at hardware stores and Radio Shack. He replaced the old leather straps with quick-release seatbelts. He offered complete electric chair systems for $35,000 each.

"As someone who believes in capital punishment but does not believe in torture, I sleep well knowing that as a result of what I do, fewer people are tortured," he said in early 1990, adding that he liked traveling around to prisons across the country.

Among his innovations was an electronic mechanism designed to conceal which of two executioners, each with his own control, actually administers the fatal jolt. He said he planned to replace the old leather straps on the chairs with seat-belt-like quick-release buckles and nylon straps. To maximize the inmate's comfort in his hour of death, Leuchter used adjustable arms on the chair to accommodate different sized people. His helmet featured a denim face mask that could be snapped across the inmate's face.

"This allows the executee to enjoy some degree of privacy during execution," Leuchter said with an apparently straight face. He sold his equipment and training programs at conventions of correctional institution personnel at which he passed out pens advertising "Execution Equipment and Support" with his name and address.[6]

During the 1980s the death penalty became a hot political issue. Republicans Ronald Reagan and George Bush used their strong support for it against Democrats who were opposed or lukewarm on the issue. Opposition to the death penalty came to be interpreted as "soft on crime" and became a losing issue with the voters. At the state level candidates often debated each other over who would execute more criminals. By the 1992 campaign even most Democrats had become death penalty advocates. A Gallup poll in 1983 found that 72 percent of Americans favored capital punishment, up from 42 percent in 1966. Meanwhile, the electric chairs continued to malfunction.

John Louis Evans, Alabama State Prison, April 22, 1983

During the execution of Evans, sparks and flames erupted from the leg electrode, which burst from its strap and caught on fire. White smoke leaked from around his hood. When the chair was shut off the doctors checked for a heartbeat. Finding one, they ordered the chair turned on again. They had to reattach the leg electrode because the strap had burned off.

When the chair was turned on again there was more smoke and burning flesh. When the current was turned off, doctors still heard his heart beating. At this point, Evans's attorney, who was a witness at the execution, asked the commissioner of corrections to halt the execution, claiming that what he was witnessing was "cruel and unusual punishment." The commissioner spoke with Gov. George C. Wallace by telephone. Before the governor could make a decision on the request, prison guards turned on the current a third time, and there was still more smoke and small flames erupted. Finally, 14 minutes after the current had first been turned on, Evans was pronounced dead. Witnesses walked away from the execution convinced that Evans had been burned alive in the chair.

"Based on what I saw, I would think that everybody would rather have a different [execution] method," said Ron Tate, a spokesman for the Department of Corrections, who saw Evans's charred body after the execution. "It wasn't a pretty sight to see, I'm sure, but it's the only thing we have."[7]

Alpha Otis Stephens, Georgia State Prison, December 12, 1984

The current was first turned on for two minutes and, as expected, Stephens's body slumped against the straps when the current was turned off. Then one of the witnesses noticed that Stephens was still breathing. The doctors waited six minutes until Stephens's body cooled off enough so that they could examine it. At that point a doctor said that he was still alive. During this period one witness counted 23 breaths taken by Stephens. He finally died after the current was turned on a second time.[8]

On April 25, 1985, the U.S. Supreme Court denied a petition from a death row inmate named Jimmy L. Glass, who claimed, as many had before, that electrocution was a violation of the Eighth Amendment. Glass used the many well-publicized cases of electric chair malfunctions to support his case. Although the Court denied this request, Justice William Brennan wrote a long dissenting opinion in which he attacked the electric chair as "nothing less than the contemporary technological equivalent of burning at the stake."

Of the 41 executions that had been carried out since the death penalty was reinstated, he said, 31 were killed in the electric chair. Since the Court ruled that the electric chair was neither cruel nor unusual in the case of Kemmler in 1890, new evidence shows that "death by electrical current is extremely violent and inflicts pain and indignities far beyond the mere extinguishment of life" and causes "unspeakable pain and suffering."

"It's an inescapable fact that the 95-year history of electrocutions [in] this country has been characterized by repeated failures swiftly to execute and the resulting need to send recurrent charges into condemned prisoners to assure their deaths." Electrocution, he said, was "a barbaric torture device," and the process had become a "gruesome ritual."

Justice Thurgood Marshall was the only other justice who shared this opinion, however, and the electric chair continued to operate.[9]

William E. Vandiver, Indiana State Prison, October 16, 1985

Indiana's 72-year-old electric chair took 5 jolts and 17 minutes to kill 37-year-old Vandiver. He was still breathing after the first jolt of 2,300 volts for 10 seconds and 500 volts for 20 seconds. After the fifth jolt, a spokesman for the Department of Corrections said the chair, "was not malfunctioning in any way."[10]

Ted Bundy, Florida State Prison, January 24, 1989

The scariest thing about the case of Ted Bundy, one of the most famous serial killers of the 1970s, was the way he could appear to be so normal. A former Boy Scout and law student, Bundy was a member of the Seattle Crime Prevention Board and wrote a pamphlet instructing women on how to avoid rape. He was a member of the Young Republicans at Washington State. He was handsome and smart and may have lured as many as 50 young women in five states to their deaths between

1973 and 1978. He carefully selected victims with long, dark hair parted down the middle.

In December 1977, while he was in jail in Colorado for killing a nurse, he asked prison officials which state was mostly likely to execute a killer. When he escaped he headed directly for the Sunshine State and was arrested for killing three women in the Chi Omega Sorority House in Tallahassee.

In all of his court trials he chose to act as his own attorney. During the long appeals process, courts refused to call him insane. A federal judge in 1987 called him "the most competent serial killer in the country ... a diabolical genius." The appeals resulted in three stays of execution and cost the state of Florida $6 million. While in prison he married a woman and fathered a child in the visiting room.

In the hours before his execution, Bundy taped an interview with the Rev. James C. Dobson, a California religious broadcaster, in which he said that violent pornography had shaped his behavior and warned society that it would produce other killers like him.

On the day before his execution in February 1989, Bundy, 42, said, "I don't want to die, I kid you not, but I deserve the most extreme punishment society has."

Five hours before his execution, in a call to his mother, Bundy said, "I'm so sorry I have given you all such grief ... but a part of me was hidden all the time." In reply, his mother said, "You'll always be my precious son."

On the morning he died, 200 people gathered around the Florida State Prison to light sparklers, cheer and wave signs that said "Burn Baby Burn" and "Roast in Peace" as he was strapped into the chair and killed with 2,000 volts of electricity.[11]

Horace E. Dunkins, Alabama State Prison, July 14, 1989

It took two jolts, nine minutes apart to kill Dunkins, a mentally retarded inmate. The botch was later found to have been caused by faulty cable hookups. The next prisoner in line to sit in this same chair, an inmate named Thomas, filed a petition in U.S. District Court asking for a stay of execution until the state installed a new chair to replace the defective one. Thomas contended that Dunkins was physically and psychologically tortured and that he was likely to undergo the same torture if the same chair was used.

The judge ordered a hearing to assess how well Alabama's chair was functioning and later determined that even though the chair was old it was in proper working condition and that "the likelihood of an error similar to that which occurred during the Dunkins's execution is remote" and Thomas's appeal was denied. He died in the chair the same year.[12]

In 1990 Fred Leuchter's term as "Dr. Death" came to a sudden end after the publication of a book he had written that offered evidence that the Holocaust could not have occurred because he found no evidence of poison gas at concentration camp sites. Jewish groups and others responding to this book discovered that Leuchter, who had been offering expert testimony based on his knowledge as an engineer, was in fact not an engineer. He had no degree and no license. One by one states canceled their contracts with him. In Massachusetts he was charged with practicing engineering without a license. In the settlement of this case, Leuchter admitted that he had misrepresented himself as an engineer to various states he had consulted with or sold equipment to.

Leuchter's withdrawal left electric chair states with no source of information about how to fix the chairs, how to prepare prisoners for execution or how much voltage to use, knowledge that previous executioners like Davis and Elliott had protected as trade secrets. There is a direct connection between this lack of expertise and the increased number of botched executions, according to law professor Deborah Denno.[13]

On August 6, 1990, the electric chair celebrated its one hundredth anniversary. Many national newspapers carried articles about the history of electrocutions and noted that they seemed to be losing favor to the lethal injection method. *American Heritage* ran a birthday piece noting Edison's role in the development of the chair but underestimated the number of people killed in it by 3,000. The *Washington Post*'s birthday article was more thorough, reflecting on the long history of the device, but also erred in reporting that Ruth Snyder was the first woman to die in the electric chair. Even after a century of experience, however, and over 4,000 victims, electrocutions were still botched.

Jesse Joseph Tafero, Florida State Prison, May 4, 1990

Just months before the chair's one hundredth birthday, the state of Florida attempted to electrocute Tafero in a chair in which the natural "elephant ear" sponge that was normally used inside the head electrode to keep the flesh from burning had been replaced with an artificial sponge. When the current was turned on smoke and six-inch flames erupted from the head electrode and three jolts were required to kill him.

The use of the synthetic sponge apparently reduced the current to less than 100 volts and ended up torturing him to death. One observer said it was like watching a man be charred alive. Frank Kligo, the prison medical director, said the execution was "less than esthetically attractive."

Based on the news reports of Tafero's death, several Florida death row inmates filed requests for a stay of execution based on the condition of Florida's electric chair. The U.S. District Court ordered a hearing to look into the matter and found that the report that the problem had been caused by a defective sponge was supported by expert testimony and that the sponge had since been replaced. The inmates, however, claimed that the sponge was not the only problem with the chair. This claim was supported by testimony of a private consulting engineer who examined the chair.[14]

Wilbert Lee Evens, Virginia State Prison, October 17, 1990

During the execution of Evens, blood spewed out of the right side of his face mask, drenching his shirt. Evens continued to moan after the first jolt was applied. The autopsy showed that the bleeding had been caused by elevated blood pressure during the execution.[15]

Derick Lynn Peterson, Virginia State Prison, August 22, 1991

At the execution of Peterson, the first jolt of electricity failed to kill the prisoner, and a second jolt was required. The authorities in Virginia announced that in the future they would routinely use two jolts before checking for a heartbeat.[16]

During the 1990s support for the death penalty in public opinion polls increased to nearly 80 percent, but most of the electric chair executions actually took place in only one region, the South. By the mid-1990s two-thirds of all executions that had taken place since the death penalty was restored took place in only five states: Texas, Florida, Virginia, Louisiana and Georgia. Three of the four states that still used the electric chair in

1998 were also in the south: Florida, Georgia and Alabama. The other was Nebraska. All the states in the East and West that once used electric chairs have shut them down for good.

Louisiana's electric chair, which was last used for executions in 1991, has become one of the most popular exhibits in the Angola Prison Museum in West Feliciana Parish.

In Sydney, Australia, the electric chair has become a mall amusement-center ride. For $2 children can sit in the chair, grab the two metal arms and feel a vibration as the "voltmeter" needle moves from 300 volts to 1,000 volts to "smoke" accompanied by the whirring noise of simulated electric current. Those who stay on to the end of the ride get a certificate certifying that they have survived an execution. The "Original Shocker Electric Chair," made by Nova Productions, assures parents that the amusement is "totally safe, great fun and challenging." The sign on the front reads "see if you can make it smoke" and "insert coins to experience the chill of the electric chair."

The New South Wales Federation of Parents and Citizens was not amused and asked that the machine be removed because it was "horrific and quite barbaric" and "adds nothing to the lives of young people. It's commercialism gone crazy. For people to profit from something offensive like the electric chair is perverse."[17]

In the late 1990s opposition to the electric chair fell into a blind spot in activists' agendas. The ACLU refused to lobby for more humane methods of execution for fear of dividing support for the outright abolition of capital punishment. Their position is that all executions are inhumane. Conservative groups refuse to oppose the electric chair for fear that if one method is abolished the others might be abolished as well. This blind spot, as well as the majority view on the Supreme Court that electrocution is a painless and humane death, has allowed the electric chair to survive as states slowly pull the plug one by one.

"Having abstained from considering the hard questions relating to electrocution for so long, courts bear the onus of re-examining the constitutionality of the century-old method," concluded legal scholar Lonny L. Hoffman in 1992. "The judiciary cannot only pronounce sentence; it must also monitor how the sentence of death is carried out.... It is a sobering reminder in this age of weapons of mass destruction and killing that how we exact the ultimate sanction of the law matters. Not only for the prisoner, but for ourselves as well."[18]

The American Veterinary Medical Association's guidelines for animal euthanasia require that for an animal to be killed humanely it must be rendered unconscious before it is electrocuted. No state requires that for human beings, although some states reportedly offered opiates to condemned prisoners before they went to the electric chair.

During the summer of 1997, a Broward County, Florida, polling organization asked 600 registered voters whether the state should switch from the electric chair to lethal injection. The survey found that 34 percent favored keeping the electric chair, 44 percent favored lethal injection, 7 percent were opposed to capital punishment, 7 percent were undecided and several suggested such things as pulling the legs and arms off condemned prisoners.

"What's driving these results is the perception that the electric chair is an inhumane way to end the lives even of serial killers and others who have committed heinous crimes," said Jim Kane, head of the organization that conducted the poll. During 1997, 37 people died in Florida's electric chair.

The Florida legislature refused to pass a bill designed to pull the plug on the state's electric chair and resumed executions in 1998. When a Florida inmate appealed to the U.S. Supreme Court early in 1998, four justices said they would be willing to take another look at the issue.

"This is a clear signal that the Supreme Court may well take a case to consider at least Florida's electric chair, if not the issue of electrocution in general," said Richard Dieter, executive director of the Death Penalty Information Center in Washington.

The four justices who have indicated a willingness to look into the issue are John Paul Stevens, David Souter, Ruth Bader Ginsberg and Stephen Breyer.[19]

Meanwhile, early in 1998 the Kentucky House Judiciary Committee voted 17 to 2 for a bill that would replace the state's 87-year-old electric chair with lethal injection. The change came after a poll conducted by the *Louisville Courier Journal* found that 63 percent of the state's voters wanted to pull the plug. On July 1, 1997, Kentucky used its chair for the first time in more than 35 years when it killed Harold McQueen for the 1980 murder of Rebecca O'Hearn.

In Alabama in 1998 Rep. Paul Parker introduced a bill in the state legislature to switch from the electric chair to lethal injection and it passed 73 to 11 in the House, but the Senate Governmental Affairs Committee voted 6 to 0 in April to delay action on the bill, which killed it for that session.

"I don't want Alabama to be the last," Parker said of his bill.[20]

But as it has done from the very beginning, the electric chair tends to divide those who oppose the death penalty. Most of the large organizations, such as the American Civil Liberties Union, want the death penalty abolished entirely and do not want to get involved in disputes over the method of execution. The ACLU's "Briefing Paper Number 8" maintains that no matter what process is used, execution is "often an excruciatingly painful and always degrading process."

Other opponents, including many legislators and jurists, take the "one step at a time" approach and want the electric chair abolished as one more step on the road to eliminating the death penalty. Although 11 states still permit the use of the electric chair, only 4 of them actively use it, and in each of these states bills have been introduced to switch to lethal injection.

"It's only a matter of time," said Deborah Denno.[21]

One by one the plugs are likely to be pulled for good in each of the remaining states, ending a most peculiar chapter in the story of American criminal justice. Long after their deaths, the work of Thomas Edison and Harold Brown went on to kill 4,300 people. The electric chair survived from the gaslight era to the computer era, a remarkable record for any invention. Although Edison and Brown must take responsibility for the original invention, the nation's courts, especially the Supreme Court, are responsible for letting such a barbaric device exist in opposition to the Constitution's clear ban on cruel and unusual punishment.

It is likely that one of the condemned men currently on death row will become the last person to be killed in the electric chair. Like the chair's first victim, William Kemmler, the last victim will probably also secure a place in the history of criminal justice, and only then will the final chapter be written.

Notes

Preface

1. *New York Times*, March 25–26, 1997.
2. *Christian Science Monitor*, July 28, 1997.
3. *Gainesville Sun*, Oct. 21, 1997.
4. *USA Today*, March 28, 1997.
5. Temporary State Commission on the Revision of the Penal Law (New York) Final Report, 1962.
6. Bedau, Hugo A. *The Death Penalty in America: An Anthology*. Rev. ed. Garden City, N.Y.: Anchor Books, 1967.

Chapter 1: The Genie of the Gilded Age

1. *Buffalo Commercial Advertiser*, Aug. 8, 1881.
2. *Buffalo Evening News*, Aug. 9, 1890.
3. *Buffalo Courier*, June 12, 1898.
4. Southwick, Alfred P. "Anatomy and Physiology of the Cleft Palate," in *Transactions of the Dental Society of the State of New York*, 1877, pp. 50–61.
5. Sanford, Charles L. "Technology and Culture at the End of the Nineteenth Century: The Will to Power," in Kranzberg, Melvin, and Pursell, Carroll W. (eds.) *Technology in Western Civilization*. New York: Oxford University Press, 1967, pp. 726–743.
6. Hughes, Thomas P. *American Genesis: A Century of Innovation and Technological Enthusiasm, 1870–1970.* New York: Viking, 1989, pp. 13–40.
7. Oliver, John. *History of American Technology*. New York: Ronald Press pp. 346–361.
8. Byrn, Edward W. "The Progress of Invention During the Past Fifty Years," *Scientific American*, July 25, 1896, pp. 82–83.
9. Rowbottom, Margaret, and Susskind, Charles. *Electricity and Medicine: History of Their Interaction*. San Francisco: San Francisco Press, 1984, pp. 103–116.
10. Oliver, *History of American Technology*, p. 346.

11. Oliver, *History of American Technology*, pp. 347–348.
12. *Buffalo Evening News*, Aug. 9, 1890. See also *New York Times*, Aug. 2–3, 1889.

Chapter 2: The Hangman's Terrible Legacy

1. Mackey, Philip E. *Hanging in the Balance: The Anti-Capital Punishment Movement in New York State, 1776–1861*. New York: Garland, 1982, p. 108.
2. Mackey, pp. 124–263.
3. *New York Times*, July 22, 1882.
4. *St. Paul Pioneer Press*, July 13, 1882.
5. *New York Times*, July 2, 1882.
6. *New York Times*, March 20, 1882.
7. *Weekly News of London*, June 22, 1885.
8. *New York Times*, Feb. 29, 1887.
9. *New York Herald*, Aug. 2, 1890.
10. *Harper's Magazine*, vol. 52, p. 462.

Chapter 3: The Death Commission

1. *New York Tribune*, Jan. 4, 1885, p. 4.
2. *New York Tribune* editorial, Jan. 13, 1885, p. 4.
3. *New York Tribune*, editorial, Feb. 25, 1885, p. 4.
4. *The Lancet*, June 1885, reprinted in Commission to Investigate and Report the Most Humane and Practical Method of Carrying into Effect the Sentence of Death in Capital Cases, "Report of the Commission," January 17, 1888. Troy: Troy Press, 1888, p. 83. (In New York State Library, Albany, subsequently referred to as Commission.)
5. *New York Tribune*, July 19, 1889.
6. *Commission*, p. 87.
7. *Commission*, pp. 81–86.
8. *Commission*, p. 82.
9. The letters from Southwick to Edison are in the Edison Archives, as is the second letter from Edison to Southwick. The first Edison reply has apparently been lost but can be inferred from the others. For a discussion of this see Reynolds, Terry S. and Bernstein, Theodore, "Edison and the Chair," *IEEE Technology and Society Magazine*, March 1989, pp. 19–28.
10. Reynolds and Bernstein, "Edison and the Chair," p. 21.
11. *Commission*, p. 75.
12. *Commission*, p. 73.
13. *Commission*, pp. 80–81.
14. *Commission*, p. 90.
15. The interviews with Grant, Stevens, Walsh, Lyon and Hewitt are in the *New York Tribune*, Jan. 22, 1888.
16. *American Law Review*, quoted in *Criminal Law Magazine*, 1888, p. 581.

17. Howells, William Dean, *Harper's Weekly*, vol. 32, Jan. 14, 1888, p. 23.
18. Henry, John O. "Action of the Current on the Human Body" *Electrical World*, March 15, 1890.
19. Lockwood, Thomas P. "Electrical Killing," *Electrical Engineer*, March 1888, p. 89.
20. *Scientific American*, Jan. 5, 1889, p. 2
21. *Scientific American* Aug. 16, 1890. See also Bernstein, Theodore, "A Grand Success," *IEEE Spectrum*, Feb. 1973, pp. 54–58.

Chapter 4: The Battle of the Currents

1. *New York Times*, April 18, 1888. For a summary of the political tactics used on the electric chair bill see the *Utica Morning Herald*, Aug. 6, 1890.
2. *New York Times*, April 26, 1888.
3. *New York Times*, May 9–12, 1888.
4. The "battle of the currents" is described in one way or another in most of the biographies of Edison and Westinghouse and was well documented in its own era. Among the best descriptions of it are those in Conot, Robert, *A Streak of Luck: The Life and Legend of Thomas Alva Edison*. New York: Seaview Books, 1979; and Reynolds and Bernstein "Edison and the Chair." See also Silverberg, Robert, *Light for the World, Edison and the Electric Power Industry*. Princeton: Van Norstrand, 1967, pp. 229–243.
5. Platt, Harold L. *The Electric City: Energy and Growth in the Chicago Area, 1880–1930*. Chicago: University of Chicago Press, 1991. Chapter 3, "The Crisis of Urban Politics, 1880–1893."
6. Hughes, Thomas P. "Harold P. Brown and the Executioner's Current: An Incident in the AC-DC Controversy." *Business History Review* 32 (1958): 143–165.
7. The exact nature of the relationship between Brown and Edison remains unclear. The correspondence between the two shows it was much closer than they maintained at the time. Many historians take it for granted that Brown was Edison's employee. See *American Heritage*, July-Aug. 1990.
8. *New York Times*, May 12, 1888.
9. Rybak, James P. "AC or DC?" *Popular Electronics*, Sept. 1994, pp. 42–48.
10. Edison to Johnson, undated 1886 memorandum, Edison Archives.
11. Josephson, Matthew. *Edison, A Biography*. New York: McGraw-Hill, 1959, p. 347.
12. Harold P. Brown's letter to the *New York Evening Post* is reprinted in "The Admission of Alternating Current into New York City," *Electrical World*, July 12, 1888, p. 40.
13. *New York Times*, June 5, 1888.
14. *Albany Times*, June 5, 1888.
15. Hughes, "Harold P. Brown and the Executioner's Current" (1958) is the source of much of the information about Brown's activities in 1888. Brown's experiments are described in New York newspaper accounts and in his own article "Death Current Experiments in the Edison Laboratory," *Electrical World*, Aug. 11, 1889, p. 69. He also published his own summary, "The Comparative Danger

to Life of the Alternating and Continuous Electrical Currents" in book form in 1889. This was reprinted in the transcript of Kemmler's appeal to the state court of appeals.

16. *New York Times* and *New York Herald*, July 21, 1888, and *Electrical Engineer* 7 (1888): 369.

17. *Electrical Engineer*, Aug. 1888, p. 375.

18. Brown to Kennelly, Aug. 4, 1888, Edison Archives.

19. *Electrical Engineer*, Sept. 1888 pp. 451–454.

20. *New York Times,* Dec. 6, 1888.

21. The Medico-Legal Society's report on electrocution is in its journal, printed Dec. 12, 1888, and reprinted in *Electrical World*, Dec. 18, 1888.

22 F. S. Hastings to Thomas Edison, Jan. 21, 1889, reprinted in the *New York Sun*, Aug. 25, 1889.

23. *New York Times*, Jan. 7, 1889.

24. MacDonald to Brown, March 19, 1889. Reprinted by the *New York Sun*, Aug. 25, 1889.

Chapter 5: The People v. William Kemmler

1. The 226 cases were counted by Denno, Deborah, in "Is Electrocution an Unconstitutional Method of Execution? The Engineering of Death over the Century," *William and Mary Law Review* 35 (1994): 551–692.

2. Details of Kemmler's early life before his trial were not immediately known but were revealed in newspaper reports before his execution. See *Utica Saturday Globe* Aug. 2 and Aug. 9, 1890, *New York Times*, May 24, 1890, *Buffalo Evening News*, April 1, 1889, *Utica Daily Press*, Aug. 6, 1890, *New York Herald*, Aug. 7, 1890.

3. The transcript of *The People of the State of New York v. William Kemmler* has not survived. There are no known copies of trial notes or exhibits from either the prosecution or the defense. The only source of information about the actual testimony during the trial is newspaper accounts in the Buffalo daily newspapers, which gave the event extensive coverage before, during and after the trial. My account in this chapter closely follows the reports in the *Buffalo Evening News*, which seemed to be the most complete and accurate account.

Chapter 6: Westinghouse's Counterattack

1. Many of Harold P. Brown's negotiations and business dealings in the spring of 1889 were conducted in the utmost secrecy; however, some of them can be pieced together through statements made by others and especially by a packet of 45 letters that were apparently stolen from his desk and published in the *New York Sun* on Aug. 25, 1889. Historians who have compared these letters to originals in the Edison Archives are convinced that they are genuine. These letters show that Brown stayed in close contact with Edison throughout this period,

seeking advice and keeping Edison informed about his dealings. See Hughes, "The Executioner's Current," and Reynolds and Bernstein, "Edison and the Chair."

2. MacDonald to Brown, *New York Sun*, Aug. 25, 1889.

3. See Hughes, "The Executioner's Current."

4. Brown to Edison, *New York Sun*, Aug. 25, 1889. In 1892 the Edison company and Thomson-Houston merged to form General Electric.

5. *New York Tribune*, Aug. 7, 1890. See also Hughes, "The Executioner's Current."

6. Brown to Edison, *New York Sun*, Aug. 25, 1889.

7. *New York Times*, May 12, 1889.

8. *Albany Evening Times*, June 7, 1889.

9. Kennelly to Brown, June 29, 1889, Edison Archives.

10. The details from the Becker hearings are from the *New York Times*, *New York Herald* and *New York Tribune*, July–August 1889, all of which gave them extensive coverage.

11. Brown to Insull, July 17, 1889, Edison Archives.

12. *Albany Journal*, July 24, 1889.

13. *Wilkes-Barre News*, July 25, 1889.

14. *New York Times*, Aug. 7, 1890.

15. *New York Herald*, Aug. 22, 1889.

16. *Scientific American*, Oct. 19, 1889.

17. *New York Times*, Aug. 6, 1889.

18. Proceedings of the National Electric Light Association at its Tenth Convention, vol. 7, New York, 1890.

19. *New York Tribune*, Sept. 18, 1889.

20. *New York Times*, Oct. 10, 1889.

21. *Albany Evening Times*, Oct. 10, 1889.

22. Brown, Harold P. "The New Instrument of Execution," *North American Review* (Nov. 1889): 587–593.

23. Edison, Thomas A. "The Dangers of Electric Lighting," *North American Review* (Nov. 1889): 625–634.

24. Westinghouse, George, "A Reply to Mr. Edison," *North American Review* (Dec. 1889): 653–664.

Chapter 7: Cruel and Unusual Punishment

1. *New York Times*, Feb. 12, 1890.

2. New York Court of Appeals, case 119 New York—74 Sickels, People ex rel. *Kemmler v. Durston*.

3. *New York Times*, March 22, 1890.

4. *New York Times*, March 22, 1890.

5. *New York Times*, April 29, 1890.

6. *New York Times*, April 28–29, 1890. See also *Electrical World,* May 3, 1890, p. 296.

7. Accounts of preparations for the aborted execution are from the *New York Times*, *New York Tribune*, *New York Herald*, *Auburn Advertiser* and *Utica Daily Press*, April 28–29, 1890.

8. *Port Arthur Weekly Sentinel*, May 2, 1890.
9. *New York Times*, April 30, 1890.
10. Westinghouse later admitted that he had hired Sherman. See *New York Tribune*, Aug. 9, 1890.
11. *New York Tribune*, May 1, 1890.
12 *New York Times*, May 1, 1890.
13. *Albany Law Journal*, May 10, 1890.
14. *New York Times*, May 6, 1890.
15. The aborted attempt to abolish capital punishment in May 1890 is described in the *New York Tribune*, May 1–5, 1890.
16. *Albany Law Journal*, May 5, 1890.
17. IN RE KEMMLER, 119 US 584, 1890.
18. *New York Tribune*, May 24, 1890.
19. *New York Tribune*, May 24, 1890.
20. *New York Times*, May 24, 1890.
21. *Albany Law Journal*, July 5, 1890.

Chapter 8: The Human Experiment

1. The minute-by-minute details of Kemmler's final days in Auburn were described by nearly every paper in New York. The information in this chapter comes from the *New York Times*, *New York Tribune*, *New York Herald*, *Auburn Advertiser*, *Albany Evening Journal*, *Saturday Globe* and *Utica Daily Press*, Aug. 2 to Aug. 8, 1890. Many of these stories are identical and were no doubt originally part of wire service stories filed from Auburn.
2. Warden Durston's report to the Department of Prisons has not survived, but portions of it were reprinted in "First Execution" *Corrections* [published by the State Department of Corrections] vol. 14, no. 6 (June 1949): 8–10.
3. *Albany Evening Journal*, Aug. 7, 1890.
4. MacDonald, Carlos F., "Report on the Execution by Electricity of William Kemmler, Alias John Hort," Presented to the Governor, Sept. 20, 1890. Albany: Argus, 1890.
5. Attributed to Marty Johnson, as quoted in "Verse and Worse," *Elmira Star Gazette*, Nov. 21, 1966.

Chapter 9: The Reaction: "A Thrill of Indignation"

1. Newspaper reactions to Kemmler's execution were reprinted in the *New York Times*, the *New York Tribune*, *New York Herald*, *Utica Daily Press*, *Albany Times*, *Saturday Globe*, et al., Aug. 6 to Aug. 18 1890.
2. *New York Tribune*, Aug. 8, 1890.
3. *New York Tribune*, Aug. 7, 1890.
4. *New York Tribune*, Aug. 7, 1890.
5. Quotes from Dr. Spitzka, Dr. MacDonald, Dr. Shrady, Dr. Daniels, and Southwick: the *New York Tribune*, Aug. 7, 1890.

6. *Buffalo Evening News*, Aug. 7, 1890.
7. *Utica Daily Press*, Aug. 8, 1890.
8. *New York Herald*, Aug. 7, 1890.
9. *New York Tribune*, Aug. 8, 1890.
10. *New York Tribune*, Aug. 8, 1890.
11. *New York Herald*, Aug. 8, 1890.
12. *New York Tribune*, Aug. 8, 1890.
13. The post-execution editorials were printed on Aug. 7 and 8, 1890. The *Utica Saturday Globe* editorial is reprinted in *Corrections* [published by the State Department of Corrections] vol. 14, no. 6 (June 1949): 8–10.
14. *New York Tribune*, Aug. 8, 1890.
15. *New York Tribune*, Aug. 8, 1890.
16. *Buffalo Evening News*, Aug. 8, 1890.
17. *Buffalo Evening News*, Aug. 8, 1890.
18. *Medical Record of New York*, Sept. 1890.
19. *Scientific American*, Sept. 27, 1890.
20. MacDonald, Carlos F. "Report on the Execution by Electricity of William Kemmler."
21. *Albany Law Journal*, Aug. 16, 1890, p. 121.
22. *New York Times*, July 6, 1891.
23. *New York Times*, July 7, 1891.
24. MacDonald, Carlos F. "Infliction of the Death Penalty by Means of Electricity, a Report of Seven Cases, "*Department of Prisons Annual Report*, 1892.

Chapter 10: The First Era: 1892–1974

1. Bowers, William J. *Legal Homicide: Death as Punishment in America, 1864–1982*. Boston: Northeastern University Press, 1984. See also the up-to-date statistics provided by the Death Penalty Information Center: <http://www.essential.org/dpic/>
2. Denno, "Is Electrocution an Unconstitutional Method of Execution?"
3. Weisberg, J. "This Is Your Death," *New Republic*, July 1, 1991, p. 23.
4. Miller, Arthur S. and Bowman, Jeffery H. *Death by Installments, the Ordeal of Willie Francis*. New York: Greenwood Press, 1988.
5. Hoffman, Lonny L. "The Madness of the Method: The Use of Electrocution and the Death Penalty," *Texas Law Review*, 70 (1990): 1039–1062.
6. For more information about Davis see his file in the Corning Historical Society, which contains undated clippings and personal recollections. See also *Elmira Star Gazette*, Nov. 21, 1966, *Corrections*, June 1949; *Corning Leader*, May 26, 1923; *Corning Leader*, Aug. 18, 1987; *Utica Herald*, March 30, 1908, p. 5. U.S. Patent No. 587,649 "electrocution chair," Aug. 3, 1897. See also the personal memoirs of a man who knew him: Elliott, Robert G. *Agent of Death: The Memoirs of an Executioner*. New York: E. P. Dutton, 1940. See also his obituary: *New York Times,* May 27, 1923, and from "Auburn State Prison, Its History, Makeup and Programs," published by the New York State Department of Corrections, June 1949.

7. MacDonald, "Infliction of the Death Penalty by Means of Electricity."

8. Annual Report of the Superintendent of State Prisons, Albany, N.Y., 1894, pp. 3–4.

9. Hearn, Daniel A. *Legal Executions in New York State, A Comprehensive Reference.* Jefferson, N.C.: McFarland, 1997. See also Elliott, *Agent of Death.*

10. Elliott, *Agent of Death*; *New York Times*, 28–29, 1901; Hearn, *Legal Executions.*

11. Hearn, *Legal Executions.* See also Elliott, *Agent of Death.*

12. Brandon, Craig. *Murder in the Adirondacks.* Utica, N.Y.: North Country Books, 1986.

13. Hearn, *Legal Executions*; *New York Times*, March 29–30, 1909.

14. Hearn, *Legal Executions.*

15. Hearn, *Legal Executions.*

16. Elliott, *Agent of Death.* See also Lawes, Lewis. *Twenty Thousand Years in Sing Sing.* New York: R. Long & R. R. Smith, 1932.

17. Jones, G. R. N. "Judicial Electrocution and the Prison Doctor," *The Lancet*, March 24, 1990.

18. Elliott, *Agent of Death.* See also, Lawes, Lewis, *Twenty Thousand Years.*

19. Marquart, James W., Ekland-Olson, Sheldon, and Sorensen, Jonathan R. *The Rope, the Chair and the Needle: Capital Punishment in Texas, 1923–1990.* Austin: University of Texas Press, 1994.

20. Elliott, *Agent of Death.* Russell, Francis, *Tragedy in Dedham: The Story of the Sacco-Vanzetti Case.* New York: McGraw-Hill, 1962.

21. Lawes, *Twenty Thousand Years.*

22. Hearn, *Legal Executions*; *New York Times*, Jan. 13–15, Feb. 8, 1928.

23. Elliott, *Agent of Death.*

24. Marquart et al. *The Rope, the Chair and the Needle.*

25. Hearn, *Legal Executions*; Frazier, David K. *Murder Cases of the Twentieth Century.* Jefferson, N.C.: McFarland, 1996.

26. Fisher, Jim. *The Lindbergh Case.* New Brunswick: Rutgers University Press, 1987; Frazier, *Murder Cases.*

27. Hoffman, "Madness of the Method."

28. Hearn, *Legal Executions.*

29. Hearn, *Legal Executions.*

30. Hearn, *Legal Executions.*

31. Miller and Bowman. *Death by Installments.*

32. *Charleston Gazette*, March 26–27, 1951.

33. Wexley, John. *The Judgment of Julius and Ethel Rosenberg.* New York: Cameron & Kahn, 1955. *New York Times*, June 20, 1953.

34. Frazier, *Murder Cases.*

35. Hearn, *Legal Executions.*

36. Hearn, *Legal Executions.*

37. Blaustein, Susan, "Witness to Another Execution," *Harper's*, May 1994.

38. Temporary State Commission on the revision of the Penal Law (New York) Final Report, 1962.

39. *New York Times*, June 30, 1972.

Chapter 11: The Electric Chair Reborn: 1976–1998

1. *New York Times*, July 3, 1976.
2. Bedau, Hugo. *The Death Penalty in America, Current Controversies.* New York: Oxford University Press, 1997.
3. *New York Times*, May 26, 1979.
4. Lehman, Susan. "A Matter of Engineering," *Atlantic Monthly*, Feb. 1990, pp. 26–29.
5. Trombley, Stephen. *The Execution Protocol.* New York: Crown, 1992.
6. Denno, "Is Electrocution…."
7. *Mobile Register*, April 25, 1983.
8. Denno, "Is Electrocution…."
9. U.S. Supreme Court, *Glass v. Louisiana* 471 US 1080.
10. Hoffman, "Madness of the Method." See also Denno "Is Electrocution…."
11. Frazier, *Murder Cases.*
12 Hoffman, "Madness of the Method."
13. Denno, "Is Electrocution…."
14. Weisberg, "This Is Your Death." See also Hoffman, "Madness of the Method."
15. Hoffman, "Madness of the Method."
16. Hoffman, "Madness of the Method."
17. Evans, Michael, "Electric chair game…" *Sydney (Australia) Morning Herald*, June 10, 1997.
18. Hoffman, "Madness of the Method."
19. *St. Petersburg Times*, April 1, 1998.
20. Associated Press, April 8, 1998.
21. Richey, William, "As Execution Evolves, Electric Chair Is on Trial," *Christian Science Monitor*, July 28, 1997.

Bibliography

Books

Acker, James R., Bohm, Robert M., Lanier, Charles S., eds., *America's Experiment with Capital Punishment*. Durham: Carolina Academic Press, 1998.

Bedau, Hugo A. *The Death Penalty in America: An Anthology*. Rev. ed. Garden City, N.Y.: Anchor Books, 1967.

_____. *The Death Penalty in America, Current Controversies*. New York: Oxford University Press, 1997.

Bowers, William J. *Legal Homicide: Death as Punishment in America, 1864–1982*. Boston: Northeastern University Press, 1984.

_____. *Executions in America*. Lexington, Mass.: Lexington Books, 1974.

Brandon, Craig. *Murder in the Adirondacks*. Utica, N.Y.: North Country, 1986.

Brown, Wenzell. *Women Who Died in the Chair*. New York: Collier Books, 1963.

Canby, Edward Tatnall. *A History of Electricity*. New York: Hawthorn, 1963.

Clark, Ronald W. *Edison: The Man Who Made the Future*. London: Macdonald and Jane's, 1977.

Conot, Robert. *A Streak of Luck: The Life and Legend of Thomas Alva Edison*. New York: Seaview Books, 1979.

Drimmer, Fredrick. *Until You Are Dead: The Book of Executions in America*. New York: Carol Publishing Group, 1990.

Elliott, Robert G. *Agent of Death: The Memoirs of an Executioner*. New York: E. P. Dutton, 1940.

Engel, Howard. *Lord High Executioner: An Unabashed Look at Hangmen, Headsmen and Their Kind*. Willowsdale, Ontario: Firefly Books, 1996.

Espy, M. Watt. *Executions in the United States, 1608–1987*. Ann Arbor, Mich.: Inter-university Consortium for Political and Social Research, 1987.

Fisher, Jim. *The Lindbergh Case*. New Brunswick: Rutgers University Press, 1987.

Frazier, David K. *Murder Cases of the Twentieth Century*. Jefferson, N.C.: McFarland, 1996

Gillespie, L. Kay. *Dancehall Ladies: The Crimes and Executions of America's Condemned Women*. Lanham, Md.: University Press of America, 1997.

Gray, Ian, and Stanley, Moira. *A Punishment in Search of a Crime*. New York: Avon Books, 1989.

Guernsey, Joann Bren. *Should We Have Capital Punishment?* Minneapolis: Lerner, 1993.

Habakkuk, H. J. *American and British Technology in the Nineteenth Century.* Cambridge: Cambridge University Press, 1962.

Hearn, Daniel A. *Legal Executions in New York State: A Comprehensive Reference.* Jefferson, N.C.: McFarland, 1997.

Hood, Roger. *The Death Penalty: A Worldwide Perspective.* New York: Oxford University Press, 1996.

Horwitz, Elinor L. *Capital Punishment USA.* Philadelphia: Lippincott, 1973.

Hughes, Thomas P. *American Genesis: A Century of Invention and Technological Enthusiasm, 1870–1970.* New York: Viking, 1989.

_____. *Networks of Power: Electrification in Western Society, 1880–1930.* Baltimore: Johns Hopkins University Press, 1983.

Josephson, Matthew. *Edison, A Biography.* New York: McGraw-Hill, 1959.

Laurence, John. *History of Capital Punishment.* New York: Citadel Press, 1960.

Lawes, Lewis. *Life and Death in Sing Sing.* Garden City, N.Y.: Sun Dial, 1937.

_____. *Man's Judgment of Death: An Analysis of the Operation and Effect of Capital Punishment Based on Facts, Not on Sentiment.* New York: G. P. Putnam's Sons, 1925.

_____. *Twenty Thousand Years in Sing Sing.* New York: R. Long & R. R. Smith, 1932.

Leupp, Francis E. *George Westinghouse: His Life and Achievements.* Boston: Little, Brown, and Company, 1918.

Mackey, Philip English. *Hanging in the Balance: The Anti-capital Punishment Movement in New York State, 1776–1861.* New York: Garland, 1982.

_____, (ed.) *Voices Against Death: American Opposition to Capital Punishment, 1787–1975,* New York: B. Franklin, 1976.

MacLaren, Malcolm. *The Rise of the Electrical Industry During the Nineteenth Century.* Princeton: Princeton University Press, 1943.

Marquart, James W., Ekland-Olson, Sheldon, and Sorensen, Jonathan R. *The Rope, the Chair and the Needle: Capital Punishment in Texas, 1923–1990.* Austin: University of Texas Press, 1994.

Mencken, August. *By the Neck: A Book of Hangings.* New York: Hastings, 1942.

Metzger, Thom. *Blood and Volts: Edison, Tesla and the Electric Chair.* Brooklyn Autonomedia, 1996.

Millard, Andre. *Edison and the Business of Innovation.* Baltimore: Johns Hopkins University Press, 1990.

Miller, Arthur S. and Bowman, Jeffery H. *Death by Installments: The Ordeal of Willie Francis.* New York: Greenwood Press, 1988.

New York Edison Company. *Thirty Years of New York, 1882–1912; Being a History of Electrical Development in Manhattan and the Bronx.* [New York]: Press of the New York Edison Company, 1913.

Oliver, John W. *History of American Technology.* New York: Ronald, 1956.

Passer, Harold C. *The Electrical Manufacturers, 1875–1900.* Cambridge: Harvard University Press, 1953.

Platt, Harold L. *The Electric City: Energy and Growth in the Chicago Area, 1880–1930.* Chicago: University of Chicago Press, 1991.

Prejean, Sister Helen. *Dead Man Walking.* New York: Vintage Books, 1994.

Prout, Henry G. *A Life of George Westinghouse.* New York: C. Scribner, 1922.
Rowbottom, Margaret, and Susskind, Charles. *Electricity and Medicine: History of Their Interaction.* San Francisco: San Francisco Press, 1984.
Russell, Francis. *Tragedy in Dedham: The Story of the Sacco-Vanzetti Case.* New York: McGraw-Hill, 1962.
Scott, George Ryley. *The History of Capital Punishment.* London: Torchstream Books, 1950.
Sharlin, Harold I. *The Making of the Electrical Age: From the Telegraph to Automation.* New York: Abelard-Schuman, 1964.
Silverberg, Robert. *Light for the World: Edison and the Power Industry.* Princeton, N.J.: Van Nostrand, 1967.
Trombley, Stephen. *The Execution Protocol.* New York: Crown Publishers, 1992.
Vanderbilt, Byron M. *Thomas Edison, Chemist.* Washington: American Chemical Society, 1971.
Wachhorst, Wyn. *Thomas Alva Edison: An American Myth.* Cambridge, Mass.: MIT Press, 1981.
Wexley, John. *The Judgment of Julius and Ethel Rosenberg.* New York: Cameron & Kahn, 1955.

Articles and Reports

Albany Law Journal. "Capital Punishment," April 12, 1888.
_____. "Current Topics," May 10, 1890; July 5, 1890; Aug. 16, 1890.
_____. "The Kemmler Case," May 10, 1890.
American Heritage. July-August 1990.
American Law Review. "A Substitute for Hanging," Feb. 1888.
Anderson, Kurt. "An Eye for an Eye." *Time,* Jan. 24, 1983, pp. 28–39.
Annual Report of the Superintendent of Prisons. Albany, N.Y., 1894.
Beichman, Arnold. "The First Electrocution." *Commentary* 35 (1963): 418–419.
Bell, Clark. "Electricity and the Death Penalty." *Medico-Legal Journal,* N.Y., 1889.
Bernstein, Theodore. "A Grand Success." *IEEE Spectrum,* Feb. 1973, pp. 54–58.
Blaustein, Susan. "Witness to Another Execution." *Harper's,* May 1994.
Bleyer, J. Mount, M.D. "Best Method of Executing Criminals." *Medico-Legal Journal,* Feb. 1888.
Brown, Harold P. "The New Instrument of Execution." *North American Review,* Nov. 1889, pp. 587–593.
Byrn, Edward W. "The Progress of Invention During the Past Fifty Years." *Scientific American,* 75 (July 25, 1896).
Caher, John. "Lemuel Smith killed the state's death penalty." *Albany Times Union,* Feb. 13, 1995.
Case, Dick. Column item, *Syracuse Herald American,* March 7, 1965.
Commission to Investigate and Report the Most Humane and Practical Method of Carrying into Effect the Sentence of Death in Capital Cases. "Report of the Commission," January 17, 1888. Troy: Troy Press, 1888. (In New York State Library, Albany.)
Corrections (magazine published by the State Department of Corrections), vol. 14, no. 6, June 1949, pp. 8–10.

Denno, Deborah. "Execution and the Forgotten Eighth Amendment," in Acker, James R., et al. eds. *America's Experiment with Capital Punishment*. Carolina Academic Press: Durham (1998), pp. 547–577.
_____. "Is Electrocution an Unconstitutional Method of Execution? The Engineering of Death over the Century." *William and Mary Law Review* 35 (1994): 551–692.
Devlin, Lucinda. "Death's Doors," *Time,* June 16, 1997, pp. 38–40.
Edison, Thomas A. "The Dangers of Electric Lighting," *North American Review*, Nov. 1889, pp. 625–634.
Electrical World. "Action of the Current on the Human Body," March 15, 1890.
_____. "The Apparatus for Electrical Executions," May 3, 1890, p. 296.
_____. "Effects of Currents on the Human Body," April 26, 1890.
Ellsworth, Phoebe L., and Gross, Samuel R. "Hardening of the Attitudes: Americans' Views on the Death Penalty." *Journal of Social Sciences* 50, no. 2 (1994).
Evans, Michael. "Electric chair game mocks youth suicide," *Sydney (Australia) Morning Herald*, June 10, 1997.
Gromer, Jonathan. "Machines of Death," *Popular Mechanics*, Jan. 1998, pp. 52–56.
Henry, John O. "Action of the Current on the Human Body," *Electrical World,* March 15, 1890.
Hoffman, Lonny L. "The Madness of the Method: The Use of Electrocution and the Death Penalty." *Texas Law Review* 70 (1990): 1039–1062.
Howard, Lucy. "Pulling the Plug," *Newsweek*, Aug. 5, 1991, p. 4.
Hughes, Thomas Parke. "Harold P. Brown and the Executioner's Current: An Incident in the AC-DC Controversy." *Business History Review* 32 (1958): 143–165.
_____. "Thomas Alva Edison and the Rise of Electricity," in Pursell, Carroll W., ed. *Technology in America, a History of Individuals and Ideas* (1981).
Jones, G. R. N. "Judicial Electrocution and the Prison Doctor," *The Lancet*, March 24, 1990.
Laws of New York. 111th session, Chap. 489. "An Act ... relative to the infliction of the death penalty," signed by the governor, June 4, 1888.
_____. 112th Session, Chap. 36. "An act...to provide for the proper electrical apparatus...," approved by the governor, March 1, 1889.
Lehman, Susan. "A Matter of Engineering," *Atlantic Monthly*, Feb. 1990, pp. 26–29.
Lockwood, Thomas P. "Electrical Killing," *Electrical Engineer,* March 1888, p. 89.
MacDonald, Carlos F., M.D. "Infliction of the Death Penalty by Means of Electricity," a report of seven cases, prepared for *Department of Prisons Annual Report*, 1892.
_____. "Report on the Execution by Electricity of William Kemmler, alias John Hort, Presented to the Governor, Sept. 20, 1890." Albany: Argus, 1890.
Miles, William E. "The Electric Chair," *Buffalo News Magazine*, Aug. 5, 1979.
Neustadter, Roger. "The Deadly Current: The Death Penalty in the Industrial Age." *Journal of American Culture* (Fall 1989): 79–87.
New York State Court of Appeals. "People ex. rel. *Kemmler v. Durston*" (1890).
_____. *People v. Kemmler* (1890).
New York State Department of Correctional Services. "A Survey of Persons Executed by Electrocution in New York State: 1890–1963," 1976.

New York State Department of Prisons Annual Report, 1894.
Passer, N. C. "Electrical Science and the Early Development of the Electric Manufacturing Industry in the United States," in *Annals of Science*, 1951, pp. 382–392.
Penrose, James E. "Inventing Electrocution," *American Heritage of Invention and Technology*, Spring 1994, pp. 34–45.
Proceedings of the National Electric Light Association at its Tenth Convention, vol. 7, New York, 1890.
Richey, William. "As Execution Evolves, Electric Chair Is on Trial," *Christian Science Monitor*, July 28, 1997.
Reynolds, Terry S., and Bernstein, Theodore. "Edison and the Chair," *IEEE Technology and Society Magazine*, March 1989, pp. 19–28.
Rybak, James P. "AC or DC?" *Popular Electronics*, Sept. 1994, pp. 42–48.
Sanford, Charles L. "Technology and Culture at the End of the Nineteenth Century: The Will to Power," included in Kranzberg (ed.), *Technology in Western Civilization*. New York, Oxford University Press, 1967, pp. 726–739.
Schwarzschild, Henry. "Historical Sidelights on the Death Penalty," *Empire State Report*, Feb. 1983, pp. 18–19.
Scientific American. "The Electric Execution of Criminals," Oct. 19, 1889.
_____. "The Execution by Electricity," Sept. 27, 1890.
_____. "The First Electrical Execution," Aug. 16, 1890
Southwick, Alfred Porter, "Anatomy and Physiology of Cleft Palate," in *Transactions of the Dental Society of the State of New York*, 1877, pp. 50–61.
Stashenko, Joel. "Execution That Jolted World," Associated Press report in *Buffalo Evening News*, May 2, 1982.
Temporary State Commission on the Revision of the Penal Law (New York) Final Report. 1962.
U.S. Patent Office, patent number 587,649. "Electrocution Chair," patented by E. F. Davis, 1897.
U.S. Supreme Court. U.S. Reports. Vol. 136, October Term, 1889, "In Re. Kemmler, Petitioner."
_____. *Glass v. Louisiana*, 471 U.S. 1080, April 29, 1985.
Weisberg, J. "This Is Your Death," *New Republic*, July 1, 1991, p. 23.
Westinghouse, George. "A Reply to Mr. Edison," *North American Review*, Dec. 1889, pp. 653–664.

Newspapers

Albany Times, 1888–1890.
Buffalo News, 1881–1891.
Buffalo Courier, 1881–1891.
New York Herald, 1888–1890.

New York Times, 1888–1890.
New York Tribune, 1888–1890.
New York Sun, 1888–1890.

World Wide Web Sites

Death Penalty Information Center <http://www.essential.org/dpic/>

Index